the ULTIMATE guide to celebrating KIDS!

volume II

K-6th
Grade School

by
Linda LaTourelle

www.theultimateword.com
270 · 251 · 3600

For information write:
Bluegrass Publishing, Inc.
PO Box 634
Mayfield, KY 42066 USA
service@theultimateword.com
www.BluegrassPublishing.com

ISBN: 0-9761925-4-3

1st Edition
Mayfield, KY : Bluegrass Publishing, Inc, 2005

Cover Design: Todd Jones, Tennessee
Proudly printed in the United States of America

First Edition © 2005

THANK YOU

Translations from around the world

Ta
Australia

Merci
French

Danke
German

Grazie
Italian

Ukhani
South African

Gracias
Spanish

Arigato
Japanese

Spasibo
Russian

Obrigado
Portuguese

Appreciation
is a wonderful thing.
It makes what is excellent in others
belong to us as well.
-Voltaire-

THANK YOU!

Simple words I give to you with the deepest gratitude. With your love, support, prayers, writings and God's guiding, I am delighted to share with the world, this grand collection of some of the most wonderful quotes, expressions, sayings and original poetry on the planet. Please accept my utmost thanks and appreciation for sharing your talents and time in helping to create this truly amazing collection of words that is sure to inspire, delight and bless the readers of "The Ultimate Guide to Celebrating Kids II."

It is my hope that as you read it, you too, will see how your words are such a gift. May your heart be full of hope as these words reach out to others. Thank you, thank you, thank you—for these seeds that you have planted, I know that you will reap a harvest of blessings by sharing the love within your heart! You are all amazing talented people who I am honored to call friends. Thank you for using your talents for a purpose far greater than any of us can ever know. It is in giving that we ultimately receive. Your gifts are a treasure that will be forever cherished.

Thank you for your help—

Frank Asch · Brenda Ball · Dorothea K Barwick
Carla Birnberg · Jennifer Byerly · Joyce Chapman
Marcia Cruse · Rob Erskine · Nicholas Gordon
CJ Heck · Todd Jones · Lottie Ann Knox
Tom Krause · Gareth Lancaster · Lara LaTourelle
Hannah LaTourelle · Donia Linderman · Nicole McKinney
CC Milam · Jeff Mondak · Loree Mason O'Neil
Teri Olund · Patricia Osborn Orton · Robert Pottle
Shanda Purcell · Ted Scheu · Thena Smith

The fragrance always remains on the hand that gives the rose.

-Gandhi

To understand the heart and mind of a person,
look not at what he has already achieved,
but at what he aspires to.
-Kahlil Gibran

To My Dear Lord & My Daughters

Thank you for your love and faith in me. It is with great joy that I write this book for you. You have given me the inspiration and steadfastness to create this book about children. Because of you, I have a passion for children and a desire to share with the world how precious they really are and how the love of a child and the Lord will be the most tremendous gift they will ever receive.

I am so very blessed—I have a relationship with the Lord, who has loved me and believed in me all my life, even when I didn't believe in myself. From the beginning He has had such an awesome plan for my life and I am so in love with Him. He gave me the greatest gift imaginable—my incredible daughters!

My dearest daughters, I want you to know that, to me, you are such delightful, loving young ladies, who are growing into such extraordinary, beautiful people. I am so thankful for you both and filled with such gratitude that we have the Lord as head of our home. It's because of God's guidance that we have the wonderful family that we do. We have endured so much this past year and even though we have our ups and downs, the love that exists is unconditional, constant and pure. We share a faith in the Lord that carries us through every day.

There is no greater joy than to know we are walking in the Lord's will for our lives. I am so excited to dedicate this book to the best part of my life—My Lord and My Beloved Daughters.

May you be blessed and may the words within reach out to everyone who reads it and may they see the love poured out upon the pages and realize their greatest gift is having a child to love and a Father to guide.

With all my love—
Momma

Table of Contents

Table of Contents

Table of Contents

From the first
moment I saw you,
I knew
it would be a
Grand Adventure!

♡

CHILDREN

C hildren are the essence of life. We as adults can truly learn what life is all about if we take the time to look at the world through their eyes. By example, they teach us to love one another unconditionally; they see the truth when it's right before our eyes. With enthusiasm, they teach us to share, to believe, to imagine, to trust, to wonder about creation. In quietness, they show us the importance of rest. They remind us without words the necessity of being a person of integrity, keeping a humble spirit and having a forgiving heart, no matter what.

My life was forever changed the moment my own wonderful children were born. As the years have progressed, each day has been a unique journey because of their unconditional love. There have been many other children in my life who I have sweet memories of and as I recall these experiences it brings to my heart, a smile. Children have a way of helping us to become better people just by their innocence and love.

It is my desire, that within the pages of this book, you will come to see children as the marvelous creations of a Father who loves us all. The closest thing to heaven is a child.

Children are the future that we nurture today.

Blessings and Love,
Linda

12

Children are...

AMAZING	Acknowledge them
BLESSED	Treasure them
CHILDLIKE	Play with them
DELICATE	Cherish them
EVERCHANGING	Delight in them
FORGIVING	Thank them
GENEROUS	Share with them
HEAVENLY	Honor them
INNOCENT	Protect them
JOYFUL	Laugh with them
KINDHEARTED	Praise them
LOVEABLE	Love them
MAGNIFICENT	Revere them
NOBLE	Esteem them
OUTSTANDING	Celebrate them
PRECIOUS	Pray with them
QUICK	Run with them
RESPECTFUL	Admire them
SIMPLE	Sit with them
TALENTED	Encourage them
UNIQUE	Respect them
VULNERABLE	Be honest with them
WONDERFUL	Enjoy them
XTRAORDINARY	Appreciate them
YOUNG	Grow with them
ZANY	Be goofy with them

Animals—/an´d m˘l/ any such organism other than a human

My Best Friend

I have a little doggie
He likes to wag his tail
He chases me down the stairs
But I slide down the rail
He is so very funny
When he licks me on the face
It's sticky and it's stinky
But none can take his place.
Just me and my dog...

The Squirrel

Whisky frisky, Hippity hop
Up he goes to the top!
Whirly twirly,
round and round
Down he scampers to the ground.
Furly, curly, what a tail!
Tall as a feather, broad as a sail!
Where's his supper?
In the shell, snap, cracky, out it fell!

PURR-FECT

FRIENDS!

Fish

How I wish,
I were a fish!
My day
would begin
Flapping my fins.
I'd make a commotion
Out in the ocean.
It would be cool
To swim in a sea,
I'd move so free,
With just
one thought,
Don't get caught!

Poodle-Noodle Nonsense

Hi, doodle doodle!
Peter had a poodle
He could bake
and he could stew,
He could play
the fiddle too;
What a clever poodle!
Oh, doodle oodle
doodle!

If I Were a Fish

If I could have a single wish
I'd dearly wish to be a fish
Swimming in the deep blue sea.

Always Be Kind to Animals

Always be kind to animals,
Morning, noon, and night.
For animals have feelings, too,
And furthermore...they bite!

HOOK
LINE
and
SINKER
≈
Swims
Like
A
Fish

15

- Ants in the pants
- Bad to the Bone
- Bee-u-tiful Kid
- Busy as a Beaver
- Cat Nappin'
- Dog Day Afternoon
- Frogs and snakes, oh my
- Happy as a Clam
- Horsin' Around
- Impawsible!
- It's a Dog's Life
- Mad as a Hornet
- Monkey Do
- Monkey See,
- No Dogs Allowed
- No Peeping
- One Fish, Two Fish, Red Fish, Blue Fish
- Party Animal
- Pets R' Us
- Proud as a Peacock
- Puppy Love
- Purr-fect Pals
- Purr-fect Playmate
- Quack and Yak
- Quiet as a Mouse
- Snow Bunny
- Soar Like an Eagle
- Some Bunny Loves You
- Something Squirrely
- The latest Buzz
- Toadally Terrific
- Wart's and all
- Where the Buffalo Roam
- Wild and Wooly
- Wild Thing

Child—A collector of strange and wonderful creatures that they call pets. Guaranteed not to be any trouble and easy to care for.

Arts & Crafts—/ärt/ n. human creativity; expressing oneself

- A Budding Picasso
- A Creative Mess
- A Little Dab'll Do Ya
- A Picasso In The Making
- A Picture Paints A Thousand Words
- A Pigment Of Your Imagination
- A Work Of Heart
- An Artist At Heart
- Art From The Heart
- Artist At Work
- Artist In Training
- Be Bold, Color Outside The Lines
- Caution: Artist At Work
- Chalk It Up To Talent
- Chalk Talk
- Color The World With Love
- Crafty Kid
- Creating a Terrific Masterpiece
- Creativity Runs In The Family
- Cut And Paste
- Doodle Bug
- Drawn With Heart
- Every Child Is An Artist
- Handprints Of Love
- Imagination Station
- It's Color Time
- Just Add Water
- Just Doodling
- Just My Imagination
- Little Master
- Little Picasso
- Look What I Made
- Masterpiece Under Construction
- Mom's Treasured Masterpiece

17

- My Little Picasso
- My Many Colored Days
- My Masterpiece
- One Child's Art Is His Mother's Treasure! -Linda LaTourelle
- Painting Up A Storm
- Strokes Of Genius
- The Imagination Factory
- The Magic Of Markers
- The Magic Paintbrush
- The World Is But A Canvas To Our Imaginations. -Suzanne Moore
- To Imagine Love Is Everything
- Within A Child's Thoughts Exist A Masterpiece
- You Color Me Happy
- You're My Soul's Inspiration

It's Art!

It's on the refrigerator
It's on the wall
It's by the phone
When I make a call.

It's in pencil and crayon
It's in finger paint or pen
Some make me cry
And some make me grin.

What is it you ask
That puts such emotion in my heart?
It is sweet little pieces
Of my little one's art!
-Thena

ALL
THE
COLORS
OF
THE
RAINBOW
IN A
PAINTING
JUST
FOR
YOU

Award—/ǎ wôrd´/ vt. To give as the result of judging, as in a contest; prize for achievement, talent or skill

- Best Boy/Girl
- Best of The Best!
- Brightest Star
- Champion Student
- Fastest Reader
- Good Job
- Great Work!
- Graduate with Honors
- Honor Student
- In Recognition Of
- Made the Grade
- Mr/Miss Dependable
- My Star
- Perfect Attendance

- Science Fair Superstar
- Simply the Best!
- Spelling Bee Winner
- Star Kid!
- Star Student
- Superstar Kid
- The Winner
- Way to Go!
- We Are the Champions
- What A Success!
- Won The Gold!

You're # 1

The Award

FIRST

PLACE

KID

I won this award,
and I'm feeling so proud
that I want to tell everyone,
shout it out loud.
Three cheers for me!
I cannot be ignored.
I worked hard and I won
this terrific award.

-Robert Pottle ©   19

A Child's Award

It is hereby declared and we do acknowledge that you, my child, as a member in good standing, are now and forever more entitled to the following privileges: Sing, dance, smell the flowers, fly kites, act silly, laugh, cry, wiggle and fly, build sandcastles, hop, skip, jump, daydream, run free, run barefoot, count the stars, blow bubbles, forget your troubles, be happy, ask why, give hugs, play with bugs, talk to the animals, pretend, take naps, wonder, wander, play ball, want it all, have pillow fights, sleep tight, take things apart, fall down, build a fort, a tent, or tree house, rock your baby dolls, play house, go on hikes, ride your bike, collect toys, play with girls, play with boys, tell stories, camp out, squeal and shout, skip stones, eat mud cakes, save the world, be a superhero, sing like a superstar, walk in the rain, use your brain, create your own rules, play games, read books, paint, draw, say yes, shout no, make friends, learn, grow, climb, crawl, play in the leaves, run with the wind, build a snowman, swim in a lake, stay innocent, trust God and everyone, smile daily, love freely, seek peace, be joyful, and a million, zillion other little things. These, my child, are the awesome things bestowed upon the young daily. May each day bring blessings and hope that will guide you through your childhood and leave you with memories to treasure forever.

(Feel free to share some or all of this with a child and brighten their day.)

FOREVER YOUNG

Baseball—/bàs´bôl´/ n. a game played with a rawhide covered ball and a bat by two opposing teams of nine players each, on a field with four bases forming a diamond and fans that eat hot dogs and popcorn and shout loud.

- All American Game
- All-Star in Training
- And It's Good!
- Angels in the Outfield
- Are You Game?
- Awards Night
- Baseball Fun
- Baseball is for kids.
- Batter Up
- Better at the Ballpark
- Big Time Rivalry
- Big Win!
- Cheer For the Home Team
- Dig, Dig, Dig
- Double Play
- Faster, Higher, Braver
- Field of Dreams
- Fly Ball
- Foul Ball
- Game Day

- Go (team nickname)
- Go Home
- Go Team!
- Going...Going...Gone
- Grand Slam
- Havin' a Ball
- Hero Worship
- Hey Batter Batter
- Hey Now, You're an All-Star
- Hit a Homer
- Home Team Advantage
- Home Run!
- Hooray for Our Team
- I'm convinced that every boy, in his heart, would rather steal second base than a car
- In a league all your own
- Instant Replay
- Is that your boy?

21

ITS OUTTA HERE!

Putting on the helmet and picking up his bat, he saunters up to the plate, grabs hold tight and swings. "Strike one!" the ump shouts. Nervous as he listens to the crowd, he swings again and misses. Now the crowd is really roaring as he takes his stance toward the pitcher. The pressure is on and the game is on the line. It's all up to him. This could be the winning hit. With sweat clouding his eyes, he holds his breath and with one fierce crack of the bat, the ball soars, up, up, up, out of the park. What a rush as the crowd starts to cheer. In shock, he just stands there. It was the last inning of the season, the game was tied. Suddenly he feels the exhilaration of the moment as he hears his Dad shouting, "Go for it, son! You're a winner!" Coach hollers, "Run Home". As he slides into home plate he hears his teammates chanting "Hero, hero, hero"! Oh, what a moment! Years from now, when he is grown with children of his own, he will remember the cheers, the friends and the fun. And he too, will encourage his children, as they build memories of their own. So cheer him on and help to hit a home run that will last for generations to come.

–Linda LaTourelle

WRITE YOUR CHILD'S STORY!

Baseball

It doesn't take a baseball game
To make you a big star
It only takes a great young man
And that's just what you are
So if you're disappointed
I thought that you should know
You're still an All-star to me
No matter where you go!

-Jennifer Byerly © 2004

- It ain't nothin' till the umpire calls it!
- It's All in the Game
- Let the Games Begin
- Little Babe
- Little Big League
- Lil' Slugger
- Little Slugger
- Major League Fun
- MVP
- No harassing the Ump!
- Oh! What A Night!
- On To Victory
- Our Home Run Hitter
- Outta the Park
- Pitching In
- Play ball
- Playing by the Book

The ball is coming
And coming fast
Yippee! Hooray!
A hit at last!!
Run! Run! Run! RUN!
I think my baseball career
Has finally begun!

-Thena

- Practice makes perfect
- Prime Time Sports
- Rookie of the Year
- Runnnnnn!
- Safe!
- Score
- Season Opener
- Seventh-inning Stretch
- Shut-out
- Stealing Second
- Striiiiiike!
- Step Up to the Plate
- Take Me Out to the Ballgame
- Take State
- Taste of Victory
- The Agony of Defeat
- The Best in the West
- The Last Hit
- The Rookie
- The Underdogs
- Three Strikes, You're Out
- Today's Heroes
- Triple Play
- Undefeated

Play Catch With Me Dad

"Play catch with me-Dad?"
I hope you don't forget-
about the small kid at home
with the baseball and the mitt.
I know that you've been busy
with important things all day-
but it makes me feel so special
when you take some time to play.
Learning how to throw and catch
don't mean that much to me.
It's just being with you
that makes us family.
So even if you are feeling tired
from the day that you just had
Please don't forget to
play catch with me-Dad.
-Tom Krause ©

24

Field of Flowers

Picking flowers for my mommy
Forget the baseball game I am playing
These pretty flowers she would love
I'm sure she won't really mind the bugs
There's pretty yellow powdery ones
Fluffy furry ones to blow
Purple sticky stemmed ones too
I'm sure she would love the blue
They grow a- plenty behind home plate
I'm sure coach won't mind the wait
I will just take them up to mom
She's sitting in the stands yelling "RUN!"
So I hurry up the stands
Place the flowers in her hands
Run back down and pick up the bat
I miss the ball 'cause all I hear
Is mommy sneezing as she cheers!!!
-Teri Olund ©

- ⓘ Unsportsmanlike Conduct
- ⓘ Varsity
- ⓘ Victory Seekers
- ⓘ Way to Go!
- ⓘ We Are the Best
- ⓘ We Are the Champions
- ⓘ Whose kid is that?
- ⓘ Winning with Style
- ⓘ Wow!
- ⓘ You're Outta here!

AND THE BALL FLIES UP, AND THE BALL COMES DOWN, HE SWINGS HIS BAT ALL THE WAY AROUND

25

Basketball—/bas'kit-bôl/ a game played by two teams five players each, in a zoned floor area points are scored by tossing a ball through a basket

- Above the Rim
- Around the Rim
- Baskets of Fun
- B-Ball
- Bubba Luvs B-Ball!
- Crashing the Boards
- Dishin' & Swishin'
- Dribble & Score
- Foul
- Free Throw
- Hang Time
- Hittin' the Shot
- Hoop Dreams
- Hoop It Up
- Hoops, Anyone?
- H-O-R-S-E
- Hot Shots
- In the Air Tonight
- In the Paint
- In the Zone
- In Your Face
- Intentional Foul
- Jam Session
- Jump Shot
- Last Second Shot
- Nothin' But Net
- Open Shot
- Overtime
- Shootin' Hoops
- Slam Dunk
- Space Jam
- Swish!
- Swoosh!
- Take It To The Hoop
- The Hoopster
- Time Out
- Whoop It Up
- Zero Gravity

I LOVE BASKETBALL

Basketball

Dribble, dribble, shoot, miss.
I'm gonna try again.
Dribble, dribble, shoot, miss.
I gotta score to win.
Dribble, dribble, blocked shot.
I'm knocked onto the ground.
Dribble, dribble, blocked shot.
The clock is counting down.
Dribble, dribble, shoot, score!
I think we're gonna win.
-Robert Pottle ©

- ⊕ Shoot for 2
- ⊕ Up, Over and In
- ⊕ 3 Point Line
- ⊕ Whoosh!
- ⊕ No Net
- ⊕ Backboard Bounce
- ⊕ D-E-F-E-N-S-E
- ⊕ Mopping the floor
- ⊕ Guard your Man
- ⊕ Bring it down the floor
- ⊕ Double Dribble
- ⊕ Foul Shots

The basketball court is my favorite place.

I love to make a difficult shot
Even with guards right in my face.
Intruding on my spot!
I love to dribble right past the ones
Who don't want me to succeed
And I love the chance to show
My knowledge, skill and speed

27

Bath Time— /bäth/ *n.* The act of soaking or cleansing the body, in water or steam; a time for splashing and playing; Mother's punishment for children; it's rubber ducky time

Rub-a-
dub-dub
_____ kids
in the tub
splishing and
splashing
with glee.
Soap on
the floor
Dirt on
the towels
And the
water is all
over me.

I Love My Bath

I love my bath and playtime,
I splash the whole time there.
I get my Mom and Dad all wet,
But they don't seem to care.
I kick and squirm, squeal, and splash,
It's fun to make them laugh,
So I don't cry or fuss one bit,
When they tell me... time for bath!
My duck swims gently by me,
The bubbles itch my nose,
My mom and dad say see
We wash ten tiny toes!
I love to kick, squirm and splash,
It makes a mess, I know,
But look at all the fun we have,
All seven days in a row!
-Donna Linderman ©

- All Wet
- Bath and Body Works
- Bath Time
- Bath Time is Splash Time
- Bubble Bath Time
- Bubble Boy/Girl
- Bubble Buddies

- Bubble Time
- Bubble, Bubble Whose Got the Bubble?
- But Mom... It's Not Saturday yet!
- Clean as a Whistle
- Cowboy's don't take baths, we just dust off

28

- Bubble Bash
- Bubble's Galore
- Clean, Clean, Clean
- Conserve water - Bathe with a friend
- Country baths...used water 5 cents, fresh water 10 cents
- Don't wash my hair
- Don't throw the baby out with the bath water.
- Even princesses have to take a bath sometimes
- Getting Wet
- Got Bubbles?
- Got Dirt?
- Hair So Fresh
- I Like Dirt
- In the tub NOW!
- Kid Overboard
- Lifeguard Needed—Call Mom
- May your day bubble over with fun
- Me and my ducky
- Mermaid on Duty
- Rub a dub dub, fun in the tub
- Rubber Ducky—I Love You
- Scrub, Scrub, Scrub
- Slippin' and a Slidin'
- Smells so sweet
- Squeaky Clean
- Soap Gets in My Eyes
- Tugboat Captain
- Will you please sit down

In the Bath

How do the fishes know how to steer
When they're swimming around in the sea?
Why couldn't I have a nice fish here
To swim in the bath with me?
Why do my feet go up, do you s'pose,
While my head goes bobbling about?
Why don't I go where the water goes
When the stopper is taken out?

Beach– sand, sun and surf; a place for fun and relaxation; swimming, fish, seaweed; waves and seashells; family vacation

Do I Like To Be Beside The Seaside?

We went off to the seaside
For a walk along the beach
It's only fifteen miles away
So it's not too far to reach
And when we walked upon the shore
There, much to our dismay
It wasn't just sand, sea and shells
But rubbish all the way
There was old tin cans and chip bags
Bottles by the stack
And some things that Mum and Dad said
Would have stopped me in my tracks!!
Old fishing line washed up at night
Oil flushed out from boats
Two pallets and some milk crates
A tattered Army coat
We never seem to cherish
The simple things we've got
And the people who are dumping this
Do you think they care a jot?
So please be careful with our world
Or soon the day will dawn
That when our children's children play
The good stuff will be gone
-Rob Erskine ©

Bedtime — /bed-tim/ n. one's usual time for going to bed; a time avoided by children;

THE CASTLES OF DROWSY TOWN

Away in the castles of drowsy town,
The lights are twinkling high,
The fays are pulling the curtains down,
And the winds are wandering by.
The Giant Night in his robe of dusk,
Is coming over the hills,
Bringing an odor of rose and musk,
And a ripple of distant rills
This black man is as high as the sky,
And his eyes shoot starry gleams,
And his pockets are ready to burst, well nigh,
With bundles of children's dreams.

He moves with a soft, mysterious tread,
Through the scented dusk and damp,
And he carries the moon upon his head,
As a miner carries a lamp.
And straight for my little ones cometh he
When twilight is dropping down,
And bears them swiftly away from me
To the borders of Drowsy Town.
Oh the gates are open on ev'ry side,
And the children are trooping in.
With dainty cap strings cunningly tied,
Right under each dimpled chin.
-Carrie Shaw Rice

SWEET DREAMS

Up All Night

Yes it's past my bedtime
I'm not going to sleep tonight
I'm staying up 'til morning
Because Daddy says it's all right
I get to stay in my bedroom
No one's going to look in on me
The light is out which makes it fun
To imagine instead of to see
Tomorrow I'll tell all my friends
About the special time I had
They'll all wish they lived with me
And with my wonderful Dad
No kid's ever been up this late
It's so quiet and dark outside
All my toys are in bed with me
We're waiting for the sun to rise
It must be eighteen o'clock
I'm not...going...trr...swepp...tu...nonnnny
I'm...mmm...Hmm? What?
Oh—good morning, Mommy!
-Jeff Mondak ©

Sleepy Harry

"I do not like to go to bed!"
Said sleepy little Harry
"Go, naughty Betty, go away,
I will not come at all, I say!"
Oh, silly child! What is he saying
As if he could be always playing!
Then, Betty, you must come and carry
This very foolish little Harry.
-unknown

Bedtime

Goodnight daylight
And having fun,
Goodnight toys,
The day is done.
Goodnight friends,
And sister and brother,
Goodnight dog
And father and mother.
Goodnight God
And everyone
Time for sleep
Bedtime's come.

-Linda LaTourelle

- ☺ Beautiful Dreamer
- ☺ Bedtime for Bonzo
- ☺ Caught Napping
- ☺ Counting Sheep
- ☺ Down for the Count
- ☺ Dream Sweet Dreams
- ☺ Dream Time
- ☺ Dreamland Express
- ☺ Finish the Chapter
- ☺ Golden Slumbers

Sweet Son of Mine

Sweet son of mine
my heart, my pride
So tired you seem
Rest now, dream
As the sun rises,
a new day for you
Happiness awaits
in the sweet morning dew.

-Teri Olund ©

- Good night Sweetheart
- Good night, sleep tight, don't let the bed bugs bite
- Goodnight Sweetie
- Here comes the night
- Hit the Sack
- I don't want to sleep
- I'm Thirsty
- I want water
- Life is But a Dream
- Mr. Sandman
- Nightie, Night
- Night-light Please
- No More Water
- One More Page?
- Only in My Dreams
- Peace and Quiet
- Saturday Sleep-in
- Say your Prayers
- Sleep Tight
- Sleeping Beauty
- Sleepovers
- Sleepy Head
- Sleepy time Gal/Guy
- Slumber Party
- Snoozin'
- Snug as a Bug in a Rug
- Strangers in the night
- Sweet Dreams
- Things that Go Bump in the Night
- Time for a Nap!
- Time for Bed, Sleepy Head
- Too beat to sleep
- Too Late for Reading
- Turn off the Light
- Walking after midnight
- What A Dream!
- When I Dream
- When in doubt, take a nap
- While You Were Sleeping
- Who Needs Some Sleep?
- Zonked out
- Zzzzzz

SLEEPY

HEAD

Brotherly Warning

Brother says the bugs come out
When it's time for bed
They hide beneath my pillow
Where I lay down my head
He says they crawl when I'm asleep
Exploring everything
Turns out the crumblies in my eyes
Are actually beetle wings!
He tells me that they like to peer
Up inside my nose
He says I'd better cover up
So they won't bite my toes
He also says to close my mouth
So now I've taped it shut
In case one tries to crawl inside
And exit out my gut
I've also placed this old cork top
Inside my naval hole
So I don't have to wake and find
I have a tummy full!
I'm just so very thankful
That my brother cares for me
If he hadn't warned me
Then imagine where I'd be!
-Jennifer Byerly © 2004

SLEEP GETS IN MY EYES

Monsters under the bed
Monsters in the closet
Sometimes it is scary
Sometimes it is fun
But oh how I am happy
When I see the morning sun
Cause then the monsters are gone

Being A Kid—The time when you have fun; your parents yell; laughter is abundant and you can't wait for tomorrow; you never want to grow up, but can't wait until you do

Just a Boy	Simply a Girl
Adventurous	Adorable
Belong	Bubbly
Catastrophic	Chatty
Daring	Divine
Eager	Extraordinary
Fearless	Fashionable
Growing	Gentle
Handsome	Hormonal
Inventive	Intuitive
Jet-propelled	Jazzy
Knights	Kindred
Loud	Lovely
Monsters	Matronly
Negotiator	Nurturing
Orangutan	Observant
Presidential	Precious
Quick	Quintessential
Remarkable	Rambunctious
Strong	Savvy
Thinker	Tough
Unique	Ultra-special
Victorious	Vibrant
Whiz	Wonderful
Xtraspecial	Xhilarating
Yang	Yin
Zooby Do	Zensational

What's a Kid to Do?

Girls or Boys
Play with Toys
Walks along
Singing a Song
Always asks why
Ready to try
Riding a Bike
Go for a Hike
Paints and Colors
Loves you like no others
Collects frogs
Kisses Dogs
Jumps and shouts
Laughs and pouts
Full of wonder
Scared of thunder
Crawls on your lap
To take a short nap
Daydreams
Noisy screams
Climbing Trees
Wild and free
Hard to wait
Often late
Ever growing
Always knowing
Hard to scold
Easy to hold
Everything Love
A Gift from Above

Think of all the things your child does in a day, in a month, over the course of a year. Take the time to sit back, relax and reflect upon the wonder of your child. He or she is truly a miracle growing bigger and wiser, day by day. The things children say and do, think and learn are absolutely amazing sometimes. It is all the little things that happen day to day that help grow them into the unique and wonderful people they are. The things they see us, as parents, do and say will have a profound impact upon their lives. May you take the time to ponder the memories. And as you do, create a list about what makes your child special, then add these reflections to your scrapbooks. These little details will be a treasure chest of memories that can be Shared for generations to come. What a blessing!

Best Friends—/best/ adj. of the most excellent sort; above all others in worth or ability /frend/ n. a person whom one knows well and is fond of; someone to share your laughter and your tears with

My Childhood Friend

When I was a child I had a horse
He had a painted mane.
He had rockers underneath
And his saddle was painted green.
I guess I rode that rocking horse
At least a million miles
From the coast of California
To the South Pacific Isles.
I wore the paint off of him
I wore his rockers thin.
I rode him morn and evening
'Cause he was my best friend.
When I was sad he cried with me
When happy, he laughed too.
I know I just imagined it
But then it all seemed true.
Each child should have a rocking horse
To be a childhood friend
So he could ride a million miles
And then ride home again.
-Patricia Osborn Orton ©

- 2 Peas in a Pod
- A Friend Like You
- Best Friends Forever
- Bestest Buddies
- Cooties
- Forever Friends
- Friends Forever
- Friends in Sunshine and in Shade
- Friends Through Thick and Thin
- Friends 'Till the End
- Friendship in Bloom
- Girlfriends forever
- Girl's Club
- Girl's World
- Gossip Gossip Gossip
- Great minds think alike
- I'd Give You the Shirt Off of My Back
- Just the Two of Us
- Lean on Me
- Love One Another
- Me and My Shadow
- My Circle of Friends,
- No Boys Allowed
- No Girls Allowed
- Sidekicks
- The Best of Friends, The Best of Times
- The Buddy System
- Three's Company
- Treasured Friend
- True blue, love you
- Two of a Kind
- Two's Company
- Yakity-Yak
- You and Me Against the World
- You and Me, Buds Forever
- You Gotta Have Friends!
- You Make Me Smile

4-EVER FRIENDS

Best friends,
me and you
Everyday just us two
Playing and singing
Laughing and dreaming
Sharing together
Loving forever
-Linda LaTourelle

39

Bicycles—/bī'si k'l/ n. a vehicle consisting of a metal frame on two wheels, one behind the other, and equipped with handle bars, a saddle-like seat, and usually foot pedals

My Radio Flyer

It's a rocket ship
For a ride to Mars
It's a racing machine
It's the fastest of cars...

It's a stallion
only ridden by medieval knights
It's a time machine
Or a capsule for space flights.

It can do anything
That I want it to do
It just looks like
A Radio Flyer to you...
-Thena Smith ©

For a child, riding a bike is kind of like life. A child needs to know that you are there for support and encouragement. To ride smoothly they need a guiding hand and a soft shoulder when they fall down, a loving heart to comfort the pain ,kind words and cheers of praise when they accomplish each step and even when the training wheels are off, they need to know you're always there

Big Kid Now—/big/ adj impressively /kid/ n. child or young person; a person of small stature; with a big heart and wisdom beyond their years.

I'm Growing

Teacher measured us today
And I'm getting really tall
I think that of all the feet in class
Mine are the biggest of them all!
My hands are growing bigger
And can hold so much more stuff
Over all, I'd say I'm perfect
Just exactly big enough!

-Thena Smith ©

I'm the biggest in my class. Does that mean for sure I'll pass?

My Super Hero

Close to your heart you held him tight
A bundle of pure joy and delight
Now within arms reach
You struggle to keep him
Morning, noon and night.
No longer is he your baby
Or toddler even still
He holds the world in his hand,
His imagination overfilled.
A ball of pure excitement
Enough energy to explode
A stream of endless questions
With answers you'll never know.
What is in store, one never knows
For this compact little man
Is constantly filled with wonder,
Something by himself or brand new
He is a super hero through and through.

-Shanda Purcell © 2005

41

Big Wild World—/big/ n. of great size/ wild/adj. living or growing in its natural state /würld/ n. the planet earth

Children Thank God

ALL
Creatures
Great
And
Small
GOD
Made
Them
One
And
All

Children thank God for these great trees,
That fan in the land with every breeze;
Whose drooping branches form cool bowers,
Where you can spend the summer hours
For these thank God.
For fragrant sweets of blossoms bright,
Whose beauty gives you such delight;
For the soft grass beneath your feet,
For new mown hay, and clover sweet,
For all thank God.
The very cows that lie and doze
Beneath the trees in glad repose;
The birds that in their branches sing,
And make the air with music ring,
All these thank God.
Oh, thank God for the radiant sky,
Whose varying beauty charms the eye,
Now gray and dark, now blue and bright,
Unfailing source of pure delight,
For this thank God.
He gives the life to every thing,
To beasts that roar,
and birds that sing,
But thought and speech
he gave to men,
While beasts are dumb,
O children, then,
For this thank God!
-The Rhyming Story Book

Big Yellow School Bus—

n. of great size /yel'ò/ of the color gold or ripe lemons /skòòl/ a place for teaching; bus/ n. large coach to carry kids

The Bus

Sixty kids and one adult,
you gotta love those odds.
The perfect place for pulling pranks
and throwing paper wads.
Hank is standing on his head.
Billy's playing ball.
Peter wet his pants again.
Tasha pushes Paul.
Steven steals. Kevin cries.
Millicent is missing.
Katie punched her cousin Keith.
Ben and Jen are kissing.
Me, I'm taking lots of notes
on public transportation.
I think the bus provides me
With the finest education.
-Robert Pottle ©

HONK!

- ⑩ Bus Stop
- ⑩ Big Yellow Taxi
- ⑩ Magic School Bus
- ⑩ I Love My Bus
- ⑩ Riding the Bus
- ⑩ The Wheels on
  the Bus Go
  Round and Round
- ⑩ The Bus Stops Here
- ⑩ Bus Drivers Rule
- ⑩ Bus Drivers are
  big wheels

DOWN AT THE BUS STOP

Down at the bus stop,
early in the morning,
little children dressed up
warm as can be.

Takes a half an hour
just to get 'em bundled.
Oh no! One yells,
"Have to pee!"

-Robert Pottle ©

Birthdays—/bùrth-dà/ n. the day of a person's birth; a time to celebrate your special day; it's your day

- ☆ A pinch to grow an inch
- ☆ Birthday Bash
- ☆ Birthday Bonanza
- ☆ For me?
- ☆ Happy Birthday to You
- ☆ I wish for...
- ☆ Isn't it fun ?
- ☆ My big day!
- ☆ One to grow on!
- ☆ Birthday Boy/Girl

FELIZ CUMPLEAÑOS

Spanish: Happy birthday to you

Happy Birthday

Chocolate ice cream up my nose.
Frosting ear to ear.
Feeding candles to the cat.
Party time is here.

Funny hats on all the pets.
Soda on the floor.
Although I'm turning eight today,
I'm acting like I'm four.

-Robert Pottle ©

ONE

- ♡ One year in a million
- ♡ Fun to be One
- ♡ I'm One-derful
- ♡ The Wonder of One

TWO

- ♡ Totally Two
- ♡ Two-rific
- ♡ Look who's 2
- ♡ I'm 2—so much to do

THREE

- ♡ Look at me now I'm 3
- ♡ Three big candles
- ♡ Thrilling Threes

FOUR

- ♡ 4 You are Fabulous
- ♡ Fantastic Four
- ♡ 4 Years Big
- ♡ More with four

FIVE

- ♡ Just Look Who's Five
- ♡ I've arrived—I'm 5

SIX

- ♡ Turning Six—good trick
- ♡ Silly Sixes

SEVEN

- ♡ Simply Seven
- ♡ Seven is Heaven

EIGHT

- ♡ Eight is Great
- ♡ 8 and truly great

NINE

- ♡ Nine is fine
- ♡ Now I'm 9—the world is mine

The Pinata

The pinata is hung in the air
With only moments to spare
Before the kids are blindfolded
And led into the room
To a pinata which is
Unaware of its doom.
It stays happily aloft
Until the hits start to come
And down it comes
With treats for everyone!

-Thena

Spanish Party Words

Celebre
Celebrate

Golpee el pinta
hit the pinta

Es un partido
It's a party

Ten

I think there is a magic age,
And that it might have been,
When you felt you were grown up,
Though you were only ten.
Cane pole held tightly in your hand,
You headed for the creek,
Barefoot with faded overalls,
Straw hat to shade your cheek.
Part of the fun was getting there,
While walking down the path,
Time suspended hung in space,
No need to hurry back.
Seated on the old wood dock,
A can of worms close by,
Overhead white fluffy clouds,
Adorned a bright blue sky.
But still the best was yet to come,
When you stretched out to rest,
Old Rover was your pillow,
As the sun moved toward the west.
And when long shadows told you,
Time to head home again,
That had to be the best of times,
When you were only ten.
-Loree Mason O'Neil ©

CELEBRATING YOU!

Happy Birthday

- ♡ Birthday's R' Us
- ♡ Bring on the presents
- ♡ Gifts and cake and ice cream, oh my!
- ♡ Happy Birthday to Me
- ♡ It's a cele-birthday
- ♡ It's great - I'm 8
- ♡ It's My Birthday
- ♡ It's My Party
- ♡ Just what I've always wanted
- ♡ Let's All Sing
- ♡ Let's Party
- ♡ Let Them Eat Cake
- ♡ Make a Wish
- ♡ M'm! m'm? Good
- ♡ My Wishes Came True
- ♡ Party Girl
- ♡ Present Time
- ♡ Ready, Set, Blow
- ♡ So many candles!
- ♡ Surprise!
- ♡ That Takes the Cake
- ♡ They grow up so fast
- ♡ Time for Cake
- ♡ Today Is Your Day
- ♡ Too Much Cake
- ♡ Under Wraps
- ♡ We need more candles
- ♡ We're having a party and you're the present
- ♡ We're havin' some fun now
- ♡ What a celebration!
- ♡ What a party!
- ♡ Wrapped With Love
- ♡ You Take the Cake
- ♡ You're how old?
- ♡ You're not getting older, you're getting better

MAKE A WISH

Blue Jeans—/blōō jēnz/ Pants usually made of blue denim; rugged, rough and tumble clothes for kids; daily wear for kids; all tattered and torn makes them a favorite

Little Boy in Denim

Little Boy in Denim
What do your pockets hold
Is there a wiggly worm inside
Or something you can fold?

I see your pockets bulging
And I hesitate to give you a hug
Lest in my show of affection
I would swish a frog or bug!

I love the way your eyes light up
As you play the whole day through
My dear little boy in denim...
It looks so wonderful on you!!

-Thena Smith

- Angel in Blue Jeans
- Baby's Got Her Blue Jeans On
- Bell Bottoms
- Blue Jean Baby
- Blue Jean Jammin'
- Denim Days
- Fashionably Torn
- Forever in My Jeans
- Frayed and Frazzled
- Mr. Blue Jean
- My Old Blue Jeans
- Overall Cute
- Ragged Edge
- Riveting Details
- Rough and Tumble
- Saggy, Baggy Baby
- Stiff and Stinky

48

Body—/bŏdē/ head, shoulders, knees and toes and everything in between; a human, a kid; a child in all his glory; ever-growing

- A head start
- A heart of gold
- A kick in the pants
- Above my head
- Absence makes the heart grow fonder
- Adam's apple
- Air-head
- All ears
- All thumbs
- All talk—no action
- All thumbs
- An ear for music
- Arm in arm
- As cute as a bug's ear
- As mad as a hornet
- Baby Blues
- Bad hair day
- Bare bottoms
- Bat your baby blues
- Break a leg
- Brothers in arms
- Button your lip
- Cat got your tongue?
- Change of heart
- Cold hands warm heart
- Cry your heart out
- Dancing cheek to cheek
- Down in the mouth
- Elbow room
- Eye-catching
- Eye to eye
- Eyes in the back of your head
- Fight tooth and nail
- Finger-lickin' good
- Follow your nose
- Foot in mouth
- Footloose and fancy free
- From the bottom of my heart
- Grin from ear to ear
- Grit your teeth
- Hair-raising

- Hand in hand
- Hand me downs
- Hand-picked
- Have a heart
- Head first
- Head in the clouds
- Head in the sand
- Head over heels in love
- Heart to heart
- Head to head
- Heads up
- Heart warming
- Heartbreak Hotel
- Here's mud in your eye
- High five
- Hit the nail on the head
- Home is where the heart is
- In my heart of hearts
- Keep your chin up
- Keep your eye on the ball
- Knuckle down
- Laugh your head off
- Lend a helping hand
- Lend an ear
- Let your hair hang down
- Look, Ma, no cavities!

- Melts in your hands, not in your mouth
- Mouth watering
- Neck and neck
- Open wide
- Open your heart
- Out of hand
- Out on a limb
- Pull your hair out
- Put your foot down
- Ringing in your ears
- Shake a leg
- Sink your teeth into it
- Sleepyhead
- Stiff upper lip
- The sparkle in your eye
- Twinkling of an Eye
- Tongue in cheek
- Tongue-tied
- Too big for his boots
- Twisted around your little finger
- Young at heart
- Your best foot forward
- Your eyes are bigger than your stomach

Boo-Boos—/bōō-bōō/ abrasion, black eye, black-and-blue mark; fall down and get hurt; injury; owie; something Mommy kisses and makes better

Kiss and Make It Well

I sit at my window and sew and dream,
While my little boy at play
Bewilders my thoughts from hem and seam
As he frolics the live-long day;
But time and again he comes to me
With a sorrowful tale to tell,
And mother must look at the scratch or bump,
Then kiss it and make it well.

So I kiss his head, and his knee, and his arm,
And the dear little grimy hand;
And who can fathom the magic charm,
And who can understand?
For I even kiss when he bites his tongue,
And love works its mystic spell,
For there's never a cut, nor a scratch, nor a bump,
But mother can kiss it well

'Tis a foolish whim, do you say? Ah, yes!
But the foolish things of earth
Have taught the wise, since a little child
In Bethlehem had his birth.
And we know that many an older hear—
We know, but we do not tell—
Will never be free from its bitter smart
'Til kisses have made it well.

Mommy—Kiss it and make it better!

Boogers—/bŭgrs/ excess nose goo; a curious treat for little fingers; a no-no; one way to get Mom's attention when trying to choose one; can cause sticky fingers; a natural inclination for children

Mum's Been Zapped By A Boogie

As I was walking down the road
I gave a mighty sneeze
Then the biggest boogie I have seen
Shot off on the breeze
It skipped along the pavement
And bounced back off a wall
We have to catch it very soon
Or it will slime us all
It hurled back towards me
I just had time to duck
Then it landed in my Mother's hair
I guess that was bad luck
But not for me, you understand
I grin with silent glee
As Mum's been zapped by a boogie
While I got off scott free

-Rob Erskine ©

Hey Mr. Boogie Man

You can't scare me!
I'm not afraid of the dark
As you can plainly see!
But I turn on the light
So that when darkness comes
You don't sneak in the house
And scare my MOM!

-Thena

Books ARE Fun—Travel the world, find a best friend, adventures and stories

A Book

There is no frigate like a book
To take us far away,
Nor any show horse like a page
Of prancing poetry.
This journey may the poorest take
Without the fear of tolls;
How frugal is the chariot
That carries human souls!
-Emily Dickinson

There is more treasure in books than in all the pirate's loot on Treasure Island.
-Walt Disney

The Alphabet

Long is the Alphabet
In my blue reading book:
There is each letter set,
With its peculiar look—
Some seeming fat and glad,
Others a little sad.
Some seeming very wise,
Some with a roguish look,
Making all kinds of eyes
In my blue reading book!
While a few seem to say,
"Shall you know us to-day?"
-Maud Keary

TODAY A READER, TOMORROW A LEADER

The Gift of a Book

The gift of a book is a present
That keeps giving each time that you read
Because with a book comes potential
Of ideas that begin with its seed
And the hours we spend with our children
Cuddled up on our laps with a book
Is time well spent on their future
And time well spent that you took!
-Jennifer Byerly © 2004

Around the world in 200 pages

- Adventure is just a page away
- Books are the bees which carry the quickening pollen from one to another's mind. -James Russell Lowell
- Everywhere I have sought rest and not found it, except sitting in a corner by myself with a little book. -Thomas Kempis
- Libraries have become my candy store. -Juliana Kimball
- Love to Read
- Reading Rocks!
- So Many Books, So Little Time
- Story Time

**THE MORE THAT YOU READ,
THE MORE THINGS YOU WILL KNOW.
THE MORE THAT YOU LEARN,
THE MORE PLACES YOU'LL GO.
-DR. SEUSS**

Boys—TWO SMALL ARMS TO HOLD YOU TIGHT, TWO SMALL FEET TO RUN, TWO SMALL EYES FULL OF LOVE FOR YOU, ONE SMALL SON.

- 100% Boy
- All American Boy
- Backyard Boy
- Boy's are a constant SON-shine!
- Boys are God's way of telling you that your house is too neat!
- Boys are like bank accounts....without much money...they don't generate much interest!
- Boys Boys Boys
- Boys are beautiful
- Boys are like dogs, if we don't take them in they run wild and are a menace to society.
- Boys are like parking spaces...all the good ones are taken.
- Boy Meets World
- I love boys, every girl should own one.
- It's a girl's world...boys just live in it!

Boys are like stars, there are millions of them— but only one can make your dreams come true!

Brothers' Day

Let's all celebrate Brother's Day,
some dreary night,
in early May.
We'll whoop and cheer-- oh, yes, we won't.
A day for brothers, and all they don't.
We'll give them gifts-- the best we couldn't.
Sing them songs-- the ones we shouldn't.
Sprinkle ants between their sheets;
bake them spinach cake with beets.
Slip some worms inside their snacks;
slap a sign across their backs.
Knot the laces
of each shoe;
squeeze in
globs of super glue.
Order extra
vaccinations;
send them all
on long vacations.
So, Hip! Hip! Hooray for Brothers Day!
I'll cheer until I'm blue!
Hey, wait...
I just remembered...
I'm a brother too!
-Ted Scheu ©

MY BROTHER AND ME
FRIENDS WE BE

A boy, before he really grows up,
is pretty much like a wild animal.

One of the best things in the world
is to be a boy; it requires no experience,
but needs some practice to be a good one.

-Charles Dudley Warner

Boys are found simply everywhere—
on top of, underneath, inside of, climbing on,
swinging from, running around or jumping to.

-Alan Marshall Beck

Today he's doing nothing—
Nothing but skipping, playing and running around.

God made little boys for fun, for rough and tumble times of play; he made their little legs to run and race and scamper through the day. He made them strong for climbing trees, He suited them for horns and drums, and filled them full of revelries so they could be their father's chums.

—Edgar Guest

Being a boy is...
catching frogs,
hugging dogs,
eating dirt, often hurt
Running in the sun
Simply having fun
Climbing a tree
Time just to be
Simply who God made him!

Bright and happy little face,
Movements quick of childish grace;
Large and speaking eyes of blue,
Silken hair of golden hue.

- Boy, Oh Boy!
- BOYS
- Boys and their toys
- Boys just want to have fun
- Boys only!
- Boys Only! No Girls Allowed!
- Boys will be boys
- Boys-n-Toys
- Boys'R'us
- Cowabunga Dude

The Boy Who Never Told a Lie

Once there was a little boy,
With curly hair and pleasant eye—
A boy who always told the truth,
And never, never told a lie.
And when he trotted off to school
The children all about would cry
There goes the curly-headed boy,
The boy who never told a lie!
And everybody loved him so,
Because he always told the truth;
But every day as he grew up
'Twas said, 'There goes the honest youth!
And when the people that stood near
Would turn to ask the reason why,
The answer would be always this—
'Because he never told a lie.'
-R Worthington 1880

Little Boys

Little boys are special
Little boys are sweet
Little boys have everything
That make life a treat.

They are bundles of energy
With feet swift and sure
Full of mischief
That is delightful and pure.

Little boys are sunshine
On a cloudy day
And having a little boy to love
Is wonderful in every way!

-Thena

- ☺ Daddy is my hero
- ☺ Daddy's little boy
- ☺ Daddy's/Mommy's little boy
- ☺ First set of wheels
- ☺ Genuine Boy
- ☺ I'm a big boy now
- ☺ I wanna be just like Daddy
- ☺ Just me and my Pa'
- ☺ Just one of the boys
- ☺ When you can't do anything else with a boy, you can make him wash his hands

TO

BE

A

BOY

Being a boy is such great fun
Splashing in the creek,
Or just soaking up sun,
Muddy, grubby hands
Or dirty, stinky feet
Exploring the world
Right here on my street
Reading adventures in wonderful books,
Playing cowboys or cops and crooks;
I dream and I wonder
Such amazing things
Like where God sleeps
Or why birds sing
I'm never bored or lonely
There's always so much to do
I can search for hidden treasure
Or climb a tree or two
My daddy is my hero
My mommy is my friend
They love that I'm still little
And wish it wouldn't end.
But soon the years will fly
And quickly I will grow
One day I'll have my own boy
And then true love I'll know
-Linda LaTourelle © 2004

BLUE
RIBBON
CHAMP!

A Boy
Will...

jump in puddles,
run in the sun,
dance in the rain,
explore the world
play with frogs,
ride his bike,
pick up snails,
pull puppy dog tails,
eat mud pies,
get dirty,
steal your heart...
AND
be forever yours!

HE'S JUST A BOY...
BUT HE'S MY BOY!

What a Boy!

- I'm the mother of boys
- It's a boy's life
- I've been working on the railroad
- Just Daddy & Me
- Just like Dad
- Like father, like son
- Little Blue Boy
- Little Man
- Little slugger
- Men At Work
- Mommy's little "Son" flower
- Mud puddles
- My Three Sons
- No girls allowed!!!
- Oh Boy!
- Oh Brother!
- Our Little Man
- Peculiarly sweet
- Praise the High One for giving me boys
- Snips and snails and puppy dog tails
- So Handsome
- Country Boy
- The Boy from New York City
- The Son also rises
- Tool Time
- Torn blue jeans, toads, whistles and worms. The furred and feathered and whatever squirms.
- Tough as Nails
- What are little boys made of?
- Wonder Boy
- You are my "Son" shine

Climbing a tree, my buddy and me—watching the clouds go by
Buildin' a fort
No girls allowed
Talking and dreaming
Tired, but happy
Playing together
This is the life
Of a boy

A boy is...
Trust with dirt on its face,
Beauty with a cut on its finger,
Wisdom with bubblegum in its hair,
and the Hope of the future
with a frog in its pocket.
                    -unknown

MY BOY

Blue jeans and trucks,
Scrapes on his knees,
Running in the dirt
Trucks and toys
Making loud noise
Stomping bugs
Giving big hugs
Oh, what a joy
That's my boy!
        -Linda LaTourelle

Dirty face
And sticky hands
Toys out of place
Ain't love grand

Animals and bugs
Snakes and frogs
Big bear hugs
And smelly dogs

He's such a sweet boy
From his head to his toes
Bringing such joy
Wherever he goes

If he will test your patience beyond your last nerve...
If he can be so wild and throw you many a curve
If he dreams of new adventures, playing 'til day is done
If he strives to do his best until that game he's won
If he will not take a bath and refuses to do his math
If he tugs at your heart and charms you with laughter
If he fills all your days with memories long after
It will be in these moments of absolute joy
That you will quickly discover he's a special little boy!
And then when he lovingly exclaims "You're the best!"
Your life will then forever, be so wonderfully blessed.
                    -Linda LaTourelle © 2004

62

Braces On

- A Smile to Beguile
- Brace Yourself
- Brace Face
- Head Gear
- I'd Rather Be Smiling
- Metal Mouth
- Million Dollar Smiles Take Awhile
- No Pain No Gain
- Train Tracks

Brace Yourself

"Brace yourself," Momma said
But it was the orthodontist
That did the bracing instead
When he did strange things
To the teeth in my head!

"Be prepared," my mom told me.
"Some strange things you are
going to see!"
And sure enough there was
measuring and molding
And when headgear wasn't
worn, a bit of scolding!

I've been pushed and prodded
and measured and seen
By orthodontists and dentists
and those in between.
And all I can do is quietly
pray for the day
When all of this metal and
plastic will go away!

-Thena

The Challenge

For ten years I was able
To eat, drink and chew
Anything I wanted
Just like you.

Now I am getting braces
That will cover my teeth
And will curb my eating
And affect my speech!

I will accept the challenge
And do the best I can
But exactly what the purpose is
I'm not sure I understand!

-Thena

Million dollar SMILE

Braces Off

- Construction is done and the view is beautiful
- Free at Last
- Metal Free
- No more pain
- See my 'New' Smile
- I have pearls where metal used to be
- From Metal to Marvelous
- My pearly whites are pearly smooth

SMOOTH

AND

SLIPPERY

Look at you!
It's been a while
But the braces are off
Of your million dollar smile!
-Thena

Un-Braced

How much time has it been
How many months have passed
Happily now my braces are off
And I'm free at last!
Look out chocolate
Look out gum
Look out Hot Tamales
Here I come!!!
-Thena

No More Braces

On my face
No more fear
Of clumsy headgear
No more unsightly
Braces gleaming brightly
No more orthodontists tightening
Braces 'til it's frightening
We are FREE
My beautiful teeth and me!
-Thena

Broken bones—owie, help, oh, my aching
bones. Wearing crutches and getting attention

I broke my little toe
There's nothing they can do
Except to wait for it to heal
So I can wear a shoe!
It really hurts a lot
Although it's very small
Sometimes the smallest owies
Are the biggest ones of all!
-Jennifer Byerly © 2004

Hunter's Arm

Hunter has a broken arm
He broke it yesterday
It happened while he was at school
As dodge ball he did play!
So many x-rays were taken
That poor Hunter was quite shaken
It seems that he has no way of knowing
That in the dark he won't be glowing.
But radioactive or not
You should see the cast he's got!
His mom has recorded it all...
Well, everything except the fall.
Soon Hunter will be well and then
He can play dodge ball again
But hopefully his arms will stay intact
And never again will they be "cracked"!
-Thena Smith © 2004
(Name can be changed to personalize)

65

Caution...Broken Bone Zone

Be careful when you ride your bike
And wear your helmet on your head
For if you hit a bump
The helmet will bounce instead!
-Thena © 2004

Sweetheart ...I'm so sorry
You took that nasty spill
It was really scary!
My goodness! What a deal!
"Not fair!" you may be feeling
"Now what do I do?"
But it's only temporary
Good times still wait for you!
Rest up! You're gonna need it
'Cause when your cast is gone
You'll be turning cartwheels
And playing on the lawn
So smile! And be happy
It's good for you to do
And always keep in mind
Your mom and dad love you!
-Jennifer Byerly © 2004

**CAST
SIGNING
WELCOME**
♡
**SIGN
HERE!**

I'm stuck in the house
With nothing to do
Because I broke my ankle
When I fell off my shoe!
Mom told me to change
Before I went out for a hike
But I wanted to impress
A cute guy on a bike!
-Thena © 2004

Oh, dem broken bones!

It was just a game of tetherball
But oh what a hum-dinger!
I may have won the game
But I also broke my finger!

-Jennifer Byerly ©

Slings and Crutches and Casts, oh my!

This tree is tall
The branches keep snapping
It's a really good thing
My mommy is napping!
Up the limbs, I climb,
I will only go half-way
Oh, what the hay
I can climb a bit more!
SNAP! CRACKLE
CRASH!!
I scream as my face hits the grass
Off to the Doctor's office I go
Mommy is crying
Daddy is grinning
I wave my cast and say
"I feel better, now let's go swimming!"

-Teri Olund © 2004

Broken

School was finally out
And summer had officially begun
I wanted to go swimming
So I began to run.
I tripped over my scooter
And landed on the ground
On top of the new swim flippers
That my Mom had found.
I knew I was in trouble
But really was aghast
When Mom rushed me to the doctor
And he put me in a cast.
So when can I go swimming?
Or go surfing with my friend
Well, according to the doctor
It will be at summer's end!

-Thena © 2004

One moment you were climbing and playing
The next you were down on the ground
Pale in your pain and confusion
I'm so thankful that I was around!
The drive to E.R. took forever
By your braveness I felt so impressed
As we sat and we waited forever
In the room where they gave you to rest
Your new purple cast will soon house
Well wishes from all of your friends
You'll wear it until x-rays tell us
Your injury has had time to mend!

-Jennifer Byerly © 2004

Broken Wrist

The doctor said a wrist
Is most common of the breaks
All I know is that it throbs
And really, really aches!

Then he put a cast on me
In a lovely shade of blue
I got to pick the color out
And that was pretty cool!

Next my mama took me out
To buy a special treat
She said to choose anything
So I chose something sweet.

When I went back to school
The teachers all said "Hey!
"I don't recall you wearing that
Just the other day!"

Soon my lovely cast of blue
Was full of scribbled notes
I can't wait to show my mom
All the nice things that were wrote!

I suppose a broken bone
Isn't that bad after all
I sure like the attention
And I'm having quite a ball!
-Jennifer Byerly ©

OH, THE PAIN!

69

Bugs—annoying little creatures, some think they are cute; pests; edible by some; chocolate covered, too; scary at times; useful some; good to feed your bird; bad for mom's garden

Bug Soup

Spiders on the wall
Mites inside the bed
What about those nasty little
Lice that gnaw your head?
Worms inside the garbage
Mosquitoes everywhere
How about those awful fleas
That live in your dog's hair?
Bugs and creepy crawlers
Are always on the loose
What if we could catch them
And make them into juice?
We could strain the hairy legs out
And blend them up 'til smooth
Fish out the antennas
And make it USDA approved!
-Jennifer Byerly ©2004

Lil' Bug

Love Bug

- ◎ Don't Bug Me
- ◎ Busy as a Bee
- ◎ Snuggly Buggly
- ◎ Ants in My Pants
- ◎ Those Darn Bugs

Snug
As
A
Bug
In
A
Rug

The itsy bitsy spider climbed up my bedroom wall
I watched as my big sister flew right down the hall
She cried and looked so very funny
Running to get help from our dear mommy
It was such a eensy bug, it wouldn't hurt a fly
But oh my poor sister, she thought that she would die.
So now when I see a spider whether it's big or it is tiny,
I call for my brave mom before sister gets too whiny.
                                        -Linda LaTourelle

Butterflies—pretty and gentle; fun to watch; a special little blessing; graceful; free

"LIVING IS NOT ENOUGH," SAID THE BUTTERFLY, "ONE MUST HAVE SUNSHINE, FREEDOM AND A LITTLE FLOWER."

–Hans Christian Anderson

- B-E-A-U-tiful Butterfly
- Butterfly, Butterfly Fly, Fly away
- Butterflies Welcome Here
- Flutter by....Butterfly
- Happiness is like a butterfly
- If wishes were butterflies...
- I'm like a butterfly because...
- Flyin' high, floating free
- Love is like a butterfly
- Come let it sit on your shoulder
- They don't butter-fly, they flutter-by

Be like the beautiful butterfly, take time to stop and smell the flowers...

There
were
days
when she ran
in a garden,
like a child of
ten, after a
butterfly.
—Alexandre Dumas

I LOVE BUTTERFLIES

Watch it flitter by
Pretty little butterfly
It is too fragile
To go very high
But it's beauty
Still makes me sigh!
-Thena

The Butterfly

I hold you at last in my hand,
Exquisite child of the air.
Can I ever understand
How you grew to be so fair
You came to my linden tree
To taste its delicious sweet,
I sit here in the shadow and shine
Playing around its feet.
Now I hold you fast in my hand,
You marvelous butterfly,
Till you help me to understand
The eternal mystery.
From that creeping thing in the dust
To this shining bliss in the blue!
God give me courage to trust!
I can break my chrysalis too!
-Alice Freeman Palmer

Camp—a parent's vacation; a child's time to explore; campfires, friendships; crafts and more

At Sugar Camp

At Sugar Camp the cook is kind
And laughs the laugh we knew as boys;
And there we slip away and find
Awaiting us the ole-time joys.
The catbird calls the self same way
She use to in the long ago,
And there's a chorus all the day
Of songsters it is good to know.

-Edgar Guest

Poison Ivy, Rainy Days

Poison ivy, rainy days,
Mosquitoes drive me mad.
I'll never get to sleep tonight.
I love to camp with Dad!

-Robert Pottle ©

S'MORES...
ONE OR
FOUR?
YOU'RE
SURE TO
WANT
MORE!

I'm so happy
To be on my way
For we're off to
Summer camp today!
The moms are watching
As the bus pulls away
The kids are shouting excitedly
My what a happy day!

Candy—a child's favorite food; sugar; bribery food; anything chocolate; sweets

Suspicious Evidence

My sister is a meanie
And now she's gone too far!
She riffled through my private stash
And ate my candy bar!
I just can't find it anywhere
Nothing! Not a trace!
Except a bit of evidence
There's chocolate on her face!
She's tells me she is innocent
But I know her much to well
And now she's gonna get it
Because I plan to tell!
But when I told our mama
She said "For goodness sakes!"
"I let your sister have a taste
Of my fresh chocolate cake!"
But I still don't believe it
And now she's on my list
'Cause that's a candy wrapper
That she's hiding in her fist!
-Jennifer Byerly © 2004

Chocolate kisses
And Peppermint Hugs
Gumdrops, cupcakes,
Sugar pie Love

Candy Galore

There are red ones and green ones
And orange ones galore!
Its my very first trip
To the Candy Store!
There's chocolate and Cherry
Vanilla and strawberry
Oh My! How these flavors vary!
Sour and Sweet
Some nutty, some creamy
I rub my eyes, for I think I am dreaming!
A little of this one
A lot more of that one!
Just one more taste
A lick or two!
Just one more mom, well, maybe a few!
Before I knew it
My tummy was achy!
-Teri Olund ©

Candy is my favorite food

Though Mom says it's a snack
But when I go to school
I love to have it in my pack.

It doesn't seem fair
To put it down
And say it isn't "healthy"
I would eat it all day long...
If only I were wealthy!
-Thena Smith

Cars & Trucks—big boy toys and girls, too; just like dad; can't wait to run with the big kids

- A Day at the Races
- A Need for Speed
- A Red Flag Warning
- A Track Record
- Along for the Ride
- And awaaay he/she goes
- And the winner is...
- At the Track
- Away He Goes
- Baby, You Can Drive My Car
- Back on Track
- Balancing act
- Born to Bike
- Born to Race
- Born to ride—forced to work!
- Breaking Away
- Breakneck Speed
- By a Length
- Caution - Yellow Flag
- Choo-Choo Kid
- Chug Chug Chug
- Chuggin' Along
- Danger: Boy At Work
- Danger: Kid Drivin'
- Demolition Dude/Darlin'
- Diggin' the Dirt
- Don't Like My Driving; Get Off the Road
- Drivin' me crazy
- Driver Wanted
- Dump Truckin' Kid
- Easy Rider
- Enjoying the Ride
- Fast, Faster, Fastest
- First set of wheels
- Get ready, get set, go
- Go Fast! Turn Left!
- GO GO GO!
- Go speed racer
- Going the Distance
- Good to Go
- Go on Green
- Go for the finish

- Life in the Fast Lane
- Little boys grow up to be bigger little boys.
- Little Big Man
- Little Captain
- Look Out World
- Look Out...Here I come
- Loop the Loop
- Makin' tracks
- Me and my Dad
- My Partner & Me
- Next stop: candy store
- No training wheels
- Not So Fast
- On a bicycle built for ___
- On the Fast Track
- On the Road Again
- On your mark
- Pace Car
- Pedal Practice
- Pit Crew & Boss
- Peddle to the Metal
- Race to the Finish
- Ready for the Pro-Circuit
- Road Adventures USA
- Road Hog
- Road Racer
- Rockin' and a Racin'
- Rollin'-rollin'-rollin', keep those wheels rollin'
- Simply Roaderiffic
- Speed Racer
- Speed Sweetheart
- Spin-Out
- Survival of the Fastest

DRIVE MY CAR

Look up at the airplane
Smoothly gliding in the sky
When I grow up I'll be a pilot
And a big ole plane I'll fly!

- Oh, what a ride!
- Take it to the Limit
- Taste of Victory
- The Competition
- The Driver's Seat
- The Finish Line
- Thrill of Victory
- Thrill Ride
- Top Speed
- Two, three, four wheelin'
- Unrivaled Competition
- Up, Up, Up and Away
- Victory Lap

- White Knucklin' It
- Where the Rubber Meets the Road
- Wipe-out
- Young Kid Driving
- Youth in the fast lane

ON YOUR MARK, GET SET, GO

Get Out Of My Way!

Dad has a car
Mom does too
Dad's car is red.
And Mom's car is blue.
Sis got a car for her birthday
Her's is a bright yellow bug,
And all I got for my birthday
Was a wallet and a hug!.
-Thena

I want to drive a car
I want a big ole car for me
But I must wait awhile
Because I'm not old enough, you see...

Cheerleaders—jump and shout; turn about; cheer today; hip, hip hooray

A - Agile
B - Believe in your team!
C - Cheers
D - Determination
E - Energy
F - Fans and Fun
G - Games
H - Half-time
I - I Love Cheerleading
J - Jumping for Joy
K - Kick 'em up
L - Losses
M - Megaphones
N - Never Quit
O - Overtime
P - Pom-Poms
Q - Quick on the feet
R - Rallies
S - Sportsmanship
T - Teamwork
U - United
V - Victorious
W - We've Got Spirit
X - X-citing
Y - Yelling
Z - Zantastic

My daughter as I watch you
My heart fills up with pride
Your spirit and your dance moves
Simply brings the crowd alive!
Jennifer Byerly ©

- A jump above the rest

- Athlete by nature, cheerleader by choice!

- CHEER the game! WORK the crowd! BUILD the spirit!

- Cheerleaders-another word for LOUD!

- Go, Fight, Win

- Go, Team, Go

- Hold That Line

- I Inspire

- I don't play the field I rule the sidelines.

- It's hard to be humble when you can jump, shout, and tumble!

- I Love Cheerleading

- Jump, Shout, Yell!

- Let's Go

- Pep Rally

- Pom-poms and Ponytails

- Push 'em Back, Push 'em Back, Waaaaay Back

- Stand Up and Cheer

- Pom Pom Girls can sing and shout!

- We Got Spirit

- Cheerleader lead

- Yeah Team!

- You make the touchdown, we'll make the noise!

The sport of cheerleading
Is one that requires agility,
Dedication and spirit,
Hard work and ability
-Jennifer Byerly ©

I love to watch you cheering
Kicking up your feet
Cheering for the home team
Through their victory or defeat!
-Jennifer Byerly ©

HEY HO... LET'S GO!

Children—A person between birth and puberty; can be very intelligent or immature; will test your patience; guaranteed to steal your heart

A child is a handful sometimes;
a heartful all the time

♡

Bed & Breakfast:
two things kids never make

♡

In the eyes of a child,
Love is spelled T-I-M-E

♡

Housecleaning Hint:
A child will not spill on a dirty floor

♡

If you think it is impossible to love
someone more than yourself, have a child

♡

If only my kids were sleeping
instead of recharging!

♡

Nothing you do for a child is ever wasted
Real peace in this world begins with the children. –Gandhi

♡

Anyone who ever walked barefoot into his
child's room understands the value of shoes!

Oxymoron
Child: Clean Room

It's funny how when we're children,
all we want to do is grow up,
but when we're older and grown up,
we wish the world was as simple and innocent
as it were when we were a child. -Tim Hussar

**Tell me, I will forget. Show me, I may remember.
Involve me, I will understand.**

Some Proverbial Reminders...

- ☺ When in doubt, don't
- ☺ School lunches stick to the wall
- ☺ If at first you don't succeed, go ask Dad
- ☺ Never underestimate the power of a boy
- ☺ You can't teach an old dog new—Math
- ☺ Better to be safe than punch a fifth grader
- ☺ Children should be seen and not grounded
- ☺ Never ask your 3 year old brother to hold a tomato
- ☺ The most wasted of all days is one without laughter
- ☺ When Mom is mad at Dad, don't let her brush your hair
- ☺ Every accomplishment large or small begins with the same decision: I'll try
- ☺ You can lead a kid to the bath, but you can't make him wash
- ☺ Once you've heard oops...it's already too late
- ☺ Love all—trust your child

Out of the mouths of children...

The four seasons are
salt, pepper, mustard and vinegar
♡
The people who followed the Lord
were called the 12 opossums
♡
The climate is hottest
next to the Creator

Things I've Learned

Don't build an ant farm in a paper sack
Let dogs lick you, but don't lick them back
Your pants won't fall down if your belt is tight
Never try to kiss your goldfish goodnight
Throw your ball inside and something will break
Make lots of mud pies, but eat Mommy's cake
Don't push chewing gum up inside your nose
Don't paint anything on your nicest clothes
Never, ever try to cut your own hair
That laughing might mean your pants have a tear
Although he acts rotten he's still your little brother
Hug him when he cries, and love him like no other
-Jeff Mondak ©

Things I Learned too Late

Never try to kiss a snake
Or ask your mom if she's gained weight.
Never use Mom's panty hose
To wipe off baby's runny nose
And no matter how hungry you are
Always share your candy bar.
Be kind to animals great and small
And standing on a rocking chair--
Guarantees you will fall!
Kiss Aunts and Uncles if they ask
And do each chore and other assigned task
For rewards will come to a good little kid
For every single kind thing you did!
-Thena ©

How bright is the moon?
How far to the west?
How much sand on the beach?
Oh, when does God rest?

How many stars in the sky?
How hot is the sun?
How deep is the ocean?
Ah, look what God's done!

At the end of the rainbow
Or up in the clouds
The world in its wonder
Shows God's love abounds.

-Linda LaTourelle

Things Mom Should Know

I didn't want to go to school today
You would think Moms would know
That kids don't want to go to school
If there's new fallen snow!
I didn't want to eat my dinner
No kid wants veggies to eat
When there is left over cake
Or something else that's sweet.
I told my Mom some of these things
To help her understand my view
But I found out that mom's of kids
Have their own ideas
Of just what kids should do...

-Thena

84

I can do some really great things
That only I can do
For I can make the special sound
That monkeys make at the zoo!

I can do some really fun things
Like swing way up high in the sky
So very far that I can see each car
That is out on the street driving by!

I can do some very smart things
That no one but me can do
I can add and subtract and divide
And I know my "tables" too!

I can do some very exciting things
That I know are special to do
For I can dream my very own dreams
And only I know when they have come true!
-Thena

I dreamed about the mountains
I dreamed about the snow
I dreamed about the whole big world
And the places I'd like to go!
-Thena

THE SEASON OF CHILDHOOD:
CAREFREE AND FULL OF WONDER

Boys are much more fun than girls
And if I had my way
I'd tell the schools to change their rules
And send all the girls away!

Girls have no sense of humor
About things that boys find fun
But I'll have to change my mind someday
'Cause I'll have to marry one!
-Thena

To become a real boy, you must prove
Yourself brave, truthful and unselfish
-from "Pinocchio"

A boy is the only thing
that God can use to make a man.

A boy between birth and puberty;
can be very intelligent or immature;
will test your patience;
guaranteed to steal your heart

Of all the animals,
the boy is the most unmanageable

A child is an island of curiosity
Surrounded by a sea of question marks

B Blessing
O of
Y Yours

The Five Senses of Childhood:

1. Smell—Mom's fresh baked cookies
2. Sight—The smile of a friend
3. Sound—Laughter from the soul
4. Taste—Snowflakes on your tongue
5. Touch—A hug full of love

♡

Kids know what is really important in life:
Family, Friends, Fun, Food, Faith

Children live up to what you believe of them.

A child is fed with milk and praise.

**In Childhood, we can dream big,
with little doubt for success.**

In Childhood our wishes are grand,
our life is simple and our trust is immeasurable

**We must laugh and we must sing
We are blest by everything.**
-W.B. Yeats

Life's most delicious moments
come in all flavors:
Lollipops, popsicles, lemon drops,
peppermint, bubble gum and chocolate

Top Ten Reasons Childhood is Fun:

10. You don't have to wear a watch
9. Taking a bath isn't really a priority
8. You can change the rules whenever you want
7. You can act silly and no one thinks you're weird
6. You can run through the sprinkler when it's hot
5. You get the whole summer to play and sleep late
4. Friends are easy to be found
3. You don't have to work or pay bills
2. Your imagination is your best friend
1. Someone can kiss your owie's and it works!

**When I grow up I'm going to be
A teacher, a doctor, or simply just me!**

I got a brand new pair of roller skates
That came with a brand new key

**Jesus said, "Let the little children
come unto me..." –Matthew 19:14**

Those were the days...
Skipping rocks upon the water
Chasing fireflies with my father
Staying out late
Leaving food on my plate
Hop, roll and run
What life, what fun!

HOPE IS
THE HEART OF A CHILD

- Praise your children and they will blossom
- Raising kids is part joy and part guerilla warfare
- The handwriting on the wall means kids found the crayons
- There are two things a child will share willingly: chicken pox and his mother's age
- To be in your children's memories tomorrow, you have to be in their lives today
- Unattended children will be sold as slaves
- We teach children to love by first loving them
- You can't scare me, I have kids!
- Lord, grant me the patience to endure my blessings
- Out of the mouths of babes come words we should have never said
- A child to love is a gift from above
- We can handle any problem—we have kids
- Celebrate Children—Celebrate Life!
- I Celebrate You
- I am a child of God
- It must be a kid thing
- So much homework—so little time!
- Caution: Children at play

GOD'S BIGGEST TREASURES ARE CHILDREN

Hannah said, "I asked the Lord to give me this child, and he has answered my prayers.. –1Samuel 1:27

THE HEART OF A CHILD IS LOVE

- Lord, give me strength
- Thou shalt not whine
- To the world...you may be one person, but to your child you are the world
- Who takes a child by the hand, takes the mother by the heart
- Little girls are precious gifts, wrapped in love serene. Their dresses tied with sashes and futures tied with dreams
- The Bigger They Come, the Harder They Fall
- The essence of love is found in a child
- Girls just like to accessorize
- 7 going on 17
- Did I say cute?
- Hold on—I'm in charge!
- Occasional Angel
- Kid with Class
- Head of the Class
- BEWARE: You are now entering—the Kid Zone
- Personality Plus
- Radical Dude
- Kid with a Million Faces
- New Kid on the Block
- When I was your age
- When you view the world through a child's eyes, magic happens
- The best security blanket for a child is parents who love each other.

Children live up to what you believe of them.
-Lady Bird Johnson

The Master's Recipe

God uses different recipes
For every girl and boy
First He starts with angel dust
And mixes it with joy

Some receive a heaping mound
Of freckles on their face
While some don't get any
Others just a trace

He mixes hues from rainbows
For their skin, their eyes, their hair
Some get extra pigment
Some turn out quite fair

In each He places happiness
By folding smiles in
Then adds a sparkle to their eyes
Puts silly in their grins

He uses curiosity
Imagination for their play
Questions to fill up their minds
Every single day

For God makes every girl and boy
Uniquely it is true
Each recipe a masterpiece
And that's including you!

© 2005 Jennifer Byerly

I AM NEITHER ESPECIALLY CLEVER, NOR ESPECIALLY
GIFTED, JUST VERY, VERY CURIOUS. -EINSTEIN

- ABCDEG..Tell Me What You Think of Me
- A Face Only a Mother Could Love
- All About Me
- All My Children
- Barefoot in the Park
- Blooming Beauty
- Bottomless Pit
- Bless This Child
- Bully Who?
- Child Crossing
- Clownin' Around
- Crimes & Misdemeanors
- Danger: Boys at Work
- Diva Darling
- Do It Yourself Haircut
- Drama Queen
- Express yourself
- Fussy Little Princess
- Grease Monkey

- Hangin' With the Boys
- Here's Looking at You, Kid
- Just Hangin' Out
- I am the BOSS
- I Walk the Line
- I Love You 'Beary' Much
- I'm A Big Kid Now
- In My Father's Arms
- In My Mother's Smile
- In My Father's House
- In the News
- In The Spotlight
- Inside the Mind of a Child
- Inside, Outside, Upside Down
- It's All Small Stuff
- It's Mine!
- It's Not Easy Being a Princess
- Just Me and My Mom
- Just One of the Girls

Child: a lot of love in a little package

- I'd Rather Be In Recess
- I'd Rather Be _____
- Kids will be Kids
- King of the Playground
- King/Queen of Recess
- Kindergarten Graduate
- Look, No Hands
- Love Me... Love My Messes!
- Me and My Teddy Bear
- Me and My Dad
- My Hero, My Dad
- More, More, More
- Mug Shots
- Picture Perfect
- Practically Perfect
- Practice Makes Perfect
- Pretty as a Picture
- Saturday in the Park
- Shoe Princess
- Smart as a Whip
- Star Light, Star Bright
- Prince Alarming!
- Prince Charming ???
- Princess in Training
- The Line Starts Here
- The Princess Sleeps Here
- The Star of the Show!
- The Usual Suspects
- We are Family
- Raised in a Barn
- When I Count My Blessings, I Count You
- You Can't Always Get What You Want
- You're One in a Million

The Thinker

The Leader

The Singer

The Love Bug

The Joker

The Dreamer

Wonder Kid

The Book Worm

The Dancer

The Class Clown

To be a kid you must...

**To be a kid you must
walk through many mud puddles**

To be a kid you must climb the tallest tree

A child's delights in the simple things

How do you like to go up in a swing,
Up in the air so blue?
Oh, I do think it the pleasantest thing
Ever a child can do!
-Robert Louis Stevenson

**We find delight in the beauty and
happiness of children that makes
the heart too big for the body.**
-Ralph Waldo Emerson

**A child's wish...
To see the world
Through loving eyes**

Alice had begun to think
That very few things indeed
Were really impossible.
-Lewis Carroll

**A child's prayer...
A family to love**

**THERE IS MAGIC
IN THE MEMORY
OF SCHOOLBOY
FRIENDSHIPS**
-DISRAELI

**My Best
Friend**

Christmas—the happiest day in the life of a child; visions of candy and toys; payday for parents; family day

- 100 % pure Christmas
- A Caroling We Will Go
- A Good Girl/Boy Am I
- A Visit With St. Nick
- A White Christmas
- A Caroling We Will Go
- A Merry Little Christmas
- All I Want For Christmas Is My Two Front Teeth!
- All I Got For Christmas Was...
- All Is Merry and Bright
- All The Trimmings...
- All Through The House
- All Wrapped Up!
- Baking For Santa
- Beary Kiss-Mas
- Believe
- Candy Cane Kids
- Christmas Blessings
- Come Let Us Adore Him
- Down the chimney
- Elf Crossing
- Expect a Miracle
- I Break for Reindeer
- Kringle Crossing
- Oh Christmas Tree
- North Pole
- Naughty Or Nice?
- Property of Santa
- Santa and Co.
- Sleigh Parking
- Wrapped in Love

God's Crown

How still the night,
How still the stars,
How still that little
sleeping town,
How like a jewel in
God's crown
That Star of stars
That shines so bright.

Candles and stars
And Christmas tree lights
Twinkle and glow
In the velvety night

FATHER CHRISTMAS, will you please
Bring us lots of books and toys,--
Fill our stockings, deck the trees
With all sorts of shining joys,
So that every child who sees
Makes a loud and happy noise!
Come with merry sound of bells
Breaking through our midnight sleep,
Rousing hamlets, citadels,
Prompting little heads to peep--
If they see you, no one tells,
'Tis a secret that we keep.
Come with snowy coverlet,
Spread it over field and town
When the hasty sun is set,
And the night drops softly down;
Little children don't forget
Your rosy face and holly crown!
-Maude Keary

A Christmas Prayer

God Bless Mummy and Daddy
And my little sister too
I hope you will take care of them
Don't let them get the flu
Can you tell Father Christmas
That I've been good this year
And could I have a Barbie doll
That talks and cries real tears
Can my sister have a coloring book
She'd really find that fun
And can you say a Happy Birthday to
Jesus, who's your Son
-Rob Erskine ©

Dear Santa,
I want it ALL!
I really have been good!

The True Meaning of Christmas

At church they asked what Christmas meant.
I knew that. Up my hand went.
When I was asked, I said with glee,
"On that day I get gifts. You see,
my family loves me - I'm so great -
they buy me gifts to celebrate."
At least that's how it seems to me.
The preacher seemed to disagree.
-Robert Pottle ©

- Christmas Cookies And Holiday Hearts...
- Christmas Cuties
- Christmas In _____
- Christmas is sharing
- Christmas Joy
- Christmas love and all the trimmings
- Christmas is Love
- Christmas Memories
- Christmas shimmer
- Chopping down our tree
- Cookies for Santa
- Dear Santa, I want one of everything
- Dear Santa, I've been soooo good
- Desperately seeking Santa
- Do you recall...the most famous reindeer of all?
- Family is the best part of Christmas
- Happy Birthday Jesus
- His name is Rudolph
- Holly-Daze
- Holly Jolly Daddy
- Holly Jolly Santa
- Home for the Holidays
- I Believe in Santa Claus
- I Love Christmas
- I saw Mommy Kissing Santa Claus
- Love-Peace-Joy
- No Humbugs Allowed
- Snowy Days
- The Christmas Star
- Trimming the Tree
- Twas The Night Before Christmas
- Village Toy Shoppe
- 'Tis the Season
- Twinkle, Twinkle Christmas Star
- Winter Wonderland

Christmas is: family near Words of cheer Memories dear

- Ho, Ho, Ho Merry Christmas
- HO HO HO to You
- Hooray for Christmas
- Hooray for the Holidays
- Here's to Christmas Future
- How _____ Stole Christmas

I will honor Christmas in my heart and try to keep it all year

- It's a Jolly Holiday with...
- It's Christmas All Over!

Dear Santa

Dear Santa,
I love all the new toys
I have just one complaint
I didn't get the big screen
But I got this silly paint!
Mommy said it wouldn't fit
"Down the chimney with care"
But all you had to do was yell
'Cause Daddy was here!
The bike I got was pretty cool
I can try to ride it to school
I asked my mommy, she started to cough
She laughed and said
"Maybe after the trainers come off!"
It's ok, maybe next year
I know your getting older
And its harder for you to hear
So next time, I will write down model numbers
So you can get it right!
-Teri Olund ©

Snowman

I'm a little snowman white and fat
I can wear a scarf or even a hat
My eyes are shiny
and my nose may be too long
However they make me really isn't wrong.
I love to stand and glisten in the sun
But when it gets too hot, oh, no, I'll be gone.
- Linda LaTourelle

OVER THE RIVER
AND THROUGH THE WOODS
TO GRANDMOTHER'S HOUSE WE GO

Jingle Bells

- Jingle all the way
- Love, Joy, Hope, Peace
- No Peekin' 'til Christmas
- O Holy Night
- Oh Tannenbaum
- Reindeer Crossing
- Santa Delivers
- Santa Express
- Santa please stop here!
- Santa was here
- Santa, I want it all
- Santa's elf
- Santa's little helper
- Silent Night
- Santa's Workshop
- Who needs Santa—we have Grandma

At Christmas, Play &
Make Good Cheer,
For Christmas
Comes But
Once A Year

100

He's checking his list and counting it twice

Here's a little "head's up"
Just to let you know
Santa has been watching you
Everywhere you go!
At times you have been naughty
That's why this gifts for you
Some coal made out of bubble gum
To remind you as you chew
Santa's always watching
And he's not gonna quit
So if you want some presents
You'd better not blow it!
-Jennifer Byerly © 2004

Santa Claus

Was tired
As tired as can be
Today about a million children
Climbed upon his knee

They asked for dolls and tea sets
Racing cars and trains
They asked for books and crayons
And pin-striped candy canes

"I'll do my best" said Santa
With a twinkle in his eye
Just promise me you'll be asleep
When I come flying by!
-Jennifer Byerly © 2004

**We gather round
the Christmas tree
to thank with grate-
ful thoughts of thee**

- The perfect tree
- The spirit of Christmas is the laughter of children
- Toys, toys, and more toys!
- Tree-mendous
- Unto us a child is born
- Up on the rooftop
- Waiting for Santa
- We believe in Christmas
- We love Christmas
- Who needs Santa...I have my Grandma and Grandpa
- Wow! Thanks Santa!
- Wrapped up with care
- Yes,_____, there is a Santa Claus
- You'd better not pout

While visions of

Sugar plums

**Danced in their
heads**

So Talk To Me Of Christmas

So talk to me of Christmas
This special time of year
Where the noble pub is set on fire
And we're stuffed full of cheer
Where dear old Father Christmas
Goes flying on his sled
Then zips on down your chimney
While you're asleep in bed
But surely that's December
When snow is on the street
Not here now in August
While we shelter from the heat
But yes, there are Christmas crackers
And I'm sure I saw mince pies
Here's a box of Christmas cards
I don't believe my eyes
What happened to religion?
Has it been swept away?
The story of the Christ child
Not relevant today?
The ad-men spin a different tale
They give it all they've got
But if the truth were really known
I think they've lost the plot
So at this sacred time of year
Where retail reigns supreme
Think upon the little child
He's real and not a dream
-Rob Erskine ©

Circus—A show under the big top,
lions, tigers and clowns, oh my, our family
fun time, riding the elephants, dancing
ponies, cotton candy, popcorn and music

Oh the Circus-Day parade!
How the Bugles played and played!
And how the glossy horses
Tossed their flossy manes, and neighed,
As the rattle and rhyme of the tenor-drummer's time
Filled all the hungry hearts of us with melody sublime!

The Merry-Go-Round

I choose a flying horse, a horse of dapple gray
Right next to you upon your horse of shiny bay,
We ride around the merry-go-round,
The whirling, whirling merry-go-round,
The merry-go-round, hurrah!
Oh, let us go round again.
The merry-go-round, hurrah!
Oh let us go round again!
-unknown

**AND THE
PAINTED PONIES
GO UP
AND DOWN**

- ⊚ The Circus is in Town
- ⊚ Three Ring Circus
- ⊚ Hip-Hip-Hoo-Ray!
- ⊚ Monkey'n Around
- ⊚ A car full of Clowns
- ⊚ Horsin' Around
- ⊚ Just Lion Around

- ⊚ Monkey Business
- ⊚ Elephant Brigade
- ⊚ Wild Thing
- ⊚ Trapeze Artist
- ⊚ Clowning Around
- ⊚ Don't feed the animals
- ⊚ Roarin' Like a Lion

- ⊙ Acrobats Galore
- ⊙ Audience Applause
- ⊙ Balancing Act
- ⊙ Balls of Fire
- ⊙ Comical Clowns
- ⊙ Cotton Candy Kisses
- ⊙ Dancing Bears
- ⊙ Enormous Elephants
- ⊙ Fire Breathing Man
- ⊙ Get Your Peanuts
- ⊙ Human Cannonball
- ⊙ Hoops of Fire
- ⊙ Leaping Leopards
- ⊙ Lions and Tigers and Bears, Oh, My
- ⊙ Lion Taming
- ⊙ Midway Music
- ⊙ Monkey See—Monkey Do
- ⊙ Popcorn and Peanuts
- ⊙ Send in the clowns
- ⊙ The Flying Trapeze
- ⊙ Three Ring Circus
- ⊙ Whistle While You Work
- ⊙ Zany Tight Rope Walker

Merry-Go-Round

The rollicking, frolicking merry-go-round
Goes around and around and around,
And the tinkly, twinkly music plays
With a gay and a silvery sound.
The ponies kick their frisky heels
At the tinkly, twinkly sound,
At the rollicking, frolicking merry-go-round
Goes around and around and around.
If I had my choice each summer day
Of the spot where I'd like to be,
The rollicking, frolicking, merry-go-round
Would be the place for me.
And all of the time that the music played
With its tinkly, twinkly sound,
I'd go riding around and around,
On the rollicking, frolicking merry-go-round.
-unknown

Circus-Day Parade

Oh the Circus-Day parade! How the Bugles played and played!
And how the glossy horses tossed their flossy manes, and neighed,
As the rattle and rhyme of the tenor-drummer's time
Filled all the hungry hearts of us with melody sublime!

How the grand band-wagon shone with a splendor all its own,
And glittered with a glory that our dreams had never known!
And how the boys behind, high and low of every kind,
Marched in unconscious capture, with a rapture undefined!

How the horsemen, two and two, with their plumes of white and blue,
And crimson, gold and purple, nodding by at me and you,
Waved the banners that they bore, as the Knights in days of yore,
'Til our glad eyes gleamed and glistened like the spangles that they wore!

How the graceless-graceful stride of the elephant was eyed,
And the capers of the little horse that cantered at his side!
How the shambling camels, tame to the plaudits of their fame,
With listless eyes came silent, masticating as they came.

How the cages jolted past, with each wagon battened fast,
And the mystery within it only hinted of at last
From the little grated square in the rear, and nosing there
The snout of some strange animal that sniffed the outer air!

And last of all, The Clown, making mirth for all the town,
With lips curved ever upward and his eyebrows down,
And his chief attention paid to the little mule that played
A tattoo on the dashboard with his heals, in the parade.

Oh the Circus-Day parade! How the Bugles played and played!
And how the glossy horses tossed their flossy manes, and neighed,
As the rattle and rhyme of the tenor-drummer's time
Filled all the hungry hearts of us with melody sublime!

-James Whitcomb Riley

I LOVE A PARADE

- 76 Trombones
- The Big Parade
- Bands and Horses and Floats, Oh My!
- Banner Moments
- Class Parade
- Dancing Ponies
- Don't rain on my parade
- Drum Major
- Easter Parade
- Everybody loves a parade!
- Floating Along
- Forward, March!
- Keep in Step
- Life is a Parade
- Light Parade
- Marching Bands
- Marching to the beat
- Parade of Athletes
- Parade of Nations
- Pomp and Circumstance
- Rose Parade
- Thanksgiving Day Parade
- View from the Boulevard

RAT-A-TAT-TAT

The Circus

The trumpets blow, the bugles play,
The circus is coming to town today!
With a big elephant and a jolly old clown,
A really live circus is coming to town!
With lions and tigers and monkeys, too,
It's hard to believe that it's really true!
Oh, the animals roar, and they chatter and scream;
It seems like a wonderful magical dream.

-Alice C. D. Riley

Class Fun—Concerts, plays, programs, class parades, celebrations together, these are the fun memories of being in school

The Kindergarten Concert

The kindergarten concert was an interesting show.
Peter walked onto the stage and yelled,
"I have to go!"
Katie was embarrassed,
but she had nowhere to hide.
She raised her dress to hide her face.
Her mother almost died.
Keith removed his tie and said,
"It's ugly, Dad. I hate it!"

David picked his nose on stage.
What's worse is that he ate it.
They sang their song, and Wyatt burped,
then he did a dance.
Michael fell while spinning round.
Peter wet his pants.
The music teacher, at the end, said,
"There, I'm glad that's done."
The kindergarten bowed and said,
"Let's sing another one!"
-Robert Pottle ©

Be sure to read more about
this great poet in our biography section.
We Love Him!

The Christmas Play

We had a Christmas play
To celebrate the birth
Of precious baby Jesus
When God sent Him to earth.

I wanted to be an angel
And brother wanted to be a sheep
And little baby sister
Curled up in the manger and went to sleep.

Mom was playing Mary
And Dad was one of the kings
With special gifts in his hands
That to baby Jesus he would bring.

All in all it went real well
Until the very end of the play
When baby sister woke up in the cradle
And ate a handful of the hay!

-Thena

Parade Day

Our teacher said it was parade day
And everyone should portray
By a float, costume, or skit
A special hero in some way.

Some dressed up as firemen
And some as men in space
But the costume that I wore
Put a smile on teacher's face.

I dressed up as a teacher
And decorated brother's wagon as my desk
Although I'm not usually one to boast
Teacher liked my costume the best!

-Thena

Clubhouse—Kids only, no grownups allowed; it's our place to hide away

Mobile Clubhouse

I pulled the sheets and blankets
From my tidy bed
And used a couple thumb tacks
To pin them overhead
I propped my wicker desk chair
Against my bedroom wall
And made myself a clubhouse
Then welcomed one and all
I play there with my dolls
Because we all agree
It's the nicest place for us
To share a spot of tea!

-Jennifer Byerly © 2004

Girls Club

I formed a club
That is for girls alone
No boys are allowed
Not even on the phone.
They can't come inside
Because it seems to me
That boys are mean
And love to disagree!

-Thena

NO GIRLS KEEP OUT BOYS ARE WHAT THIS CLUB'S ABOUT

Country Kids

- A Country Mile
- Back in the Saddle
- Baling Hay
- Best Kid in the West
- Chickens and Ducks
- Come and Get It
- Country Bumpkin
- Country Sunshine
- Country-fied
- Cowboy Dreams
- Cowtown Cuties
- Don't Fence Me In
- Down on the Farm
- Farm livin' is the life for me
- Get Along Lil' Doggies
- Giddy Up Horsey
- Going to the Farm
- Green Grass Growing
- Happiness is Being a Cowgirl/Cowboy
- Harvest Time
- Head Em Up—Move Em Out
- Hitch Your Wagon
- Hitching Post
- Home, Home on the Farm
- Home on the Range
- How the West Was Fun
- I Got Spurs that Jingle Jangle Jingle
- I Was Country When Country Wasn't Cool
- Just me and Bubba
- Kindly Keep It Country
- Momma Don't Let Your Babies Grow Up to be Cowboys
- Old MacDonald Had a Farm
- Park Your Boots
- Planting the garden
- Ride a Fast Horse
- Ridin' a Big Tractor
- The Simple Life
- Sittin' round the campfire
- The Lady Takes the Cowboy
- The Reins Stop Here
- Wah-Hoo
- W-A-N-T-E-D
- Where's the Beans?

Oh give me a home, where the buffalo roam
And the deer and the antelope play
Where seldom is heard a discouraging word
And the skies are not cloudy all day.

Just Relaxing

Sing to me mister cricket
Chirp your happy song!
I'll be glad to listen
And perhaps I'll sing along
Flitter Madame Butterfly
Dance and catch the breeze
I like the way you land about
Then fly off as you please
Buzz off! Mr. Honey bee
Please leave me alone!
Gather up your pollen
To make honey in your home
Sway on happy flowers
I see you on that hill!
I spy your sunny faces
Even though you won't hold still
Float by fluffy white clouds
Yesterday you were black
But now I can enjoy you
As I lay here on my back!
Slow down mid-day sun
I know there're chores to do
I promise I'll get moving
In an hour or two!
-Jennifer Byerly © 2004

- ⓘ Bubba and Me
- ⓘ Buckin' Bronco
- ⓘ Cattle Drive
- ⓘ Cowgirl Blues
- ⓘ Cow Pies!
- ⓘ Dusty Old Trail
- ⓘ Happy Trails
- ⓘ Howdy Ya'll
- ⓘ Lil' Cowpoke
- ⓘ Lil' Buckaroo
- ⓘ Ride 'Em Cowboy
- ⓘ Ropin' the Wind
- ⓘ Tan Your Hide
- ⓘ The OK Corral

HE WAS JUST A LONELY COWBOY WITH A HEART SO BRAVE AND TRUE

New Boots

Now I lay me down to sleep
With my new boots still on my feet
At the rising of the sun
I'll get up and have some fun
I've got puddles to wade in
When the day begins again
Please Lord let it rain tonight
So I can splash in
morning's light!
-Jennifer Byerly ©

Broom Stick Cowboy

Dream on, little broomstick cowboy,
Of rocket ships and Mars,
Of sunny days, and Willie Mays,
And chocolate candy bars.
Dream on little broomstick cowboy,
Dream while you can,
Of big green frogs,
And puppy dogs,
And castles in the sand.
-unknown

RIDIN' THE WIND

You Are my Sunshine My Only sunshine

Country Living

Now I lay my sleepy head
With my boots beside my bed
I keep them close so I can play
As soon as it's another day
I simply pull them on my feet
When it's light so I can greet
The crowing rooster in the morn
Then chase the chickens in the corn
Later when the day turns night
I place them there 'til morning's light!
-Jennifer Byerly © 2004

- ☺ Raised in a Barn?
- ☺ Thrown For a Loop
- ☺ Trail of Tears
- ☺ Way Out Yonder
- ☺ Wild Wild West
- ☺ Yee Haw!

RIDE 'EM COWBOY

Dancing—/dans 'ing/ to move the body and feet in rhythm, ordinarily to music

- A Born Dancer
- Beautiful Ballerina
- Bee bop
- Boogie down
- Boogie fever
- Born to Dance
- Dance all night
- Dance fever
- Dance is a work of heart
- Dance is life, everything else is just details!
- Dance to the music
- Dance, dance, dance
- Dancer dreams
- Dancin' feet
- Dancing Princess
- Do the locomotion
- Dressed to dance
- En Pointe
- Flash Dance
- God danced the day you were born
- Gotta dance
- Happy feet
- Happy tappin'
- Hip Hop
- I dance—therefore I am
- I love to dance
- I've got rhythm
- Jazz Dancin'
- Jitterbug girl
- Keep on dancin'
- Let's dance
- Of course I've got attitude, I'm a dancer!
- Once a dancer, always a dancer
- Our hearts and feet dance today
- Practice makes perfect
- Put on your dancing shoes
- Rock Around the clock
- Save the last dance

113

- ⓘ Shall we dance
- ⓘ Something in the way she moves
- ⓘ Steppin out
- ⓘ Tappin'
- ⓘ Tiny Dancer
- ⓘ Toe shoes and Tutus
- ⓘ Tutu cute
- ⓘ Tutu much
- ⓘ Twinkle toes
- ⓘ Two to tango
- ⓘ We got the beat
- ⓘ We've got Rhythm
- ⓘ You should be dancin'

Anyone who thinks sunshine is happiness has never danced in the rain

Little Ballerina

Little ballerina
Dancing on tippy toes
Concentrating intently
Wrinkling up her nose.

Little tutu of pink
With dainty little shoes
Painting a precious picture
That always chases away my blues!

-Thena

TWINKLE TOES

Tiny Dancers

The tiny little dancers
Were all so very proud
Parents in front row seats
Applauded nice and loud.
One little dancer
Suddenly felt ill at ease
And hid behind a nook
The others all stopped dancing
And went to take a look.
The parents watched with love
And hearts stuck in their throats
When a wee one tumbled
But teacher said nothing broke.
Soon the dance was over
And everyone left again
And on every single face
There was a happy grin.

-Thena

Daydreams—Thinking about so many things; dreaming about wishes and hopes

Houses Of Dreams

You took my empty dreams
And filled them every one
With tenderness and nobleness,
April and the sun.
The old empty dreams
Where my thoughts would throng
Are far too full of happiness
To even hold a song.
Oh, the empty dreams were dim
And the empty dreams were wide,
They were sweet and shadowy houses
Where my thoughts could hide.
But you took my dreams away
And you made them all come true--
My thoughts have no place now to play,
And nothing now to do.
-Sara Teasdale

☆

Day Dreamin' about you

You're makin' my dreams come true

All I have to do is dream

Dream Girl/Boy

I was trying to daydream,
but my mind kept wandering
-Steven Wright

Did You Know?

Thirty days hath September,
April, June, and November;
all the rest have thirty-one,
Excepting February alone,
Which has just eight and a score,
'Til leap-year gives it one day more.

Give a Boy a Cookie

Give a boy a cookie
and he will have a feast
Give a boy a pocket
and he'll fill it with treasures
Give a boy a book
and he'll travel the world
Give a boy your time
and he'll learn to love
For a lifetime.

-Linda LaTourelle

The word

"LISTEN"
contains the same
letters as the word
"SILENT"

☆

The names of the
continents all end
with the same
letter with which
they begin

Mr. Know-It-All

Mr. Know-It-All knows it all
all in his head.
He knows what you will say
before it is said.
If at knowing things Know-It-All's
simply the best
then why doesn't he know
he's a Know-It-All pest.

-Robert Pottle ©

Dinosaurs

A dinosaur lived long ago,
A dinosaur that I did know.
He was clumsy as could be.
He often walked into a tree.
He'd blow his nose, and it would bleed.
He tripped and fell on every weed.
He cut his foot. He bumped his head.
He sometimes fell right out of bed.
He had a rather nasty cough.
His belly button fell right off!
And it should come as no surprise,
He had not one but two black eyes.
What kind of dinosaur was he?
What kind of creature could he be?
A sore-o-saurus
Of course
-Robert Pottle ©

**Land
Before
Kids**

I ♡

T-REX

Dinosaurs are funny
At least they were, I think
But I don't really know for sure
Because they are all extinct!
-Thena

Dinosaurs lived
so long ago
They never had
a chance to know
How many kids
would love to get
A dinosaur
to be their pet!

Dinosaurs names seem
To always end in rex
And I think that's rather strange
To think about those
strange "rexes"
Grazing on the range.
-Thena

Dolls—A toy in the likeness of a human; a girl's best friend; big dolls, little dolls and everything in between

Here is my dolly all tattered and torn.
Everyone loves her even though she is worn.
Her body is floppy and her hair is a mess,
but I love her dearly, and she loves me best!

My Doll Dilemma

I got a bride doll for Christmas
But I think she is too fine
To climb the trees with brother and me
And maybe too refined!

My Raggedy doll loves climbing
While my Barbie prefers to drive
Along beside me in her special sports car
Perhaps she could give the bride doll a ride!

My brother has a GI doll
And I think he is too rough
Although my brother throws him about
And says GI's are really tough!

I doubt they will get married
For dolls don't seem to age like us
But if Barbie got married first
My bride doll might make a fuss!
                        -Thena

My Sister's Dolls

My sister says her dolls look best
when dressed in pinks and reds.
I think my sister's dolls look best
when they have no heads.
                        -Robert Pottle ©

118

Dreamland

- A Dream Is A Wish Your Heart Makes
- A Kiss To Build A Dream On
- Beautiful Dreamer
- Bedtime For Bonzo
- California Dreamin'
- Caught Napping
- Counting Sheep
- Daydream Believer
- Down For The Count
- Dream A Little Dream Of Me
- Dream Lover
- Dreams Really Do Come True
- Dream Sweet Dreams
- Dream Time
- Dream Weaver
- Dream, Dream, Dream
- Dreamin' And Hopin'
- Dreamland Express
- Field Of Dreams
- Golden Slumbers
- Good Night Sweetheart
- Good Night, Sleep Tight, Don't Let The Bed Bugs Bite
- Goodnight Sweetie
- Here Comes The Night

My Dream

I had a dream the other night
When the earth was awful still
That all I had to do to fly
Was to take a pill.
The pill was so awful big
And it took me oh so long
And when morning came
My favorite pillow was gone!

-Thena

SAY YOUR PRAYERS

- Golden Slumbers
- Goodnight Sweetheart
- Goodnight Sweetie
- Here Comes The Night
- But I'm Not Tired
- I Don't Want To Go To Sleep
- I Want Water
- I'm Thirsty
- Life Is But A Dream
- Mr. Sandman
- Nightie, Night
- No More Water
- No Sleep, No Dreams
- One More Page?
- Only In My Dreams
- Peace And Quiet
- Saturday Sleep-In
- Say Your Prayers
- Sleeping Beauty
- Sleepovers
- Sleepy Head
- Sleepy Time Gal/Guy
- Slumber Party
- Snug As A Bug In A Rug
- Some Dreams Come True
- Strangers In The Night
- Sweet Dreams
- Things That Go Bump In The Night
- Time For Bed, Sleepyhead
- To Sleep, Perchance To Dream
- Too Beat To Eat
- Too Late For Reading
- Turn Off The Light
- Walking After Midnight
- What A Dream!
- When In Doubt, Take A Nap
- When You Wish Upon A Star, Your Dreams Come True
- While You Were Sleeping
- Who Needs Some Sleep?
- Zonked Out
- Zzzzzz

Dress Up

- A Diamond Is Forever
- Ain't I Cute
- All Decked Out
- All Dolled Up
- American Beauty
- Baubles and Bangles
- Blush on My Cheeks
- Call Me Irresistible
- Chantilly Lace and a Pretty Face
- Curl My Hair
- Dress-Up Day
- Fashion Frenzy
- Funny Face
- Hello Gorgeous
- Here's Looking At You Kid
- I Like to Play Dress Up
- I'm Just a Raggedy Ann in a Barbie Doll World
- Little Lady
- Look at that Face
- Mascara Monster
- Mirror, Mirror on the Wall
- Model in the Making
- Momma's Make-up Bag
- Mommy's Shoes
- Ooh La La!
- Picture Perfect
- Pretend that I'm Mom
- Pretty in Pink
- Puttin' On the Ritz
- Rosey Cheeks
- Ruffles & Lace
- Strike a Pose
- What a Doll!
- A Girl Can Never Have Too Many Shoes

PRINCESS OF PINK

Mommy's Shoes

I like to wear my Mommy's shoes
I mean the pair she doesn't use
I pick the one's with the highest heels,
You can't imagine how it feels.
To walk around, go out the door.
Clump-clumping across the floor.

STANDIN' IN HER MOMMA'S SHOES

Earth

We studied about the earth
And how the land was made
We learned about the ocean blue
And all the things that fish and dolphins do.
Then we all went outside to play
And celebrate our earth today!

- The Good Earth
- The Salt of the Earth
- Don't Be A Litterbug
- Save the Rainforest
- Recycle
- Keep It Clean!

Earth

If the earth turns around
As fast as they say
Why don't I fall off
When I go out to play?
If the stars are so hot
And burning in the sky
Why don't birds' feathers get singed
When they start to fly?
If the ocean is so big
And the sea is so deep and wide
How come it doesn't cover us
When in comes the tide?
These thoughts perplex me-
I've questioned Mom and Dad, too
But Dad says that to wait until I'm older
Is what I must do!
-Thena Smith ©

122

Easter

- A 24 Carrot day
- A basket full of goodies
- A hunting we will go...
- A tisket, a tasket, I found my Easter basket
- A very bunny Easter
- An egg-citing resurrection story
- An eggs-stra special Easter
- Baskets and bunnies
- Baskets of Fun
- Be an eggs-pert
- Coloring eggs
- Easter Basket
- Easter bonnet
- Easter egg "dips"
- Easter egg fun
- Easter egg hunt
- Easter egg morning
- Easter egg-citement
- Easter is sharing the joys of the heart
- Easter morn
- Easter Parade
- Easter Poohrade
- Easter-ific
- Easter's on its way
- Egg hunt!

- Egg painting zone
- Egg-cited for Easter
- Eggs-actly
- Eggs-cellent
- Eggstra-special!
- Eggstravaganza
- Funny bunny
- Get crackin'
- Happy Easter
- Have a spegg'tacular Easter
- Here comes Peter Cottontail
- Hippity Hoppity Hooray
- Hippity...Hoppity Easter's on its way
- Loads of eggs
- Rotten Eggs
- What an "egg-cellent" kid
- You crack me up
- You're no-bunny 'til some bunny loves you

HE IS RISEN
HE LIVES
FOR YOU

Family—A group of relatives, especially parents and their children. A unit that works together, plays together and prays together

There is no higher calling in life than the task of bearing and raising the children whom God has trusted to our care. We are given a few brief years to love and guide them and instill the values in which we believe. —James Dobson

Love bears all things,
believes all things,
hopes all things,
endures all things.
Love never fails.
-I Corinthians 13:7-8

Family

is a precious thing
Sent from God above
Tender and so special
It's the place we learn to love

Our Family

We have a little family
It's my daughters and just me
But oh, our little family
Is just what we want it to be
God brought us all together
To love and laugh and grow
Today, tomorrow and forever
May God's love we always show.
He has a special purpose
In our precious family
'Tis for His light to shine
and tell others of His Majesty.

-Linda LaTourelle

WE ARE FAMILY

The Stick-Together Families

The stick-together families are happier by far
Than the brothers and the sisters who take separate highways are.
The gladdest people living are the wholesome folks who make
A circle at the fireside that no power but death can break.
And the finest conventions ever held beneath the sun
Are the little family gatherings when the busy day is done.

It's the stick-together family that wins the joys of earth,
That hears the sweetest music and that finds the finest mirth;
It's the old home roof that shelters all the charm that life can give;
There you find the gladdest playground, there the happiest spot to live.
And , O weary, wandering brother, if contentment you would win,
Come you back unto the fireside and be comrade with your kin.

-Edgar Guest

125

- A Child Does Not Need To Be Parented. He Needs To Be Mothered And Fathered. -Zan Thompson

- A Child Enters Your Home And For The Next Twenty Years Makes So Much Noise That You Can Hardly Stand It. The Child Departs, Leaving the House So Silent You Think You Are Going Mad. —J.A. Holmes

- A Child, Like Your Stomach, Doesn't Need All You Can Afford To Give It. -Frank A. Clark

- A Family Is a Cheering Section When a Victory Is Won

- A Family Is a Haven of Rest, a Sanctuary of Peace and Most of All a Harbor Of Love

- A Family Is Where Each Can Find Solace And Comfort In Grief, Pleasure And Laughter In Joy, And Kindness And Encouragement In Daily Living. -Manny Feldman

- A Family Stitched Together With Love Seldom Ravels

- A Lot Of Parents Pack Up Their Troubles And Send Them Off To Summer Camp. -Raymond Duncan

- A Man Soon Learns How Little He Knows When His Child Begins To Ask Questions

- All Happy Families Resemble One Another, Each Unhappy Family Is Unhappy In Its Own Way -Leo Tolstoy

- All of Us Are We...And Everyone Else Is They —Rudyard Kipling

- Although There Are Many Trial Marriages... There Is No Such Thing As A Trial Child. -Gail Sheehy

- Always End The Name Of Your Child With A Vowel, So That When You Yell, The Name Will Carry. -Bill Cosby

- Always Kiss Your Children Goodnight - Even If They're Already Asleep

126

⊕ Any Child Can Tell You That The Sole Purpose Of A Middle Name Is So He Can Tell When He's Really In Trouble. -Dennis Fakes

⊕ As A Child My Family's Menu Consisted Of Two Choices: Take It, Or Leave It. -Buddy Hackett

⊕ Ask Your Child What He Wants For Dinner Only If He's Buying. -Fran Lebowitz

⊕ Before I Got Married I Had Six Theories About Bringing Up Children; Now I Have Six Children, And No Theories. -John Wilmot

⊕ Call It A Clan, Call It A Network, Call It A Tribe, Call It A Family. Whatever You Call It, Whoever You Are, You Need One. -Jane Howard

⊕ Character Is Largely Caught, And The Father And The Home Should Be The Great Sources Of Character Infection. -Frank H. Cheley

⊕ Children Are Like Sponges: They Absorb All Your Strength And Leave You Limp, But Give Them A Squeeze And You Get It All Back!

⊕ Children Are Natural Mimics Who Act Like Their Parents Despite Every Effort To Teach Them Good Manners

⊕ Children Aren't Happy With Nothing To Ignore; That's What Parents Were Created For. -Ogden Nash

⊕ Children Grow Up To Be Adults, But Parents Are Parents Forever!

⊕ Children Need Models More Than They Need Critics. -Joseph Joubert

⊕ Don't Handicap Your Children By Making Their Lives Easy. -Robert A. Heinlein

⊕ Don't Worry That Children Never Listen To You; Worry That They Are Always Watching You. -Robert Fulghum

THE A, B, C'S FOR MY CHILD AND ME

A. **A**ccept your children
B. **B**elieve in them
C. **C**are from your heart
D. **D**o devotions daily together
E. **E**njoy each moment
F. **F**ollow your heart
G. **G**ive your all
H. **H**ug your kids every day
I. **I**nspire kids with truth
J. **J**ump and shout with your kids
K. **K**iss your children often
L. **L**ove them unconditionally
M. **M**anage your time wisely
N. **N**ever abuse your children in any way
O. **O**pen your heart and soul to your children
P. **P**ray together and Play together
Q. **Q**uality and quantity are necessary
R. **R**emember that you too were once a child
S. **S**et an example in your life
T. **T**each your children godly values
U. **U**nderstand with gentleness
V. **V**alidate your children
W. **W**orship the Lord daily
X. **X**-pect that there will be some bad days
Y. **Y**ou are the one in charge, not your kids
Z. **Z**zzz Rest in the Lord

Make each moment count—time is precious
Let go of little things—they're all little
Love like it's the first time you saw their face
Give all you've got—that's what God did!

If You Have Trouble Getting Your Children's Attention, Just Sit Down And Look Comfortable

- Each Day Of Our Lives We Make Deposits In The Memory Banks Of Our Children. -Charles R. Swindoll

- Family Faces Are Mirrors Of The Past, Present And Future

- Family Is Just Accident... They Don't Mean To Get On Your Nerves. They Don't Even Mean To Be Your Family, They Just Are. -Marsha Norman

- Family Means Putting Your Arms Around Each Other And Being There

- Give Me The Life Of The Boy Whose Mother Is Nurse, Seamstress, Washerwoman, Cook, Teacher, Angel, And Saint, All In One, And Whose Father Is Guide, Exemplar, And Friend. No Servants To Come Between. These Are The Boys Who Are Born To The Best Fortune. -Andrew Carnegie

- Happiness Is Having A Large, Loving, Caring, Close-Knit Family In Another City. -George Burns

- Hot Dogs Always Seem Better Out Than At Home; So Do French-Fried Potatoes; So Do Your Children. -Mignon Mclaughlin

- If Evolution Really Works, How Come Mothers Only Have Two Hands? -Milton Berle

- If The Family Were A Fruit, It Would Be An Orange, A Circle Of Sections, Held Together But Separable—Each Segment Distinct. -Letty Pogrebin

- If There Is Anything That We Wish To Change In The Child, We Should First Examine It And See Whether It Is Not Something That Could Better Be Changed In Ourselves. -C.G. Jung

- If You Want Children To Keep Their Feet On The Ground, Put Some Responsibility On Their Shoulders. -Abigail Van Buren

- If You Want To Do Something Positive For Your Children, Try To Improve Your Marriage

It Now Costs More To Amuse A Child
Than It Once Did To Educate His Father

- If Your Children Spend Most of Their Time in Other People's Houses, You're Lucky; If They All Congregate At Your House, You're Blessed. -Mignon Mclaughlin

- If Your Kids Are Giving You A Headache, Follow The Directions On The Aspirin Bottle, Especially The Part That Says "Keep Away From Children. -Susan Savannah

- In Bringing Up Children, Spend On Them Half As Much Money And Twice As Much Time.

- Instant Availability Without Continuous Presence Is Probably The Best Role A Mother Can Play. -Lotte Bailyn

- It Would Seem That Something Which Means Poverty, Disorder And Violence Every Single Day Should Be Avoided Entirely, But The Desire To Beget Children Is A Natural Urge. -Phyllis Diller

- Labor Day Is A Glorious Holiday Because Your Child Will Be Going Back To School The Next Day. It Would Have Been Called Independence Day, But That Name Was Already Taken. -Bill Dodds

- Letting A Child Dictate To You Is The Same As Robbing Him Of A Parent.

- Life's Golden Age Is When The Kids Are Too Old To Need Baby-Sitters And Too Young To Borrow The Family Car.

- Like Branches On A Tree, We May Grow In Different Directions, Yet Our Roots Remain As One.

- Likely As Not, The Child You Can Do The Least With Will Do The Most To Make You Proud. -Mignon Mclaughlin

- Lucky Parents Who Have Fine Children Usually Have Lucky Children Who Have Fine Parents. -James Brewer

My Family Is Really Boring.
They Have A Coffee Table Book Called
'Pictures We Took Just To Use Up The Rest Of The Film.
-Penelope Lombard

⊙ Most American Children Suffer Too Much Mother And Too Little Father. -Gloria Steinem

⊙ Most Of Us Become Parents Long Before We Have Stopped Being Children. -Mignon Mclaughlin

⊙ My Accomplishments? Let Me Show You These Pictures In My Wallet.

⊙ My Mom Used To Say It Doesn't Matter How Many Kids You Have... Because One Kid'll Take Up 100% Of Your Time So More Kids Can't Possibly Take Up More Than 100% Of Your Time. -Karen Brown

⊙ My Mother Protected Me From The World And My Father Threatened Me With It. -Quentin Crisp

⊙ No Matter How Calmly You Try To Referee, Parenting Will Eventually Produce Bizarre Behavior, And I'm Not Talking About The Kids. -Bill Cosby

⊙ Other Things May Change Us, But We Start And End With Family.

⊙ Our Family Is Like A Hand-Sewn Quilt That Grows More Precious In Time.

⊙ Our Most Basic Instinct Is Not For Survival But For Family. Most Of Us Would Give Our Own Life For The Survival Of A Family Member, Yet We Lead Our Daily Life Too Often As If We Take Our Family For Granted. -Paul Pearshall

⊙ Our Most Treasured Family Heirlooms Are Our Sweet Family Memories.

⊙ Out Of The Mouths Of Babes Come The Words We Should Never Have Said.

Summer Vacation Is The Time When Parents Realize That Teachers Are Grossly Underpaid

- ⊕ Parenthood Is The Art Of Bringing Your Children Up Without Putting Them Down.

- ⊕ Parenthood: That State Of Being Better Chaperoned Than You Were Before Marriage. -Marcelene Cox

- ⊕ Parents Are Not Interested In Justice; They Are Interested In Quiet. -Bill Cosby

- ⊕ Parents Can Give Children Things Or Time—Time Is Better!

- ⊕ Parents Often Talk About The Younger Generation As If They Didn't Have Anything To Do With It. -Haim Ginott

- ⊕ Raising Children Is Like Making Biscuits: It Is As Easy To Raise A Big Batch As One, While You Have Your Hands In The Dough. -E.W. Howe

- ⊕ Reasoning With A Child Is Fine, If You Can Reach The Child's Reason Without Destroying Your Own. -John Mason Brown

- ⊕ Remember As Far As Anyone Knows, We're A Nice Normal Family. -Homer Simpson

- ⊕ Setting A Good Example For Your Children Takes All The Fun Out Of Life!

- ⊕ Simply Having Children Does Not Make Mothers. -John A. Shedd

- ⊕ Sing Out Loud In The Car Even, Or Especially, If It Embarrasses Your Children. -Marilyn Penland

- ⊕ Some Times We're So Concerned About Giving Our Children What We Never Had Growing Up, We Neglect To Give Them What We Did Have Growing Up. -James Dobson

- ⊕ Television Has Changed A Child From An Irresistible Force To An Immovable Object.

There Are Three Ways To Get Something Done: Do It Yourself, Hire Someone, Or Forbid Your Kids To Do It

- The Beauty Of "Spacing" Children Many Years Apart Lies In The Fact That Parents Have Time To Learn The Mistakes That Were Made With The Older Ones - Which Permits Them To Make Exactly The Opposite Mistakes With The Younger Ones. -Sydney J. Harris

- The Best Way To Keep Children At Home Is To Make The Home Atmosphere Pleasant - And Let The Air Out Of Their Tires. -Dorothy Parker

- The Child Supplies The Power But The Parents Have To Do The Steering.

- The End Product Of Child Raising Is Not The Child But The Parent.

- The Essence Of Childhood, Of Course, Is Play, Which My Friends And I Did Endlessly On Streets That We Reluctantly Shared With Traffic. -Bill Cosby

- The Family—That Dear Octopus From Whose Tentacles We Never Quite Escape, Nor, In Our Inmost Hearts, Ever Quite Wish To. -Dodie Smith

- The Family—We Were A Strange Little Band Of Characters Trudging Through Life Sharing Diseases And Toothpaste, Coveting One Another's Desserts, Borrowing Money, Inflicting Pain And Kissing To Heal It In The Same Instant, Loving, Laughing, Defending, And Trying To Figure Out The Common Thread That Bound Us All Together. -Erma Bombeck

- The Guys Who Fear Becoming Fathers Don't Understand That Fathering Is Not Something Perfect Men Do, But Something That Perfects The Man. -Frank Pittman

- The Happiest Moments Of My Life Have Been The Few Which I Have Passed At Home In The Bosom Of My Family. -Thomas Jefferson

The One Thing Children Wear Out Faster Than Shoes Are Their Parents!

- The Informality Of Family Life Is A Blessed Condition That Allows Us To Become Our Best While Looking Our Worst. -Marge Kennedy

- The Only Rock I Know That Stays Steady, The Only Institution I Know That Works Is The Family. -Lee Iacocca

- The Problem With Children Is That You Have To Put Up With Their Parents. -Charles Delint

- The Quickest Way For A Parent To Get A Child's Attention Is To Sit Down And Look Comfortable. -Lane Olinghouse

- The Secret Of Dealing Successfully With A Child Is Not To Be Its Parent. -Mell Lazarus

- One Hundred Years From Now It Won't Matter, The Sort Of House You Lived In, Or The Kind Of Car You Drove, But The World May Be Different Because You Were Important In The Life Of A Child.

- The Temptation Is To Tune Children Out; It Takes Much More Courage To Listen.

- The Thing That Impresses Me Most About America Is The Way Parents Obey Their Children. -Edward, Duke Of Windsor

- The Trouble With Being A Parent Is That By The Time You Are Experienced, You Are Unemployed.

- The Value Of Marriage Isn't That Adults Produce Children, But That Children Produce Adults. -Peter De Vries

- The Work Will Wait While You Show The Child A Rainbow, But The Rainbow Won't Wait While You Do The Work.

- There Are No Illegitimate Children—Only Illegitimate Parents. -Leon R. Yankwich

- There Are Two Lasting Bequests We Can Give Our Children. One Is Roots. The Other Is Wings. -Hodding Carter, Jr.

134

When My Kids Become Wild And Unruly, I Use A Nice, Safe Playpen. When They're Finished, I Climb Out.
-Erma Bombeck

- There Is Always A Moment In Childhood When The Door Opens And Lets The Future In. -Graham Green

- There Is Only One Pretty Child In The World, And Every Mother Has It. -Chinese Proverb

- There's Nothing Wrong With Using Four Letter Words In Explaining The Facts Of Life To Children—Words Like Love, Kiss, Help, Care, Give... -Sam Levenson

- To Be In Your Children's Memories Tomorrow, You Have To Be In Their Lives Today.

- To Bring Up A Child In The Way He Should Go, Travel That Way Yourself Once In A While. -Josh Billings

- To Show A Child What Has Once Delighted You, To Find The Child's Delight Added To Your Own So That There Is Now A Double Delight Seen In The Glow Of Trust And Affection, This Is Happiness. -J.B. Priestley

- To Us, Family Means Putting Your Arms Around Each Other And Being There. -Barbara Bush

- Too Often We Give Children Answers To Remember Rather Than Problems To Solve. -Roger Lewin

- Want Your Children To Listen To You? Speak Softly—To Someone Else!

- What Greater Thing Is There For Human Souls Than To Feel That They Are Joined For Life—To Be With Each Other In Silent Unspeakable Memories. -George Eliot

- When Our Relatives Are At Home, We Have To Think Of All Their Good Points Or It Would Be Impossible To Endure Them. -George Bernard Shaw

You Can Learn Many Things From Children. How Much Patience You Have, For Instance.
-Franklin P. Jones

When You Look At Your Life, The Greatest Happiness is Family Happiness. -Joyce Brothers

When You Were A Kid, You Never Understood What Your Parents Were Going Through. Now You'd Just Like To Know How They Got Through It.

Whenever I Held My Newborn Baby In My Arms, I Used To Think That What I Said And Did To Him Could Have An Influence Not Only On Him But On All Whom He Met, Not Only For A Day Or A Month Or A Year, But For All Eternity A Very Challenging And Exciting Thought For A Mother. -Rose Kennedy

Where Can A Person Be Better Than In The Bosom Of Their Family?

Who Of Us Is Mature Enough For Children Before They Arrive.

You Can Do Anything With Children If Only You Play With Them.

You Don't Choose Your Family. They Are God's Gift To You, As You Are To Them. -Desmond Tutu

You Have A Lifetime To Work, But Children Are Only Young Once.

You Know Your Children Are Growing Up When They Stop Asking You Where They Came From And Refuse To Tell You Where They're Going. -P.J. O'rourke

You Will Always Be Your Child's Favorite Toy. -Vicki Lansky

Your Children Tell You Casually Years Later What It Would Have Killed You With Worry To Know At The Time. -Mignon Mclaughlin

Your Children Vividly Remember Every Unkind Thing You Ever Did To Them, Plus A Few You Really Didn't. -Mignon Mclaughlin

- A Family Is A Gift That Lasts Forever
- A Family Is A Little World Created By Love
- A Family Is a Patchwork of Love
- A Happy Family Is But an Earlier Heaven
- All In The Family
- All things grow with love
- Are We Not Like Two Volumes Of One Book?
- Chip Off The Old Block
- Circles Of Love
- Don't Let Your Parents Down; They Brought You Up!
- Families Are Forever
- Families Are Tied Together With Heart Strings
- Family Matters
- Family Memories Are Held In Our Hearts Forever
- Family Ties

- God bless our family!
- Happiness Is Homemade
- I Am Now Smart, My Kids Are Grown.
- I Could Be A Perfect Parent If It Weren't For My Kids
- It Runs in the Family
- It's All In The Genes
- It's All Relative
- Kids Spell Love T-I-M-E
- Kindred Spirits
- Kinfolk
- Linked By Love
- Love Is Spoken Here
- Lucky To Have Each Other

**Bless this family
Day by day
With love and joy
And peace I
pray**

- Mom's Taxi Service
- Momma Bear, Poppa Bear And Baby Bear
- My Family, My Life
- Near And Dear
- Next Of Kin
- Personal Chauffeur
- Proud Parents
- Raising Our Sweetest Harvest
- Some Family Trees Bear An Enormous Crop Of Nuts
- Taxi Driver
- The _____ Clan
- The _____ Family
- The Best Place To Be Is In A Family
- The Family That Plays Together—Stays Together
- The Family That Prays Together Stays Together
- The First 40 Years Of Parenthood Are Always The Hardest!
- The Good Life
- The Love Of A Family Is The Essence Of Life
- The Luckiest People In The World
- The Parent Trap
- There Is Trial Marriage But No Trial Children.
- This Is No Ordinary Family
- We Are A Happy Family
- We Are Blessed
- We Are Family
- We May Not Have It All Together; But Together We Have It All
- We Put The Fun Back In Dysfunctional!
- We're A Wacky Bunch
- What A Child Doesn't Receive He Can Seldom Later Give
- You Can't Scare Us We Have Children!
- Yours, Mine, And Ours

138

English to Spanish Translations

Family	Familia
Father	Padre
Mother	Madre
Brother	Hermano
Sister	Hermana
Son	Hijo
Daughter	Hija
Grandfather	Abuelo
Grandmother	Abuela
Uncle	Tito
Aunt	Tia
Nephew	Sobrino
Niece	Sobrina
Cousin	Primo
Great Grandfather	Gran Abuelo
Great Grandmother	Gran Abuela
Love	Amor
Friends	Amigos
Children	Niños
Child	Niño
School	Escuela
Teacher	Profesor
Generation	Generación
My Home	Mi Hogar
I Love My Father	Amo A Mi Padre
I Love My Mother	Amo A Mi Madre
Families are Forever	Las familias están por

English to German Translations

Family	Familie
Father	Vater
Mother	Mutter
Brother	Bruder
Sister	Schwester
Son	Sohn
Daughter	Tochter
Grandfather	Großvater
Grandmother	Großmutter
Uncle	Onkel
Aunt	Tante
Nephew	Neffe
Niece	Nichte
Cousin	Vetter
Great Grandfather	Großer Großvater
Great Grandmother	Große Großmutter
Love	Liebe
Friends	Freunde
Children	Kinder
Child	Kind
School	Schule
Teacher	Lehrer
Generation	Erzeugung
My Home	Mein Haus

I Love My Father	Ich liebe meinen Vater
I Love My Mother	Ich liebe meinen Mutter
Families are Forever	Familien sind für immer

English to French Translations

Family	Famille
Father	Père
Mother	Mère
Brother	Frère
Sister	Soeur
Son	Fil
Daughter	Files
Grandfather	Grand-Père
Grandmother	Grand-Mère
Uncle	Oncle
Aunt	Tante
Nephew	Neveu
Niece	Nièce
Cousin	Cousin
Great Grandfather	Grand Grand-Père
Great Grandmother	Grand Grand-Mère
Love	Amour
Friends	Amis
Children	Enfants
Child	Enfant
School	École
Teacher	Professeur
Generation	Génération
My Home	Ma Maison

I Love My Father	J'Aime Mon Père
I Love My Mother	J'Aime Ma Mère
Families are Forever	Les familles sont pour tourjours

141

Dad—There's nothing quite like the love of a Dad; to lift you up when you're feeling sad or play a game or hug you tight. Only Dad's love makes life just right.

Only a Dad

Only a dad with a tired face,
Coming home from the daily race,
Bringing little of gold or fame
To show how well he has played the game;
But glad in his heart that his own rejoice
To see him come and to hear his voice.
Only a dad, but he gives his all,
To smooth the way for his children small,
Doing with courage stern and grim
The deeds that his father did for him.
This is the line that for him I pen:
Only a Dad, but the best of men.

-Edgar Guest

fat'·her: (noun) one who has begotten a child; a parent of the male species; a hero to a child; an example to many; the leader of his home; the love that never ends; a gift to a child from heaven above

- ☺ Hey Dad!
- ☺ Best DAD Award
- ☺ Dad Did It!
- ☺ Dad's Home!
- ☺ Don't Bother the Master While He Is Working
- ☺ Don't Wake Daddy
- ☺ Everything in life I'll share, except of course my Daddy
- ☺ He Who Laughs Last is Probably DAD!
- ☺ I'm Just as Lucky as Can Be, the World's Best Dad Belongs To Me!

Why are men reluctant to become fathers?
They aren't through being children.
-Cindy Garner

- Dad taught me everything I know. Unfortunately, he didn't teach me everything he knows. -Al Unser, Jr.

- My dad has always taught me these words: care and share. That's why we put on clinics. The only thing I can do is try to give back. If it works, it works. -Tiger Woods

- It doesn't matter who my father was; it matters who I remember he was. -Anne Sexton

- It is easier for a father to have children than for children to have a real father. -Pope John XXIII

- My father gave me the greatest gift anyone could give another person, he believed in me. -Jim Valvano

- It is a wise father that knows his own child. -Shakespeare

- Becoming a father isn't difficult, but it's very difficult to be a father.

- When Dad says no, go ask Mom.

- He didn't tell me how to live; he lived, and let me watch him do it. -Kelland

- A truly rich man is one whose children run into his arms when his hands are empty.

- Blessed indeed is the man who hears many gentle voices call him father! -Lydia M. Child

- Old as she was, she still missed her daddy sometimes.

- There are three stages of a man's life: He believes in Santa Claus, he doesn't believe in Santa Claus, he is Santa Claus.

The Mountain

It's big enough to block the sun
This stark, imposing mountain peak
But it's the one I'm going to climb
I'll make it if it takes all week
The foothills mark a narrow path
I slowly hike that spindly trail
Although I waiver as I climb
I dare not think that I might fail
The mountain towers high above
I dig and claw with all my might
My every muscle pleads for rest
But now, at last, the top's in sight
A rumbling leaves me terrified
A quaking makes me lose my grip
This mountain will not let me win
So back to earth I slide and slip
I'm on the ground no worse for wear
With nothing hurt except my pride
When I look up, the mountain's gone
'Cause Daddy rolled on to his side

-Jeff Mondak ©

ⓘ If at first you don't succeed, destroy the evidence—before Dad gets home

ⓘ I love to tickle Daddy's toes

ⓘ Master of His Kingdom

ⓘ My Buddy, My Dad

ⓘ My Dad's bigger than your Dad

ⓘ My Dad's never too Old to Play Cowboy

Just me and my Dad
☆
Like Father, Like Son
☆
Daddy & Me
☆
Daddy 'O Mine

My Dad

I love him so much
He's wise and he's strong
He plays with me
He teaches me
He corrects me
He lifts me up
He comforts me
There is no other
Man that I know
That loves me
Just like Jesus

DAD, I LOVE YOU

Truck Drivin' Daddy

Eighteen wheels or eighteen days
Please tell my daddy this
When he's not home to tuck me in
I miss his goodnight kiss!

Overnight or for a week
I'm happy as can be
When that stretch of highway
Brings my daddy back to me!

-Jennifer Byerly © 2004

Without Words

A father seldom speaks of love
But you can hear it in his laughter
He reaches out with tenderness
In moments when you need him
He never fails to tell you
In a hug or in a smile
But there's no doubt about it
His love makes life worthwhile

-Linda LaTourelle

Mender of toys, leader of boys
Changer of fuses, kisser of bruises,
Bless him, dear Lord.
Hanger of screens, counselor of teens,
Fixer of bikes, chastiser of tykes.
Help him, O Lord.
Raker of leaves, cleaner of eaves,
Dryer of dishes, fulfiller of wishes,
Guard him, O Lord.

-unknown

World's Best Dad

- Dad Rocks
- Daddy's Boy/Girl
- Daddy's Darling
- Daddy's Little Helper
- Daddy's Little Squirt
- Daddy's Princess
- My Daddy
- Walking in Daddy's Footsteps
- World's Best Dad

145

Three Words

I heard three words
From dad today
I didn't expect to hear.
They came,
 like thunderbolts,
Out of his mouth,
Before he could close my ears.
At first, he seemed shocked
They came from his lips,
In front of his only son.
He looked pretty sheepish
And turned sort of red,
When he realized what he had done.
I gave him a hug and said,
"That's OK, Dad,
You only just said what was true.
I knew one day I'd hear those words,
And you know what?
I love you, too!
-Ted Scheu ©

My Heart Belongs to Daddy
&
His heart Belongs to Me

MY FRIEND MY HERO MY DAD

- Like Father, Like Son
- Papa Bear
- The Apple Doesn't Fall Far From the Tree
- The Best Example a Father can give his children is a good example
- The Man of the House
- The most important thing a father can do for his children: is to Love Their Mother
- There is nothing in this world as strong as my Dad
- Time With Dad
- Whatcha Know—Daddy-O?
- When I grow up I wanna be just like you.
- Where's there's love— there's my Dad
- When all else fails—ask Dad

146

For I have chosen him so that he will command his children and his house after him to keep the way of the Lord by doing what is right and just.

-Genesis 18:19

Across the fields of yesterday
He sometimes comes to me
A little boy just back from play
The boy I used to be.
He smiles at me so wistfully
When once he's crept within
It is as though he had hoped to see
The man I might have been

-unknown

He's the Man

Daddy's Little Girl

You're the end of the rainbow
My pot of gold
You're Daddy's little girl
To have and hold
A precious gem is what you are
You're Mommy's bright and shining star
You're the spirit of Christmas
My star on the tree
You're the Easter Bunny
To Mommy and me
You're sugar you're spice
You're everything nice
And you're Daddy's Little Girl

-Donia Linderman ©

Lord every path I walked with Dad, has led to YOU

THAT'S MY DADDY!

147

Make our sons in their prime
Like sturdy oak trees,
Our daughters as shapely and bright
as fields of wildflowers.
-Psalm 144:12
♡

Just as the moon is the light of the night
And the sun of the day,
So are good children the light of their father.
♡

My father was a quiet man—
his loving care said all that was needed
♡

When Daddy stopped smiling
it was time to listen tight and fly right
♡

He who loves me teaches me to love
♡

Children are their father's riches
♡

I owe almost everything to my father

FATHER
⊚ Gentle
⊚ Humble
⊚ Kind
⊚ Loving
⊚ Patient

My Father
Is extremely tall
When he stands upright like a wall
But I am very short and small.
Yet I am growing, so they say,
A little taller every day
-unknown

Daddy, I love you
For all that you do.
I'll kiss you and hug you
'Cause you love me, too.
You feed me and need me
To teach you to play,
So smile 'cause I love you
On this Father's Day.

-Nicholas Gordon

Directly
After
God
In Heaven
Comes—

Daddy

- Dad's a Reel Catch
- Hero is spelled D.A.D.
- Dad's the Boss, Mom said so
- A father fills our lives with love
- A wise son maketh a glad father -Proverbs 10:1
- Real Dads know the value of DUCT TAPE!
- Dad: a son's first hero, a daughter's first love

My father has a gentle hand
To guide me every day
He has a very cheerful heart
That still knows how to play
My father is a source of strength
That helps me carry on
He is a loving, prayerful man
My father's number one

-Linda LaTourelle

♡

YES SIR...THAT'S MY DADDY!

- A Toast For Dad
- Berry Best Dad
- Big Daddy
- Big shoes to fill
- Celebrate Dad
- Celebrating Fatherhood
- DAD: The Man, The Myth, and The Legend
- Dad's #1 Fan
- Daddy hung the moon
- Daddy's Little Angel
- Daddy's Little Boy/Girl
- Daddy-O
- DADITUDE!
- Dear Ol' Dad
- Don't Wake Daddy
- Don't Forget Daddy
- Father Knows Best
- Father of the Year
- Go Daddy Go
- His Father's Son
- Hop on Pop
- I am Dad, hear me snore
- In my Daughter's eyes
- Just Like Dad
- Just Me And My Dad
- King of The Hill
- Life With Dad
- Life With Father
- Like Father, Like Son/ Daughter
- Man of the hour
- My Dad is the Greatest
- My Dad Rules!
- My Dad's a star
- My Heart Belongs To Daddy
- No One can Fill Dad's Shoes
- Our Dad's the Greatest
- Patio Daddy-O
- Proud Papa
- Sugar Daddy
- Super Dad
- We Love Dad
- Where's my Daddy?
- World's Best Daddy
- World's Greatest Father

When Pa Comes Home

When Pa comes home, I'm at the door,
An' then he grabs me off the floor
An' throws me up an' catches me
When I come down, an' then, says he:
"Well, how'd you get along to-day?
An' were you good, an' did you play,
An' keep right out of mamma's way?
An' how'd you get that awful bump
Above your eye? My, what a lump!
An' who spilled jelly on your shirt?
An' where'd you ever find the dirt?
Who knocked that engine on its back?
An' stepped upon that piece of track?
Who strewed those toys upon the floor,
An' left those things behind the door?
Who upset all those parlor chairs
An' threw those blocks upon the stairs?
I guess a cyclone called to-day
While I was workin' far away.
Who was it worried mamma so?
It can't be anyone I know!"
An' then I laugh an' say: " It's me!
Me did most everything you see.
Me got this bump the time me tripped.
An' here is where the jelly slipped
Right off my bread upon my shirt,
An' when me tumbled down it hurt.
That 's how me got all over dirt.
Me threw those building blocks down the stairs,
An' me upset the parlor chairs,
Coz when you're playin' train you've got
To move things 'round an awful lot."
An' then my Pa he kisses me
An' bounces me upon his knee
An' says, 'Well, well my little lad,
What glorious fun you must have had!"
-Edgar Guest

Does this sound like anyone you might know? Too Cute!!!

My Dad

I Love my Dad so very much
And it's very plain to see
That as much love as I have for him
Even more love he has for me!

He lifts me up to his shoulders
When we are in a parade or crowd
And lets me hide my head in his jacket
When noise or music gets too loud.

He buys me ice cream from the ice cream store
(I chose my favorite and then taste several more)
He's big and strong and very kind to me
Just how lucky could one kid be.
-Thena

A father can shape a child's understanding of God By the way that he shows them love

♡

My Daddy... My Hero

♡

Yankee Doodle Daddy

♡

MY HEART BELONGS TO DADDY

Moth·er-—/ *noun*/ woman who conceives, gives birth to, or raises and nurtures a child; also known as: ma, mamma, mammy, mater, matriarch, mom, momma, mommy, mum, parent, one whom a child adores; a gift from God

My Mother

I don't know where I'd be this day
If it weren't for the love that came my way
Through tears and joy and fears and love
My life was formed with care from above.

Through prayers and hopes I came to be
A world of love in my new family
There was one who above all others
Was a gift from God—I call her Mother.

With patience plenty and love divine
I am so blessed to call her mine
She knows my every joy and woe
And in all this world no love is more.

I thank the Lord for giving to me
The perfect example for my eyes to see
Unconditional love and forgiveness, too
Nothing in life can compare with you.

-Linda LaTourelle

Her children rise up and call her blessed

-Proverbs 31:28

MY MOTHER, MY FRIEND

Motherhood: God's special blessing for women...

- Adores
- Blesses
- Cares
- Cuddles
- Disciples
- Disciplines
- Fusses over
- Gives
- Hopes
- Hugs
- Inspires
- Kisses
- Listens
- Loves
- Ministers
- Nurses
- Nurtures
- Pampers
- Praises
- Prays
- Protects
- Raises
- Rears
- Rocks
- Serves
- Spoils
- Teaches
- Understands
- Waits
- Watches
- Worries

A Mother's heart
is a beautiful expression
of God's everlasting love

A Mother is
a child's first—
Heartbeat
Teacher
Friend
Preacher
Leader
Playmate
Nurse
Hug
Kiss
Gift
Smile
Tear
Joy

A Mom is Love
A Mom is everything
♡
Her Child is
Blessed!

154

Youth fades; love droops, the leaves of friendship fall; A mother's secret hope outlives them all.
-Oliver Wendell Holmes

Of all the rights of women, the greatest is to be a mother.
-Lin Yutang

I remember my mother's prayers and they have always followed me. They have clung to me all my life.
-Abraham Lincoln

I believe in you, Mom
You're strength and courage, too
I believe that God has plans
Still on earth for you
-Jennifer Byerly

Our family is like
A garden
That grows from
Day to day
Planted on
Solid ground
We laugh and
Love and pray

Nobody knows of the work it makes
To keep the home together
Nobody knows of the steps it takes,
Nobody knows but Mother

Best friends forever
mom and me
picking flowers
and climbing trees.
a shoulder to cry on
secrets to share
Warm hearts and hands
that really care

Who ran to help me when I fell,
And would some pretty story tell,
Or kiss the place to make it well?
My Mother."
-Ann Taylor

I'll smile at the simplest things, like when my daughter grabs my hand and begs for me to skip with her; even though she has so much energy stored in her that needs to be let out, I love it that she wants to let it out with me.

–Lara LaTourelle

♡

My Mother's Hugs and Kisses

My mother's hugs and kisses
Can never be replaced
Nothing feels much better
Then her breath upon my face
I think when God made mother's
He knew just what to do
So he filled her up with kisses
And hugs for me and you!

-Jennifer Byerly © 2004

♡

"M" Stands For Mom NOT Maid!

♡

Every Mother Is a Working Mother

♡

Mother said...

Just because the rest of the world is doing
Something doesn't make it right with God

♡

Mother said...

Every Job is a Self-Portrait
of the Person Who Did It
Autograph Yours
With Excellence

- #1 Mom
- A Meeting Of Mums
- A Mother Holds Her Children's Hands For A While, Their Hearts Forever
- Anyone Can Be A Mother, But It Takes Someone Special To Be A Mommy
- A Mother Is Not A Person To Lean On, But A Person To Make Leaning Unnecessary
- A Mother Understands When No One Else Can!
- A Mother's Heart Is As Big As The World
- A Mother's Love For Her Child Is Like Nothing Else In The World. It Knows No Law, No Pity, It Dares All Things And Crushes Down Remorselessly All That Stands In Its Path. -Agatha Christie
- Be A Mother—The Payment Is Pure Love
- Because I'm The Mom— That's Why!
- Caution, Mom Is Stressed
- Every Mother Is A Working Mother
- Every Mother Knows When Children Say They Are Doing Nothing, They Are Into Mischief
- Father Knows Best, But Mom Knows Better!
- Flowers Have The Sun, Children Have Their Mothers
- Food Fight—Mommy Lost
- Forever My Mom
- I am Always at Your Side
- I Love Mom
- I'm the Mom...I Don't Have to be Reasonable
- If children are the ones who take the baths, why are moms the ones who get soaking wet?

157

- If Evolution Really Works, How Come Mothers Only Have Two Hands?

- If You Want Your Kids to excel, let them hear all the nice things you say about them to others

- It's easy for a parent to hear Herself talking; all She Has to Do is listen to her Kids!

- Like Mother, Like Daughter

- Mirror, Mirror On the Wall, I am my Mother After All

- Mom - Maker Of Miracles

- Mom said there would be days like this just not so many

- When God Invented Mothers, He Gave Me the Best

- Mom taught you that the greatest leap comes with the first step

- Mom when thoughts of you are in our hearts we are never far from home

- Mom, Thank You for loving me enough to let go

- Mom, Thank You for Missing Me so Much, But Letting Go

- Mom, You Taught by Example, I Learned by Love

- Mom's Hug is Healing

- Mommy's Mess Maker

- Mom's Day Off

- Mom's Son-Flowers

- Mom's the Word

- Momma Loves Me and I Love Momma

- Mommy's Girl/Boy

- My Mom's the Best

- My Mommy Loves Me Just The Way I Am

- My Mother, My Friend

- Mother - The Heart Of The Home
- Mother And Child
- Mother Knows Best
- Mother, May I ?
- Mother's Take Care Of The Possible And Trust God With The Impossible
- Mother—A Shoulder To Cry On, A Smile To Count On, A Love To Live On
- Motherhood Is Not For Wimps!
- Mum's The Word
- My decision is Maybe and that's Final!
- My Greatest Blessings Call Me Mommy
- My Mother Had A Great Deal Of Trouble With Me, But I Think She Enjoyed It. -Mark Twain
- Mother Love Is The Fuel That Enables A Child To Do The Impossible
- My Heart Belongs to Mom!
- Mom's love Teddy Bears/Dolls, just like me
- Nobody Does It Better
- Not Made-Of-Money?
- Of all the blessings from above, the sweetest is a mother's love
- Only when I became a mother did I learn to be a daughter
- Please understand that no matter how big I get, I will always be a kid at heart
- Real Mothers Don't Walk; They Run All Day
- Real Mothers Have Sticky Doors, Dirty Laundry And Happy Kids
- Real Mothers Know That Their Kitchen Utensils Are Probably In The Sandbox
- No One Hugs Like Mom

159

- She Who Laughs Last... Is Probably MOM!

- Super Mom

- The best things to spend on kids is time

- The Momster

- There Is No Friendship, No Love, Like That Of A Mother For Her Child.
  -Henry Ward Beecher

- To be in your children's memories tomorrow, you have to be in their lives today

- You Can Fool Some Of The People Some Of The Time, But You Can't Fool Mom!

- You Can't Scare Me...I have Children

M is for the million things she gave me,
O means only that she's growing old,
T is for the tears she shed to save me,
H is for her heart of purest gold;
E is for her eyes, with love-light shining,
R means right, and right she'll always be,
Put them all together, they spell Mother
A word that means the world to me.
-Howard Johnson

In her eyes
the look of loving,
In her smile
The warmth of caring.
In her hands
the touch of comfort,
In her heart
the gift of sharing
-unknown

Mother

You are gentleness and kindness
Warmth and security,
Love and laughter in your smile are
Making fond memories now
and for eternity.
-Marcia Cruse
♡

Just My Mom & Me

- A mother understands what a child does not say.

- On Mother's Day, your children are supposed to cater to your every whim...sort of goes against the natural order of things, doesn't it?

- The only thing better than having you for my mother, is my children having you for a grandmother.

- Sooner or later we all quote our mothers.

- You tickled my toes, checked for monsters, showed me the stars...and taught me how to reach them, I love you Mom!

Totally Mom!
- Life givin'
- Hug givin'
- Story readin'
- Great kid rasin'
- Perfect advice givin'
- Household runnin'
- Boo boo kissin'
- Dinner cookin'
- Rules enforcin'
- Carpool drivin'
- Task jugglin'
- Never restin'
- Ever lovin'

**Mother said...
The purpose of life
is a life of purpose.**

Where there is great love
There is a great child.
♡
Where there is a great kid
There is a great mother nearby.

- The power of one mother's prayers could stand an army on it's ear. –E. DeHaven

- There is no way for one to be a perfect mother— but there are a million ways she can be a good one.

- Point your kids in the right direction and when they're old they won't be lost. –The Message

No matter what my mom does to it
Spinach still tastes awful!

♡

God made mother's special
With lots of loving care
He placed in her a tender heart
Forgiveness when we err
He fashioned her with goodness
Gentleness and light
A brightness in her smile
That could light the stars at night
But first God made a woman
His most famous work of art
Because you don't have to be a mother
To have a mother's heart
-Jennifer Byerly © 2005

♡

Love never gives up, never loses faith,
Is always hopeful, and endures through
Every circumstance. –1 Cor. 13:7 NLT

Love is my Mother!

♡

When God thought of mother,
He must have laughed with satisfaction
And framed it quickly—so rich, so deep,
So divine, so full of soul, power
And beauty was the conception.
-Henry Ward Beecher

♡

Shhh...Mom is in Time-Out!

My Mother Kept a Garden

My Mother Kept a Garden
A garden of the heart
She planted all the good things
That gave my life its start.
She turned me to the sunshine
and encouraged me to dream
Fostering and nurturing
the seeds of self-esteem
And when the winds and rain came
She protected me enough
But not too much because she knew
I needed to grow strong and tough
Her constant good example
always taught me right from wrong
Markers for my pathway
that will last a lifetime long
I am my Mother's garden
I am her legacy
And I hope today she feels the love
reflected back from me.

-unknown

♡

If you bungle raising your children, I don't think whatever
else you do well matters very much. -Jacqueline Kennedy

♡

Youth fades; love droops; the leaves of friendship fall: a
mother's secret love outlives them all. -Oliver Wendell Holmes

Attention Children:
Mom's spit never hurt a bit!

163

Her love is like an island in life's ocean, vast and wide; a peaceful, quiet shelter from the wind, the rain, the tide. 'Tis bound on the north by Hope, by Patience on the west, by tender counsel on the south and on the east by rest. Above it like a beacon light shine Faith, and Truth, and Prayer; and thro' the changing scenes of life I find a haven there. —unknown

♡

For the mother is and must be, whether she knows it or not, the greatest, strongest, and most lasting teacher her children have. -Hannah Whithall Smith

Only One Mother

Hundreds of stars in the pretty sky,
Hundreds of shells on the shore together,
Hundreds of birds that go singing by,
Hundreds of birds in the sunny weather.
Hundreds of dewdrops to greet the dawn,
Hundreds of bees in the purple clover,
Hundreds of butterflies on the lawn,
But only one mother the wide world over.
                            -unknown

♡

My Mother, my friend so dear
throughout my life you're always near
A tender smile to guide my way
You're the sunshine to light my day

♡

I'm the Mom...
I Don't Have to be Reasonable

To the world you might just be one person,
but to your mother you are the world

-Linda LaTourelle

♡

Mother's Song

Songs my mother taught me,
In the days long vanished.
Seldom from her eyelids,
Were the teardrops banished.
Now I teach my children,
Each melodious measure.
Oft the teardrops flowing,
Oft they flow from my memory's treasure.

♡

Life doesn't come with an instruction book
—that's why we have Mothers

♡

If I had a flower for each time I thought of My Mother,
I could walk in my garden forever

♡

Someone's in the kitchen with Mommy,
Someone's in the kitchen I know,
Someone's in the kitchen with Mommy,
eating all the cookie dough!

Once upon a memory,
Someone wiped away a tear
Held me close and loved me
Thank you, Mother dear

M agnificent

O ustanding

M arvelous

Others throw their faith away,
but Mothers always pray and pray
—Linda LaTourelle
♡

Over the years,
I've watched
the wonderful ways
you've made life special
for our family...
the moments of love
and laughter,
the traditions
and memories
we'll carry with us
throughout our lives.
But most of all
I've watched the way
you've shown us
the true meaning of love
in everything you do.
♡

A mother is not a person—she's a miracle
♡

The toughest thing about raising kids is
Convincing them you have seniority
♡

In raising my children I have lost my mind
But haven't lost my soul
♡

My mother gave me everything that I needed
To be all that I am and ever hope to be

Thank You Mother

For the shoes that you tied
And the dinners you cooked
Always listening to whining
And never complaining

For drying my tears
And calming my fears
Your love was abounding
Your patience astounding

With your eyes on the goal
You guided my soul
Making memories complete
Our life was so sweet

For the stories you read
Each night before bed
You taught me to pray
Showing God knew the way

Your teaching me right
And forgiving my wrongs
Gave a solid foundation
Made my character strong

Playing taxi by day
And nursemaid by night
You were referee, too
When there was a fight

Time was your gift
And you gave all you had
The days flew so quick
Your love made me glad

From heaven to earth
You let Jesus shine through
No other has prayed
The way that you do

Your love was so selfless
Right from the start
Your care and devotion
Overflowed from your heart

You made life full of love
And I thank the dear Lord
For bringing from heaven
A Mother I adored
-Linda LaTourelle

Thank you from the heart
for all you've done for me
and I bless the Lord for sending
the best mother there could be!
♡

Real Mothers don't eat quiche;
they don't have time to make it
♡

Be A Mother—The Payment Is Pure Love

Siblings—hose wonderful people in your home who play with you, pray with you, get you in trouble; bug your friends; eat your food; steal your toys; annoy you; get into your stuff; but are your best friend

Don't call me GODDESS, Don't call me QUEEN,
just call me the cutest sister you've seen

♡

Brothers since the beginning—friends til the end

♡

Brotherly Love—Sisterly Hugs

♡

A Sister Understands—A Brother Annoys

- Just me and my Sissy
- The Sister Club
- Brothers in Cahoots
- My Sister, My Sister, My Friend
- When God invented brothers, He gave me the best!
- Sugar and Spice and Everything Nice that's what my sweet sister is made of

By wisdom a house is built, and
through understanding it is established
through knowledge it's rooms are filled
with rare and beautiful treasures.
Proverbs 24:3-4

Dear Little Brother

Dear Little Brother
My Sweetest Blessing
Come play with me
While Daddy's resting.
Here is a game
We both can try
Let's yell and jump
And scream and cry
Let's stomp the floor
And be our worst
We'll take turns...
You go first!
-Jeff Mondak ©

B old
R owdy
O riginal
T ender
H appy
E nergetic
R eal

I'm
Glad
God
Chose
You
To be my
BROTHER

It was nice growing up
with someone I call Brother
someone to lean on
someone to count on
someone to tell on—
but always someone to love

A brother shares
childhood memories
and grown-up dreams

I've got a brother like no other

There is no other,
like my big (or little) brother

- A Brother is a Special Friend
- Always My Brother
- I'm My Brother's keeper
- Best Buddies
- Brother, Brother
- Brotherhood of Love
- Brotherly Love
- Brotherly Ties
- Brothers are forever
- Brothers are just like sisters, only they like bugs!
- Brothers are Special— Especially Mine
- Brothers are the Best
- Brothers from the start
- Brothers in Arms
- Brothers make the best friends
- Brother's together
- First a Brother, Now a Friend
- Forever my Brother, always my Friend

- He Ain't Heavy - He's My Brother
- I couldn't ask for a better brother!
- I Love My Brother
- I'm glad God chose you to be my brother!
- My Brother, My buddy
- My Hero, My Pal
- Oh, Brother!
- There is no other, like my big/little brother!
- What a Pair!
- When I get big, I'll get even
- You were first a bother, now a friend

I love my brother
He's really neat
But he has
The biggest feet!

Sometimes my brother
I have to tell
"Your big feet
Have a stinky smell!"
-Thena

170

Life goes by so very fast
What was future now is past
Yesterday a babe so small
Now you've grown very tall

Seems we're busy everyday
Need to simply stop and play
Loving you is life for me
Let's take the time just to be

And when the day is done
After we've had lots of fun
I'll tuck you in and pray
And thank God we shared today!

-Linda LaTourelle

It was nice growing up
with a loving Sister
someone to lean on
someone to count on
someone to tell on—

♡

Little sister how I love you
You are as cute as you can be
And I am so happy
That you are a sister to be.

-Thena

Sisters are wonderful
That is so true
And no sister
Is as wonderful as you!

-Thena

♡

Sisters are special
From young ones to old
God gave me a sister
More precious than gold

- ○ I Love My Sister
- ○ Just Like Big Sister
- ○ She's My Sister
- ○ Sister Act

- ○ Sibling Rivalry
- ○ Forever my Sister
- ○ Sister's all the way
- ○ Sister of my heart

- #1 Sister Award

- A Sister to Adore

- _____'s been promoted to big sister

- A sister is a forever friend

- A sister is a gift to the heart, a friend to the spirit, a golden thread to the meaning of life   -Isadora James

- A sister is a little bit of childhood that can never be lost -Marion C. Garretty

- A sister is a special kind of friend

- A sister is a special part of all that's precious to my heart

- A sister is always close in thought wherever she may be

- A sister shares childhood memories and grown-up dreams

- A sister's love will last the years

- Big sisters are the crab-grass in the lawn of life -Charles M Schulz

- Celebrating Sisterhood

- Celebration of Sisters

- Close to my heart you'll always be, friends from the start, my sister and me

- Go sister, go sister, go sister go!

- God made you my Sister, Love made you my friend!

- God often speaks to us through a sister's love.

- God's made a Masterpiece, called Sister

- Having a sister is like having a best friend you can't get rid of. You know whatever you do, they'll still be there

- I don't know what I did to deserve a sister like you ...but whatever it was, I'm sorry!

- I Love My Sister

172

- I Love My Sissy

- I Love You Dear Sister

- If love were a color, you would be the rainbow to me!

- I'll always do my best with my sister by my side

- I'm glad God chose you to be my sister!

- I'm smiling because you're my sister...and laughing because there's nothing you can do about it!

- I'm the Big Sister

- I'm the Little Sister

- In all the world there's only one sister--that's you!

- In the cookies of life, sisters are the chocolate chips

- Is solace anywhere more comforting than that in the arms of a sister? -Alice Walker

- It was nice growing up with someone like you:

- Just Like Big Sister

- Like Two Peas in a Pod

- More than a forever friend, you are a joy to the heart and love without end

- My sister taught me everything I really need to know, and she was only in sixth grade at the time

- My Sister, My Friend

- No closer bond of friendship is to be found than the love shared between sisters

- Our roots say we're sisters, our hearts say we're friends.

- S.I.S.—Simply Incredible Sister

- Sis, I Love You with a special love that deepens throughout the years!

- Sister—I Love You

173

- Sister Act

- Sister to sister we will always be, a couple of nuts off the family tree.

- Sister, those quiet confidences we share remind me that you're always there.

- Sisterly Ties

- Sisters—Gotta Love 'Em!

- Sisters and roses are much the same.

- Sisters are a Special Hug From God!

- Sisters Are a Special Kind of Friend

- Sisters are angels on earth

- Sisters are different flowers from the same garden

- Sisters are Special—Especially Mine

- Sisters are Forever

- Sister's for Life

- Sisters Are Super!

- Sisters are the Best Kind of Friends

- Sisters are the blossoms in the garden of life

- Sisters by Chance, Friends because Mom Said So

- Sisters By Chance, Friends By Choice

- Sisters make the best friends

- Sisters Share a love tied with heartstrings

- Sisters share their inner souls

- Sisters heart to heart

- Sisters Warm The Heart

- The best thing about having a sister was that I always had a friend

- Sisters are the biggest pain and can hurt you the most, but true sister's love you anyway

- Sister—ah, the sweet memories of you!

- There is no better friend than a sister. And there is no better sister than you!

- Three things make life worth living: God, sisters and cookies

- To my sister: When I look back on our childhood, I can't help thinking— someday I'll get even!

- We acquire friends and we make enemies, but our sisters come with the territory

- I'm the hand-me-down girl

- Yes sir, that's my sister

- We laugh, we cry, we make time fly, best friends are we, my sister and me

- We share a history, we share a love, we share everything

- We still have great times together, and now, more than ever, I feel lucky to have a wonderful sister like you.

- Sister, my sister we're two of a kind

- What's the good of news if you haven't a sister to share it?

- When mom and dad don't understand, a sister always will.

- When sisters stand shoulder to shoulder, who stands a chance against us?

- In all life's treasures and blessings without end, I have the finest sister and even dearer friend.

- You can kid the world—but not your sister!

- Remember, as the little sister—I know too much, so you better treat me right or else I'll tell Mom

- Sisters by choice

Please feel free to substitute
"BROTHER" for "SISTER"
when using any quotes

Daughters

- A Daughter is Love
- Daughters are a special hug from God
- Daughters are flowers in the garden of life
- A daughter is a gift of love, given from God above
- A daughter is a joy forever
- A Daughter Is...
- A Daughter is a joy bringer, a heart warmer, a memory maker
- A Daughter is Love
- A Daughter Like You is a Very Precious Gift
- A daughter may outgrow your lap...but she will never outgrow your heart
- All the dreams I prayed you'll be are all the things you are
- Chance made you my daughter—Love made you my friend
- Daddy's Little Girl
- Daddy's Little Princess
- Daughters are little girls that grow up to be your best friends
- Daughters are Special— Especially Mine
- You're the end of my rainbow, my pot of gold. You're Daddy's little girl, to have and hold
- You were once my little girl and now my shining star

A Daughter
A bundle of joy
And bright as the sun
The beauty of springtime
And full of such fun

- As is the mother, so is her daughter. -Ezekiel 16:44
- The Joy of My Life
- Princess in Blue Jeans
- My Darling Daughter
- A Girl's Best Friend Is Her Mother

176

Daughters are always loved
In such a special way
Parents remember everything they do
And everything they say.

Daughters have a special way
Of lighting up a room
Their very presence in our lives
Chases away the threat of gloom.

Daughter dear
Daughter dear
My heart is happy
When you are near!

-Thena

That's why for them a parent
Sends Heavenward each day
Fervent prayers for all good things
To come their daughter's way!

-Thena

Daughters are wonderful
That is so true
And no Daughter
Is as wonderful as you!

A Daughter is a gift from above
Touched with beauty, filled with love

Daughters and Dandelions

How sweet to see a dandelion
In the hands of a little girl
Who delights in the simple things
That grow for free in our world.

Wishers she calls them
And she blows the bloom away
Hoping that her wishes come true
Before another day.

How lovely to be so innocent
So adorable and so sweet
And depend upon a dandelion
For a wonderful playtime treat.

-Thena

Sons

- All American Son
- 100% Stupendous Son
- A reflection of your father
- Beware of son's bearing little gifts
- Captain of my heart
- Daddy's little boy
- Dad's Big Boy
- Just Like Dad
- Like Father, Like Son
- My son you are a treasure
- My Son—Tough as Nails
- My Three Sons
- Our Little Man
- Pride hath much love for a Dad and his son
- Sons are the delight of their mother
- Son, you bring pride to the family, joy to the heart. You've been a blessing to us right from the start
- My Little Prince
- Sons are the light of their father's eyes
- Thank God for Sons
- Thank Heaven for Big Boys
- The night you were born I ceased being my father's boy and became my son's father. That night I began a new life.
- The Son Also Rises
- We Couldn't Have Picked A Better Son
- You are a perfect example of what a son should be!
- You Are My Son-shine

I'm thankful for you, my son
And I remember every day
How special is the gift of you
That the Good Lord sent my way!
-Thena

Superboy!

Look at him in his superman cape!
Look how cute my son is
All the super powers of the world
He now believes are his!

He holds out his hands and parts the sky
Making room for the wind to blow
He tilts his head and lowers his sights
To focus on the stars below!

His cape flows out from behind him
As he soars so fast and free
He is a super-duper hero
And he belongs to me!

-Thena Smith

Little son of mine
You are so delightful
And at times I find
That you are quite insightful!

- ☺ What a Son Needs—is what a Dad has
- ☺ I can't imagine a day without "Son-Shine"
- ☺ Father and Sons play best together

WHAT ARE YOU THINKING?

What are you thinking
Son of mine?
What wonderful things
Are going through your mind?

Are you dreaming
Of rockets and such
Or more tangible things
That you can touch?

Are you wishing
For a friend to come to play
Or a new baseball
Or a car someday?

I can see by your face
That you are far, far away
I hope that you will share
Your dreams with me today!

-Thena

179

Grandpa—gr·an·paw/n : the father of your father or mother; teaches you how to do things; tells you how smart you are; goes for walks with you; defends you to your parents

- ☺ Spending time, grandparents make precious moments
- ☺ The joy of grandchildren is measured in the Heart
- ☺ There's no place like home......except Grandma's
- ☺ Through Grandpa's eyes
- ☺ Two proud grandparents live here

Grandma—gr·an·maw/ n : the mother of your father or mother; bakes cookies; smells good; gives kisses; cooks Sunday dinner; sings to you; tells you stories; spoils you tons

- ☺ God couldn't be everywhere, so he invented Nana's
- ☺ Grandma's are just cute little girls
- ☺ Grandparents may be oldies... but they're goodies!
- ☺ Grandma's my name, spoilin's my game
- ☺ Great Grandpa's really are great!

G entle, joy-ful, giving
R eady-made hugs & kisses
A dored & adoring
N ice as nice can be
D ear & sweet beyond compare
M ore precious than words can say
A lways close in heart

G rand, great, goofy
R eady to go fishing
A wesome and adventurous
N ext to Dad he's the best
D elightful and daring
P lays games with me
A lways there for me

FOR SPOILING AND LOVE CALL
1-800-GRANDMA

My Grandad

My Grandad is a lovely man
But he's losing all his hair
His head gets cold in wintertime
It isn't very fair
He wishes he had something
To help him keep his locks
So I've emptied out my piggy-bank
And bought him a small box
-Rob Erskine ©

- When Grandpa Was A Boy
- The Good Ole Days
- When Grandpa Was Young...Life Was Fun
- Grandpa and Me
- My Grandfather
- Papaw Loves ME
- Papaw And Me
- Daddy and Me and Grandpa Makes 3
- How Dear to the Heart Are Grandpas
- In the Eyes of a Child... Grandpa is Everything
- Grandpa's Boy/Girl
- Papa showed me how
- Cuz Grandpa said I could
- I wanna be just like Grandpa

Grandpa & My Brother

Grandpa sure reminds me
Of my baby brother Keith
Neither one has any hair
And neither one has teeth
-Jeff Mondak ©

Papa of Mine

Grandpa is a gentleman
And jolly as an elf
He seems to talk a lot
But mostly to himself.

- Grandad is my hero
- Grandpa's are great at telling His-story (History)

Grandpa... Story Teller Happy Feller

For wisdom and love call 1-800-Grandpa

I LOVE PAPA

My Grandma

Grandma's are meant
For kisses and hugs
For watching rainbows
And catching bugs
For baking cookies
And reading to you
Grandma's are great
And mine is, too

Nana's Love Goes on forever

Grandchildren don't make a woman feel old; it's being married to a grandfather that bothers her

I LOVE NANA

- ☺ Just me and my Granny
- ☺ The day my Grandma came to visit...
- ☺ You can never have enough fun with Grandma
- ☺ Home is where my Grandma is
- ☺ Grandma loves me best
- ☺ You can never have enough Grandmothers
- ☺ No cowboy was as quick on the draw as Nana showing pictures of the grandkids

Nanny's Nest

Nanny's nest is best
But Papa rules the roost

♡

One old crow & a cute little chick live here

- ☺ Children's children are a crown to the aged
- ☺ Being with my Nana is like eating hot fudge with whipped cream everyday
- ☺ Always remember I need you, Grandma
- ☺ There's nothing that cookies from Grandma can't fix

Grandma... Cookie Baker Kiss Maker

A Grandma doesn't have to do anything; just knowing she's somewhere thinking about you means everything.

182

Fishing—involves a rod, reel and worm and sitting for hours; the perfect time to take a nap; a great opportunity to perfect your storytelling

- Go Fish!
- Early to Bed, Early to Rise, Fish All Day...Tell Big Lies!
- Fish Stories Told Here!
- Just Me and Dad
- Fishing a REEL Sport
- You Shoulda Seen Em'
- He Was SOOOO Big!
- Fish Fry
- Gone Fishing
- Smells Fishy
- Bridge over Troubled Waters
- Got One on the Hook
- Fly Fishin'
- Just the Boys
- Fishing is my life

I Like Fish

I like fish
When they're swimming up and down
I've seen them in the river
And an aquarium in town.
I like fish
We've got one in a bowl
All day he swims in circles
He's a happy little soul
I like fish
Like you see on the TV
With great big teeth and beady eyes
That's the one for me
I like fish
I really think they're great
Especially when they come with chips
Served up on my plate!
-Rob Erskine ©

Give a boy a fish and he will eat for a day.
Teach him how to fish and he will eat forever.

FOOD—gives energy and makes strong kids

Give Us A Bun

"Oh give us a bun," said Emily
An elephant big and grey
The time is nearly half past ten
And I think I'm wasting away

It's all very well to have roughage
Apples and peanuts are nice
But a nice currant bun with some jam in
Can't be bettered, no matter the price

So come on you mothers and fathers
I don't want the moon or the sun
Nor all the Crown Jewels tied up in a sack
All I want is a tasty cream bun
-Rob Erskine ©

- ① Bottomless Pit
- ① Chow Time
- ① Crunch and Munch
- ① Finger Licking Good!
- ① Food Fight
- ① Messy Marvin
- ① Mmm Mmm Good

The Burp

Pardon me for being so rude.
It was not me, it was my food.
It got so lonely down below,
It just popped up to say hello.
-anonymous

Animal Crackers

Animal crackers, and cocoa to drink,
That is the finest of suppers, I think;
When I'm grown up and can have what I please
I think I shall always insist upon these.
-C Morely

Popcorn

Popcorn is really neat
Fun to make
and fun to eat.
Popcorn is a
pop-pop,
ever poppin'
Never stopping,
show stoppin'
zany kind of treat!
-unknown

The Hot Dog Dragon

Every dragon 'round these parts
breathes a breath of flame.
But I can't even blow a spark
which brings me grief and shame.
The other dragons often tease.
They jeer and sneer and shout
'cause every time I take a breath
I'm breathing hot dogs out.
Hot dogs when I blow my nose.
Hot dogs when I snore.
Hot dogs when I go achoo.
Hot dogs when I roar.
I lived a life of misery,
agony, and woe,
until I met a girl dragon.
Our friendship seemed to grow.
I said to her one starry night,
"I love you dear the most."
We sighed a gentle sigh together
and had a hot dog roast.
-Robert Pottle ©

Mom's Café
Open
24 hours

Doughnuts

Mum, Dad and me all like doughnuts
They're better than fish, eggs or ham
They've got to be covered in sugar
And full up with strawberry jam.
When you bite them the jam squidges outwards
Then dribbles all over your chin
Mum says, "Be careful and don't make a mess"
I give her a big jammy grin
So now we're all going shopping
'Cause it's Saturday and I am glad
That today is the day we have doughnuts
A treat for Mum, me and Dad.
-Rob Erskine ©

Animal Crackers

Lions and tigers and bears (oh my!)
Tall Giraffe and fat hippopotami
All of these animals are close at hand
In my box sitting on the sand!
I show no favor to any cracker critter
I shall eat them all for I am no quitter!
Big and fat or slim and trim
I will gobble down each one of them!
I don't think the animals mind at all
But that they must think it's great
That kids love to devour them one and all
And to be a fun snack is their fate!!
-Thena

I like the giraffes, hippos and lions
And while I eat them I'm always trying
To imagine what animals like to eat
When they want a really tasty treat!

185

Football

- And He's Down
- And It's Good!
- Are You Ready For Some Football?
- Backyard Football
- Defense or Offense
- First and 10
- First Down
- Flag Football
- Football Banquet
- Football Fever
- Football Fun
- Football ROCKS!
- Fumble
- Go for the goal
- Go for the whole nine yards!
- Go For Two!
- Go! Fight! Win!
- Go Team Go
- Go the Distance
- Gridiron
- Half-time
- Homecoming
- I'm a football Dad/Mom!
- Instant Replay
- It's A First Down
- It's Overtime!
- Kicking Off the Season
- Penalty!
- Playing football is not a matter of life and death, it's more important than that!
- Powderpuff
- Quarterback Sneak
- Superbowl Here We Come
- Three Minute Warning
- Touch Football
- Touchdown!
- Varsity/Junior Varsity
- Water Boy
- We interrupt this homework for football season!
- Football hero
- Football Is A Kick
- Give Me The Pig Skin

Freckles—sweet speckles of love

- Just call me Freckles
- Freckles are fairy's kisses
- Freckles are angel kisses from God
- A girl is a giggle with freckles on it
- Angel kisses passed on through generations
- A face without freckles is like a night without stars

Angel Kisses

I have some freckles on my face
And freckles on my nose.
The only spots completely free
Are my un-freckled toes!

My mommy says I shouldn't fret
And there's not much my mommy misses...
She says I should be happy 'cause
They are angel kisses!

-Thena

I never saw a freckle I didn't like

♡

I like freckles and as you can see,
freckles like me

♡

Freckled Friends Forever

♡

Speckled and Sweet

♡

Freckles are speckles, it's easy to see,
on leopards, lizards, ladybugs and me

187

Best Friends:
A double-decker, hot fudge sundae with two spoons

There's always room in a child's heart for
a new best friend

Remember when:
sharing your heart meant sharing all your favorite stuff?

Take a child for a friend
And you will have a friend for life

A child's wish...
To discover the world
And all its joys
With their best friend

My best friend is My Dad
My best friend is My Mom
My best friend is my dog/cat

Friendship is making dandelion bracelets together
and blowing wishes on dandelion fairies.
Friendship is memories so wonderfully sweet.
Friendship is you!

Those were the days...
Skipping rocks upon the water
Chasing fireflies with my father
Staying out late
Leaving food on my plate
Hop, roll and run

From the mouths of Babes...
Works from local kids

I Like...

I like baseball,
bubble gum,
candy, racecars,
french fries,
nights without bedtimes,
Days without rules,
dessert before dinner,
And my favorite pet.
I like lollipops—
Big and swirly,
sticky and sweet.
I like sharing them
with someone,
Or even a couple of someone's.
Because finding someone
who likes what you like
Makes whatever you like
seem twice as nice!
-Kayla Carrico, age 11
St Joseph Catholic School, Mayfield, KY

Bluegrass Publishing ran a contest this past winter to give local students the opportunity to submit poetry for prizes and a chance to get published. As a result we received many works that it made it difficult to choose. We are delighted to debut these budding poets with you. We hope you enjoy the talent of these young poets.

Please visit our website often for future contests. We would love to share your writing with the world, too.

Blessings,
Linda LaTourelle

SOCCER

I smell the grass,
I feel the sun on my back,
I hear the happy birds singing a song.
I hear the crowd roaring and cheering,
                    It makes me feel glad.
I especially hear my mom
cheering and encouraging me on.
I receive a pass, I shoot the ball, I pass the ball.
So many options what should I do?
-Lawson Grider, age 10
St Joseph Catholic School, Mayfield, KY

Friends

(The four legged variety)

Are you bored?
Nothing to do,
You look down,
They're waiting for you,
An animal,
With cute little eyes,
As you stare deeper,
So do they.
What are you waiting for?
With them to play.
A ferret, dog, or maybe a cat,
Maybe a gerbil,
With a cute little hat.
They may cause mischief, pain, or trouble,
But as you think it will double,
You can't imagine what it would be like,
Without your thumb-less friend tonight.

-Conner Lee English, age 10
Lone Oak Elementary
Lone Oak, KY

There's A Monster In the Classroom

When the teacher leaves the door,
He is really scary
And has a loud roar!
But when the teacher comes back in,
He is gone in a flash!
In the black cabinet,
With a dash!

-Austin Shane Jones, age 9
South Marshall Elementary
Benton, KY

Give It Your All

School is really great
If you aren't late.
Try to always be on time
And you will have a great mind.
Give your teacher all you got
And in return, receive alot!

-Emily Baker, age 9
South Marshall Elementary,
Benton, KY

My Goal

The first time I rode a bike
I was so scared.
I thought I was going to fall
But I wasn't at all.
I felt good
that I achieved a goal.
I was told I could
do that you know.
I was surprised
when I did not fall.
I did not tip over at all.

-Miranda Prater, age 9
South Marshall Elementary
Benton, KY

Ever wanted to be published?
Send us an e-mail: service@theultimateword.com

Fruit

- A is for Apple
- Apple of My Eye
- A Slice of Life
- A Taste Of Summer
- An Apple a Day Keeps the Doctor Away
- As American as Apple Pie
- Banana Rama Ding Dong
- Banana, Banana, Fe Fi Fo Fanna, Banana
- Berry Cute
- Berry Special Friends
- Blueberry Blues
- Bushels of Fun
- Cherry Lips
- Grap-a-licious
- I Cherry-ish You
- I Love You Cherry Much
- I Love you a bushel and a peck
- Just Peachy!
- Life is a Bowl of Cherries
- Little Apple Dumpling
- Orange you glad we're buddies
- Orange you supposed to be in bed?
- Picking-N-Grinning
- Plum Gorgeous
- Plum Pooped!
- Strawberry Girl
- Strawberry Jammin'
- Sweets for the Sweet
- Sweet to Eat
- Sweets for the Sweeties
- The Apple Doesn't Fall Far From the Tree
- The Fruit of the Spirit is Love, Peace, and Joy
- The Pick of the Crop
- The Taste of Summer
- Top Banana
- Tutti Fruiti
- Yes, We Have No Bananas
- Watermelon Spittin'

Love is a fruit in season at all times
-Mother Teresa

191

Games

- A Winning Combination
- Family Fun Night
- Fun and Games
- Got Game
- And the winner is!
- Pick A Card...Any Card
- Playing With a Full Deck
- Do not pass Go...
- The Championship
- The Games People Play

Do you remember?

- I Spy
- Freeze Tag
- Slug Bug
- Simon Says
- Tag, you're it!
- Kick the Can
- Duck, duck, goose
- Mother may I?
- A tisket, a tasket
- Annie, Annie over
- Red light, green light
- Red Rover, Red Rover can my best friend come over?

**Hide and Seek
Don't you peek
Count to ten
Run after them**

Eenie meenie miney moe
Catch a tiger by the toe
If he hollers let him go;
Eenie meenie miney moe

Playing

It's finally summer
I'm happy inside!
We've all day to play
You seek and I'll hide!

We'll jump rope and hopscotch
And leapfrog all day.
And when we get tired
Some checkers we'll play!

You ask, "Mother may I?"
Perhaps I'll say, "Yes!!"
Just playing and laughing
It's what we love best!
-Carla Birnberg

CHILDREN LEARN BEST BY PLAYING

Gardens are for Kids, too!

The finest garden that I know
Is one where little children grow,
Where cheeks turn brown and eyes are bright,
And all is laughter and delight.

- Friends are the Flowers in the Garden of Life
- Gardeners Know the Best Dirt
- Gardening...Just Another Day of Planting Love
- Growing Like a Weed
- Grub Worm
- Harvest Seeds of Love!
- I Dig Gardening
- I Fought the Lawn and the Lawn Won!
- In God's Garden there is Work to be Done
- Lil' Punkin
- May All Your Weeds Be Wildflowers
- Mom's Garden—Dad's Weeds
- My Garden Grows with Love
- Peach Blossom
- Pretty as a Petunia
- Daffy-Dill Darling

The heart is a garden
That always has room
For the flowers of kindness
And friendship that blooms!
♡

The kiss of the Sun for pardon
The Song of a Bird for mirth
One is nearer God's Heart in a Garden
Than anywhere else on Earth
♡

Time began in a garden—time will grow your love!

Mud pie maker, petal taker
The sunshine is your oven
You wear a grin, above your chin
This backyard kitchen you are lovin'

You use a stick, and mix it thick
There's dirt sift on your nose
It's everywhere, but you don't care
Your faucet is the hose!

Mud pie maker, petal taker
What would your mother say?
Be sure of this, you'll share a kiss
When the sun goes down today!
-Jennifer Byerly © 2005

If you were a flower, I'd pick you!

I love it in the garden
Some plants are tall like me
The cornstalks when the season ends
Sunflowers with their seeds!

I love it in the garden
When squash grows everywhere
It's fun to visit neighbors
With mother when we share!

I love it in the garden
When tomatoes grace the vine
Everyday I go there
To see what I might find!
-Jennifer Byerly © 2005

Girls—/grlz/sweetness and joy to most; annoying to boys until they age; sugar and spice; occasional tomboy; the heartbeat of love

G racious

I nnocent

R adiant

L ove

I look in the mirror
And I have to smile
For I'm a girl now
But in a short while
I'll be a grown up
A lady for sure
Lovely, graceful
And so mature.
-Thena

- No Boys Allowed
- Little Miss Sunshine
- Our Little Princess
- Practically Perfect
- Princess in Training
- Proud Mom
- Soft and Sweet
- Sitting Pretty
- So Wonderful
- Sugar and Spice and Everything Nice
- The Girl Most Likely to...

- The Girl's Club
- The Girly Game
- Uptown Girl
- What a Girl Needs
- What a Girl Wants

Ribbons and Bows
Ruffles & Lace,
oh what a simply
beautiful face

Why God Made Little Girls

God made the world with the towering trees
majestic mountains and restless seas.
Then paused and said," It needs one more thing,
Someone to laugh and dance and sing,
To walk in the woods and gather the flowers,
To commune with nature in quiet hours!"
So God made cute little girls
with laughing eyes and bouncing curls,
With joyful hearts and infectious smiles
Enchanting ways and feminine wiles
and when He completed the task He'd begun
He was pleased and proud of the job He'd done!
For the world when seen through a little girl's eyes
Greatly resembles His own paradise!

-unknown

We're Girls

We're strong when it's right
But still gentle and kind
We always smell nice
(Well, not at sports time!)

Be our hair long or short
Whether straight or with wave
We know how to have FUN
and *sigh* when to behave.

-Carla Birnberg

I love to dance and twirl, it's all part of being a girl!

As time will come and go
Sometimes like a distant wind
My life sees so many changes
And I'm thankful for true friends
But as I long for wisdom
And search for that distant light
I think of yesterdays
When I watched you sleep at night
And nothing that I touch
In a sometimes lonely world
Will ever mean as much
As the love for my little girl.

We Shared Today
Life goes by so very fast
What was future now is past
Yesterday a babe so small
Now you've grown very tall

Seems we're busy everyday
Need to simply stop and play
Loving you is life for me
Let's take the time just to be

And when the day is done
After we've had lots of fun
I'll tuck you in and pray
And thank God we shared today!
-Linda LaTourelle

Being a girl
only gets better and better!

- 13 Going on 30
- 100% Girl
- Ain't She Cute
- Ain't She Sweet
- All-American Girl
- All Girl
- American Beauty
- American Girl
- Big Girls Do Cry
- Blondie
- Brat
- Brown-Eyed Girl
- Daddy's Girl
- Daddy's Princess
- Funny Girl
- Girls Just Wanna Have Fun
- Girl Power
- Girl Talk
- Girls Only
- Girls Rule!
- Girls Will Be Girls
- Girly Girl
- I Enjoy Being a Girl
- I'm Just a Girl
- Just One of the Girls
- Little Girls Are Heaven's Flowers
- Little Lady
- Little Miss Bossy
- Little Princess
- Little Surfer Girl
- Lookin' Good
- Material Girl
- Miss Smarty
- More Sugar than Spice
- My Favorite Brunette
- My Girl
- Perfection in Blue Jeans
- Pretty as a Picture
- Pretty Perfect
- Princess at Heart
- Princess of Quite-a-Lot
- She's a Superstar
- Thank God I'm a City Girl
- What A Doll!
- Where the Girls Are
- You Go Girl
- You Grow, Girl

Good Morning

As I was sleeping in my bed
The sunbeams danced upon my head
I threw open the blinds and said:
"Good Morning World
Good Morning today
How nice to be awakened
In such a lovely way.

-Thena

- Bed Head
- Early Riser
- Get Up
- Good Morning Sunshine
- Who Turned on the Lights!
- I'll Rise but I refuse to Shine
- I'm Awake—Now What?

- Rise & Shine
- It's Time to Greet the Day
- Sleepy Head
- The Early Bird Gets the Worm and Eats Breakfast
- Wake Up!
- Wake Up Little ––––––

It's such a beautiful day today
With sunshine and flowers
Coming out to play
To brighten every single spot
What a wonderful world we've got!

-Thena

♡

- Good Morning, Merry Sunshine
- I Don't Do Mornings
- Oh, How I Hate to Get Up in the Morning
- Oh, What a Beautiful Morning
- This is the day that the Lord has made
- Up and at 'em

199

Great Outdoors

- A Kids Backyard
- Beauty All Around Us
- Bird Watching
- Breath of Fresh Air
- Did You Hear That?
- Fishing Friends
- Hittin' the Trail
- Hunting Buddies
- Look What I Caught
- Nature Hike
- Nature Is the Art of God
- One with the World
- Quest for Fauna
- Riding the Rapids
- Rippling River
- Smells Fishy
- Stay on the Path
- Watch Out World
- Wonders of the World

The Best Kind of Friend

One friend I'll always treasure
Is the tree in my back yard
He's always there when I need him
Whenever life gets hard
On any day if I should need
A friend to lean upon
I simply climb into his arms
Outstretched above the lawn
He gives my heart a lift above
And close to yonder blue
He's often still and listens well
Just like a friend should do!
-Jennifer Byerly © 2004

A Day In The Great Outdoors

Paddling down the river
Taking in the view
Suddenly I felt cold and damp
Hole in my canoe
Frantically start bailing
Trying to save face
But too little, far too late
Sank without a trace
Got back to the surface
Thought I was alright
But heading for a waterfall
Could this be Goodnight?
Flying into orbit
Bouncing off the rocks
Which shook me from my hairline
To the bottom of my socks
Once again I surface
The shoreline's almost there
But just to round my whole day off
I'm bitten by a bear
So well chewed, ripped and tattered
I stagger to the shore
No more to roam the great outdoors
I'm coming back no more
-Rob Erskine©

- ⓘ Sunny Skies and Seas and Sands
- ⓘ The Beauty of Nature
- ⓘ The Road Less Traveled
- ⓘ This Great Land
- ⓘ Trail Blazers
- ⓘ Our Neck of the Woods
- ⓘ What Was that Noise?
- ⓘ Under the Stars
- ⓘ Where the Ocean Meets the Sky
- ⓘ Wilderness Trails
- ⓘ Wild Creatures That Go Bump in the Night

- A Cabin in the Woods
- A Camping We Will Go
- A Canoe for You
- A Hiking we will go...
- A River Runs Through It
- A Walk In The Woods
- Act Naturally
- Adventure Time
- Ah, Wilderness!
- At The Park
- Back To Nature
- Barefoot in the park
- Call Of The Wild
- Calm Waters
- Campfire Cookin'
- Camping Beneath The Moon And Stars
- Climb Every Mountain
- Did you hear that?
- Down By The Lazy River
- Drift Away
- Explorer Extraordinaire
- Fisherman's Delight
- Fishing stories told here
- Fresh Air
- Gone fishing
- Great Adventure
- Great Outdoors
- Happy Camper
- Happy Trails to You
- Hitting the Trail
- Let's Go Camping
- Nature Boy/Girl
- Nature Center
- Nature Walk
- Nature's Beauty
- On the Trail
- Our Camping Trip
- Poison Ivy
- Rod & Reel
- Sleeping Under the Stars
- Smoke Gets In Your Eyes
- S'More Camping
- Something's Fishy
- Starlight, star bright
- Survival of the Fittest
- The ants go marching one by one
- The Big Hike
- The Big One got away
- The Great Outdoors
- The Outback
- The River Is Wide
- The simple life
- Trail Blazers
- What was that noise?
- Where's my real bed

Great Ideas

Copy Cat

There's someone who looks just like me
He does what I can do.
I make these funny faces
And I watch him do them, too.
I open up my eyes real WIDE
And pull my mouth -- like this...
Then lean forward and get closer
And give a SCARY kiss!
It doesn't matter what I do
When I am sitting here...
The kid in there can do it, too!
When I play with Mommy's mirror.
-CJ Heck ©

Monkey See—Monkey Do—Just Like You

What are you thinking
Son of mine?
What wonderful things
Are going through your mind?

Are you dreaming
Of rockets and such
Or more tangible things
That you can touch?

Are you wishing
For a friend to come to play
Or a new baseball
Or a car someday?

I can see by your face
That you are far, far away
I hope that you will share
Your dreams with me today!

-Thena

I THINK-THEREFORE, I AM

Growing Up

Room to Grow

I cannot find my fingers,
I'll never touch a toe,
Because my parents always buy
New clothes with room to grow.
My saggy pants are dragging like
A tortoise in the snow,
Since everyone decided
I needed room to grow.
My shrimpy feet are swimming,
My run is sad and slow,
Because my socks and shoes
Have got some extra
Room to grow.
And way up high, above my eyes,
A final, crowing blow—
They've cut my hair so short I'm bald
So it has, (you guessed it)
Room to grow.
-Ted Scheu ©

- ⓘ Time Marches On
- ⓘ Bigger Inch By Inch
- ⓘ Growing Like A Weed
- ⓘ Growing By Leaps And Bounds
- ⓘ Sprouting Up
- ⓘ Scaling New Heights
- ⓘ Way To Grow
- ⓘ The Wonder Years
- ⓘ Growing up is tough...when will I be "grown" enough?
- ⓘ Growing Pains
- ⓘ Cherish yesterday, dream of tomorrow, live for today

Getting Bigger All The Time

When I Grow Up

When I grow up I mean to go
Where all the biggest rivers flow,
And take a ship and sail around
The seven seas until I've found
Robinson 'Crusoe's famous isle,
And there I'll land and stay a while,
And see how it would feel to be
A boy on an island in the sea

When I grow up I want to rove
Through orange and palmetto grove,
To drive a sled across the snow
Where great explorers go,
To hunt for treasures hid of old
Buccaneers and pirates bold,
And see if somewhere there may be
A mountain no one's climbed but me.

When I grow up I mean to do
The things I've always wanted to;
I don't see why grown people stay
At home when they could be away.

-Rupert Sargent Holland

204

Cherished Memories

He's eight years old, but almost nine;
he'll make that very clear.
This little man inside my home,
whom I hold close and dear.
It only seems like yesterday,
I held him in my arms.
He could wrap me around his finger,
with his innocent boyish charm.

As he began to grow into
a curious little lad,
Those were the best years, I think,
a mother could have had.
For there were always extras,
of his famous hugs and kisses,
And an over abundance in our home
of frogs and bugs and fishes.

There was never a dull moment
with my very active son.
From dusk to dawn it would wear me out
just to watch him play and run.
But late at night, tucked in -- asleep,
with his angelic face,
Memories were woven in my heart
that can never be erased.

He was always a humble child,
and still is to this day,
And he can make my heart melt
in a very special way.
It breaks my heart to see him
when he frowns, or cries or pouts,

When he gets into mischief,
and I must call "time out."

Today he's quite the little gent,
and takes care of his mom...
By being "the man of the house"
When his dad is sometimes gone.
With hugs, I'm assured emphatically,
he'll never move away--
He and his wife will come to live
"with you and dad someday!"

How I wish the hands of time,
would slow down for a while.
So I could savor every moment
of nearness to my child.
For if I could, I'd stop the
clock and keep him here with me.
But when he's gone, I'll still hold on
to cherished memories.

Brenda Ball
Copyright © 2001
All Rights Reserved

Written for:
My wonderful son, Ethan

Be sure to visit Brenda at:
http://www.geocities.com/brynnball/pagetwo.html

- ☺ 12 Going on 20!
- ☺ Looking all grown-up
- ☺ Big enough to use Daddy's tools

What a grown up young man
My little boy has become
Always looking out for others
I'm so proud you are my son!

Grumpy Gus

I'm a Grump

I'm a grouchy old
Growling grump today,
So would you, please, keep out of my way?
I woke up grumpy and I know I'll stay
Severely uncheerful for most of the day.
I don't give a happy hoot
What you say,
My grumps don't feel like going away.
My icy heart may never start
To melt its coat of gray,
But if you feel sorry for me...it may.
-Ted Scheu ©

Mom says I'm grumpy
Sis says I'm a brat
I'm not really worried-
I can live with that!

Don't Mess With Me

Mr. Attitude
He's kinda rude
Sport-a-tude
What a dude!

Sometime I wake up grouchy and sometimes I let him sleep

- ☻ Mr or Miss Grumps
- ☻ She or He's got attitude
- ☻ Poutin' and Shoutin'
- ☻ Pouty Baby
- ☻ Your face'll stick like that
- ☻ Stick out that lip
- ☻ Temper, Temper

- ☻ Little Miss Tantrum
- ☻ Havin' a Hissy Fit
- ☻ Raging Mad
- ☻ Cranky Pants
- ☻ Miss Know-it-All
- ☻ You're Not the Boss of Me
- ☻ You're Not the Mom

206

Gymnastics

- Amazing Athlete
- Back Flippin' for the Gold
- Balancing Act
- Beautiful Balancer
- Fabulous Full
- Fantastic Flipping
- Faultless Fulls
- Flip Flops
- Flying High
- Galloping Gal
- Giant Leap
- Go For the Gold
- Gym Rat
- Gymnasts Rule the Mat
- Hang-Time
- High-flying Fulls
- Lavish Layouts
- Lord of the Rings
- No fear - No gravity
- Nothing But Air
- Ouch!
- Perfect 10
- Perfect Balance
- Ride 'em Cowboy
- Sharp as a Tack

- Spoiled Rotten Gymnast
- Spot Me
- Stick It
- Straight as an Arrow
- Tape: A Girls Best Friend
- Terrific Tumbler
- Tremendous Tucks
- Tumble in Time
- Up in the Air
- Valiant Vaulter
- You CAN Do It!
- Zero Gravity

Thanks to my sweet niece,
Cheryln for your inspirations
With this section. Love you!

LOOK
MOM
NO
HANDS

It's so much fun
To spring and run
Until I hit the mat
Then all I hear is splat!

Grace in Action

A Blue Ribbon

Scarlett got a blue ribbon
For her gymnastics today!
She walked the balance beam
In the most graceful way!
Scarlett got a prize
For the wonderful rollovers she did
Front and back were both supreme
What a talented kid!
Scarlett's Dad was watching
And each time she smiled toward him
Her daddy took another photo....
He took a whole role of film!
Scarlett's mom was proud as punch
And told her friends on line
Wait until you see these gymnasts
The cutest one is mine!!
And Scarlett went home happy
And returned to her normal day
Got herself some tasty snacks
And watched tv that day!
-Thena Smith ©

I like to flip
I like to flop
I like to tumble
I like to hop

I love to spin
I love to twirl
What fun it is
For a boy or girl

Hair

- A Whole New Look
- All dolled up
- Bad Hair Day
- Buzzzz Cut
- Carrot top
- Crazy Curl
- Crazy Hair Day
- Curly Locks
- Cute and Curly
- Do It Yourself Haircut
- Frizzy or Dizzy
- Future Hair Stylist
- Glamorama Girl
- Golden Girl
- Goldy Locks
- Great Do Dude!
- Hair—larious
- Hair-raising experience
- Hair we go again
- Hair? What hair?
- Kids Kuts and Kurls
- Letting our hair down
- Locks of Love

- Name that Color
- Only my hairstylist knows for sure
- R-A-G-G-M-O-P-P— Raggmopp!
- Rag-a-Muffin
- Shave & Haircut, 2 Bits
- Sheer Delight
- Snip Snip
- Static Cling
- Super Cut
- Tress Obsessed
- Up do
- Wacky Wigs
- What's the Buzzzzz?
- Who did your hair?
- Wish you were HAIR!
- You got your ears lowered
- Your Crowning Glory
- You're lookin' good

Hair's Looking at You Kid

209

Halloween

- A big boo to you
- All dressed up
- Are you a scaredy-cat?
- Bat an eye for me...
- Bat mom
- Bats-R-Us
- Batty over Halloween
- Bobbing for apples
- Boo bash
- Boo from the crew
- Boo time
- Boo to you!
- Carving out memories
- Carving the pumpkin
- Caught in the web of friends
- Come "clown" around
- Costume parade
- Costumes and pumpkins and candy, oh my!
- Disguise the limit
- Gather a harvest of love
- Guess who?
- Halloween is a real treat
- Happy Pumpkin day
- Happy trick or treating
- Hip hip hooray! Its candy day!
- I'm a pleasing pumpkin
- In search of the perfect pumpkin
- It's pumpkin time!
- Great pumpkins, Charlie Brown!
- Jack-o-lanterns light the night
- Jazzy Jack-o-lantern
- Just a little bit corny
- Masquerade
- Master of disguises
- Mommy's lil' pumpkins
- You can count on me
- Yum, Yum, give me some!

Happy Pumpkin Hunting

Pumpkins and Kids
And Costumes, Oh My!
Spiced apple cider
And warm pumpkin pie
Bobbing for apples
And walking the street
Yummy good candy
And sore achy feet
Halloween's fun
And the treats are great
Scaring my sister
Oh, Boy—I can't wait!
-Linda LaTourelle

November 1st

Dial China on the phone.
Steal your brother's ice cream cone,
use the microwave to boil it.
Flush the car keys down the toilet.

Prance and dance. Skip and dip.
Tango, fandango, disco, flip.
Eat bananas. Eat the peels.
Bark like twenty singing seals.

Sing out silly, loud and long.
Sing a hard rock opera song.
To terrorize your dads and moms,
eat eighty super-sugar-bombs!
-Robert Pottle ©

Trick or Treat!

M&M's and Crunch bars—I will take a few!
King Size Twix or Kit Kat—those are yummy too!
I only get an hour—so lets make it fast
Fill up my bag! Come on! I gotta run!
Off I go, down the block
I will make it just in time!
I can grab a few more treats
Before the clock strikes NINE!
-Teri Olund © 2004

♡

I'm not afraid
Of people who say
"BOO"
As long as when
I'm trick or treating
I'm walking next to

you!

♡

I'm not afraid
Of ol' black cats
Scary pumpkins
Or big black bats!
I walk so brave
From door to door
Trick or treating
For candy and more!

Heritage—photos passed down over many years within a family; customs, traditions belonging to a family; things that go from generation to generation

Priceless

Upon a wooden shelf
Sits a book of old, you see
'Tis tattered and so worn
With pictures of Dad, Mom and me
Laid within these pages
Rests a part of history
The story of our family
Is to some a mystery
To me it is a tale of joy
At times a song of woe
A story that was written
So very long ago
I look back and remember
On the times that now are gone
a faded, precious memory
I cherish every one
This book is so important
It's the perfect legacy
A treasure that is priceless
A gift for you from me
-Linda LaTourelle © 2005

The Path That Leads to Home

The little path that leads to home,
That is the road for me,
I know no finer path to roam,
With finer sights to see.
With thoroughfares the world is lined
That lead to wonders new,
But he who treads them leaves behind
The tender things and true.
-Edgar Guest

212

- A book of our heritage
- A lifetime of memories
- Bits of yesterday
- Blessed be the ties that bind generations
- Dear ancestor
- Generation gap
- Heritage
- Memories
- Milestones
- My ancestors
- Our legacy
- Picture perfect memories
- Roaring twenties
- The way we were

Home is where the heart is

- God Bless Our Home
- HELP WANTED: Everyone in the House Qualifies
- I Like to Give Homemade Gifts, Which Kid Do Ya Want?
- If a Mother's Place is in the Home, Why am I Always in the Car?
- Laundry Room: Drop Your Drawers Here!
- Our Laundry Room Has the Latest Dirt!
- Thank God for dirty dishes; they have a tale to tell; while others may go hungry, we're eating very well.
- The House Was Clean Last Week; Sorry You Missed It!
- The Only Domestic Thing About ME is that I Live Indoors!
- There's No Place Like Home, Except Grammas
- Two Proud Parents Live Here!
- Use It Up, Wear It Out, Make Do, OR Do Without It
- With home and health and happiness, I shouldn't want to fuss; and by the stack of evidence, God's been good to us!

213

Homework—A teacher's pleasure, a child's least favorite thing to do; an opportunity to spend time with mom and dad

I Worked Like a Dog

I worked like a dog
on my homework last night.
I fetched all my papers,
then took a big bite.
I solved some equations.
I licked every one,
then buried the worksheet
when it was done.
My science exhibit
was finished with ease--
I got a glass jar
and filled it with fleas.
I worked like a dog
with hopes to impress,
but something went wrong
'cause my homework's a mess.

-Robert Pottle ©

- ☺ My Dog Ate It...
- ☺ The Computer Crashed
- ☺ You Mean That Was Due Today...
- ☺ I Got an A!
- ☺ UH OH a Zero!
- ☺ Perfect Score
- ☺ You Did It!

The dog ate my English
The cat ate my Math
When I told my teacher
It incurred her wrath.
She took my notebook
And wrote my mom a note
That said that I should be prepared
That school was not a joke.
Mom showed the note to Dad
And he took away my TV
As the dog spit up my English
And the cat just glared at me.

-Thena

- ☺ Homework makes you ugly
- ☺ Homework is where the heart isn't
- ☺ Homework—time to challenge Dad
- ☺ If I want to know about History I'll go ask Grandpa
- ☺ I don't have to do homework—I already know it all

I will not throw spitballs
I will not throw spitballs
I will not throw spitballs

How do I Love Thee?

- God Gave Us Kids In Order to Teach Us Love

- Happy is the Heart that Holds a Child's Love

- I Believe In Myself, Because You Do Too!

- If I Know What Love Is, It's Because of You!

- If You Walk In Love, You Walk with Angels

- Kids Grow Best Under Sunshine & Love

- Love Me—Love My Teddy

- Love Puts a Twinkle in Your Eye and a Smile In Your Heart

- Love Spoken Here!

- May Your Day Bubble Over With Love

- Mom, I'll Always Love You...But I'll Never Forgive You for Cleaning My Face With Spit!

- Mom, Your Love Tucks Me In & Keeps Me Warm

- Jesus loved you so much that He died for you

- The love of a family is life's greatest blessing

- Love gives itself; it is not bought.

- My Love is with You Always

- In dreams and in love there are no impossibilities

- Love is all there is

- Today Love smiled on me

- We can do no great things, only small things with great love

**I love you so much
More than words can say
I love you with joy
all night and all day
You're sweetness and light
And wonderful, too
I love you so dearly
my dreams have come true**

- We must love friends for their sake rather than for our own

When a Child

When a child slips his hand in yours
He's not asking for so much
Most times he's only looking for
A reassuring touch.

When a child slips his hand in yours
It's you he longs to please
So tell him that you love him
With a simple little squeeze.

When a child slips his hand in yours
It seems tiny and so meek
He doesn't want material things
Your love is what he seeks!

When a child slips his hand in yours
He just wants to be near
Reassure him that you love him
So that it's always clear.

When a child slips his hand in yours
On any given day
It speaks louder than most any word
That he might ever say!

-Jennifer Byerly © 2004

⦿ Children grow up to be the love they have known

⦿ Our family is a circle of strength and love

⦿ The love between a mother and child is a priceless treasure that nothing can compare to

How Do I Love You?

How do I love you,
Let me count the ways.
I love you for this minute
And all the rest of my days

I love you with my heart,
And know that it is true.
There is no greater joy,
Than the love I have for you.

I love you as a baby
And every day to come.
You are the greatest blessing
So awesome and such fun.

Forever I will love you
And hold you close to me
For all you are is everything
A mom and dad could need.

I love you with a love so grand
And treasure every day
When you reach out your little hand
We'll make memories and play.

For in His infinite wisdom
God brought our love together
A lifetime isn't long enough
Thank goodness we have forever.
-Linda LaTourelle ©2004

Inspired by "How Do I Love Thee?"
by Elizabeth Barrette Browning

Horsin' Around

- Back in the saddle again
- Barrel Racing
- Been there—Rode That
- Born to Rope
- Bronco Rider
- Bull Riding
- Calf Roping
- Giddy Up
- Git along little doggies
- Gone Ropin'
- Happiness is being a true cowgirl/boy
- Happy trails to you
- Hee Haw
- Hitching Post 10 cents
- Hold Your Horses
- Home Sweet Barn
- Hop-a-long _____
- Horse Parkin'
- Horse Play
- Horsin' Around
- Howdy Partner
- Hug a Horse
- If wishes were horses, beggars would ride
- It is not enough for a boy to know how to ride; he must know how to fall
- Judge not the horse by his rider
- King of the Cowboys
- Learning the Ropes
- Never trust a cowhand that doesn't know how to properly tie a horse.
- Queen of the Cowgirls
- Ready Partner?
- Ride'm Cowboy
- Ridin' the Rodeo
- Ridin' the Range
- Rodeo Champion
- Rodeo Queen
- Rodeo Rider in Training
- Round 'em Up
- Steer Wrestling
- Team Roping
- The Lone Rider

218

Hurts of Childhood

Anne

Anne is a fairy who doesn't have wings.
No one can ride to the place where she sings.
No one can know all the wonderful things
Each moment of intimate harmony brings.

(A poem by Nicholas Gordon about Autism)

♡

If I could catch a rainbow
I would do it just for you
and share with you its magic
On the days you're feeling blue.

♡

Would you feel better if I licked your face?

- A Stitch in Time
- A Time to Heal
- Accidents happen
- Chicken Pops
- Doctor, Doctor give me the news
- Laughter is the best medicine
- My guardian angel has a tough job
- On the Mend
- Saturday Night Fever
- Stitch by Stitch
- The Healing Touch

Little
Hurts
Are
Healed
With Big
Prayers
And
Lots
Of
Love

AN APPLE A DAY
KEEPS THE DOCTOR AWAY

- A kiss will make it better
- Against All Odds
- Bumps and Bruises
- Chicken Pox Kid
- Connect the Dots
- Crash and burn
- Give Me a Break
- It's tissue time!
- My Boo-boo's Better Now
- Scars are tattoos with better stories
- Someone told me to go out there and break a leg so I did!
- The leg bone's connected to the knee bone
- Time heals all wounds
- Wipe Out!

I Haven't Got Time for the Pain

I t couldn't be the ice cream
Or the soda pop
Or those little candy things
That looked like a lot of dots
It surely wasn't the hot dog
Or the yummy apple pie
Perhaps it was the burger
And the extra big french fry
But something that I ate today
Didn't settle right
But after I eat my dinner
I'll probably feel alright

-Thena

Oh
My
Aching
Head
Time
To
Go
To
Bed

I feel sick
I feel yukky
Feel sorry for me
I'm one sick puppy!!

-Thena

Trichotillomania
(trick-oh-till-oh may-nee-ah)

An impulse control disorder characterized by an uncontrollable urge, or impulse, to repetitively pull hair out at the root from places like the scalp, eyebrows, or eyelashes, sometimes causing baldness.

According to research, trichotillomania affects between 1% and 2% of the population, mainly girls, although boys do have it. It usually begins in the pre-teen years. Not much is known about this disorder, although symptoms of obsessive compulsive disorder, also known as OCD, which will, often go along with trichotillomania. Doctors feel that it often begins after an extremely stressful event in a person's life.

Treatment may involve therapy, medication, or a combination of both. Fortunately, most people with trichotillomania are eventually able to stop the impulses that lead to pulling out their hair. If you think you have trichotillomania, talk to a parent about how to get treatment. Trust in them, they love you and want to help.

(Info from internet search)

When she was only five
She'd watch me in the mirror
As I worked a satin ribbon
Through the French braid in her hair
At seven she insisted
To wear it down her back
I remember how it rested
Just about her pack
Then when she turned nine
It was pigtails every day
I still recall them bouncing
As she ran outside to play
But when she turned eleven
Something happened to her hair
She woke me and she showed me
Missing patches everywhere
And now that she is twelve
She always wears her hat
I miss the smell of shampoo
I wish she had it back
But yet I watch her playing
As if she doesn't mind
Life was meant for living
She won't be left behind
She's learned it doesn't matter
If you have hair or not.
It's the way you face your trials
When they are battles to be fought
She has no room for shame
In things she can't control
She holds tight to the blessings
That live within her soul
Yes, her beauty is within her
And was never to be found
In her simple strands of brown hair
That have fallen to the ground
-Jennifer Byerly ©

221

Ice Cream For Ice Cream

The Ice Cream Man

It's a hot summer day
And faraway
I hear...the ice cream truck
Oh what luck!
With money in hand
I ask if I can
Run fast...to wave him down
When he comes around!
I rush outside
My eyes fly wide
I can't believe...all the choices
My heart rejoices!
I stand with bare feet
And pick out my treat
I walk away...and I grin
With ice cream on my chin!
-Jennifer Byerly © 2004

- Make mine hot fudge
- With a cherry on top
- I Want Chocolate!
- Gimme a Push-Up
- I scream, you scream; we all scream for ice cream
- The Ice Cream Man
- Can I Have Some Gum?
- He's Coming...He's Coming!!
- MMM-mmm Good!
- Do you know the ice cream man? The ice cream man? I met him on my street.

222

Imagination

The Ginglewhap and the Thomble

Today I saw a Ginglewhap,
And wondered why, oh why,
Do Ginglewhaps run all about,
Whilst Thombles only sigh?
I thought they'd do things just the same,
As they look so much alike.
But you don't see Thombles run at all,
(They prefer to ride their bikes!)
I asked them to explain to me,
Why they behave so different.
But I couldn't grab the Ginglewhap,
And the Thomble shrugged, indifferent!
So I'm really none the wiser,
Why they don't just act the same.
And I suppose they'll never tell me,
But it's fun to watch their games.

-Gareth Lancaster ©

Castles in the Clouds

All you need to build
Castles in the sky
Are fluffy white clouds
And a fanciful eye
You can build rooms,
Add a tower too,
Add doors and windows
By ones and by twos.
Now imagine the tower
With a princess inside
All you really need
Is a fanciful eye.

-Patricia Osborn Orton ©

Innocence

The Lamb

Little lamb, who made thee,
Dost thou know who made thee,
Gave thee life, and made thee feed
By the stream and o'er the mead?
Gave thee clothing of delight,
Softest clothing, wooly bright?
Gave thee such a tender voice,
Making all the vales rejoice?
Little lamb, who made thee?
Dost thou know who made thee?
Little lamb I'll tell thee;
Little lamb, I'll tell thee;
He is called by thy name,
For He calls himself a lamb.
He is meek, and he is mild;
He became a little child;
I a child, and thou a lamb,
We are called by his name.
Little lamb, God bless thee!
Little lamb, God bless thee!
-William Blake

ⓘ I still get wildly enthusiastic about little things... I play with leaves. I skip down the street and run against the wind. -Leo Buscaglia

ⓘ One of the virtues of being very young is that you don't let the facts get in the way of your imagination. -Sam Levenson

224

Insects

A bee sat on my nose.
Then what do you think?
He gave me a wink
And said, "I beg your pardon,
I thought you were the garden."
-English Rhyme

- A Bug's Life
- Bee Mine
- Bee My Honey
- Bug Collector
- Busy As A Bee
- Butterflies Are Free
- Butterfly Kisses
- Buzzwords
- Cuddle Bugs
- Digging For Worms
- Don't Bug Me!
- Honey Of A Day
- Lady Of This Garden
- Ladybug , Ladybug, Fly Away Home
- Mad As A Hornet
- My "Bee-Utiful" Kids
- Our Bee-Utiful Son/ Daughter
- Our Little Love Bug!
- Pocketful Of Worms
- Snug As A Bug
- Snuggle Bugs
- Social Butterflies
- Sometimes You're The Windshield, Sometimes You're The Bug
- Spelling Bee
- The Antz Go Marching One By One...
- The Buzz
- The Flu Bug
- The Queen Bee
- Waterbugs
- We Bee-Lieve In Love

225

Inspiration

When things go wrong, and they surely will
Sit down and pray and just be still
Keep looking up and you will win
For Jesus will carry through thick and thin
Life is uncertain and sometimes tough
Just lean on Jesus for a path less rough
Look to Him with fear, not doubt
He can turn your failures inside out
Reach out and grab the victory cup
Hang on to Jesus and don't give up
The prize is worth the toil and pain
For love and peace is yours to gain.
Trials and sorrows may hurt a bit
But believe and trust—don't ever quit.
-Linda LaTourelle © 2005

DON'T QUIT

◉ You can do all things through Christ who strengthens you -Phil. 4:13

◉ Cast your burden upon the Lord and He will sustain you -Psalm 55:22

◉ Come to me ... and I will give you rest -Matthew 11:28

◉ Do not fear or be dismayed—the battle is the Lords -II Chronicles 20:15

◉ I am with you always –Matthew 28:20

◉ I haven't failed; I've found 10,000 ways that don't work. –Thomas Edison

◉ If at first you don't succeed, do it the way your mother told you to do it!

◉ If opportunity doesn't knock, then build the door.

◉ Success comes in cans—Failure in can'ts

◉ But they that wait upon the Lord shall renew their strength, they shall mount up with wings of eagles. They shall run and not be weary and they shall walk and not be faint. -Isaiah 40:31

◉ Success lies not in being the best, but in doing your best

◉ The kid who believes is the kid who achieves.

226

It Wasn't Me!

I Don't Know and Not Me

There are four kids in our family
But sometimes there are six
The other two show up
When we find ourselves in a fix

Their names are I Don't Know
The other is Not Me
Mother doesn't get it
And asks "How can that be?"

If someone leaves the lights on
Or whenever there's a mess
We can always count on
Not Me to confess

And it's Not Me who will usually
Bring I Don't Know along
(It takes courage to admit when
You need to right a wrong!)

But there are times when I Don't Know
Who should get the blame
My brother's back me up
'Cause they all think the same

Though mother cannot see them
I can assure you this
I Don't Know and Not Me
Really do exist
-Jennifer Byerly © 2004

But Mom—
I didn't do it!

It's all
Your
Fault!
♡
Who
Me?

Mom Knows

I always get in trouble
For brother's doing wrong
Mom thinks its really me
When it's him all along

He's sneaky and sly
Bad things are his fun
When mom comes round
He takes off on a run

He can cause a big ruckus
And be quiet as a mouse
He fools everyone
As he tears up our house

But I know the truth
I'm always there
I guess that's why Mom
Says we're quite a pair
-Linda LaTourelle ©

I'm Sorry

Do Unto Others

There once was a lonely, sad monster
Who sat in his swamp all alone
He just wanted someone to play with
Or someone to call him on the phone
His demeanor had been sour and selfish
Which caused him to lose all his friends
It seems that being so grumpy
Doesn't help anyone in the end
So he stopped and considered his options
As he sat there knee deep in the muck
He realized he'd made some mistakes
So he decided to turn 'round his luck
He picked up the phone and dialed
Calling every lost friend that he knew
"I'm sorry that I've been so awful
Please let me make it up to you!"
The lesson he learned he'll remember
And he'll carry it all of his days
If you treat others poorly you'll end up
With nobody who wants to play!
-Jennifer Byerly © 2004

♡

To say I'm sorry takes a lot
Of strength from up above
But doing what God wants of me
Fills me with much love
-Linda LaTourelle

Jump Rope Rhymes

Cinderella, dressed in yellow
went upstairs to kiss a 'fella
made a mistake
and kissed a snake
how many doctors
did it take?
♡

I like coffee
I like tea
I like _____
to come in with me
♡

Blue bells, cockle shell
Easy ivy over

Raspberry, strawberry,
apple jam tart
Tell me the name
of your sweet heart
♡

Bubble gum, bubble gum
in a dish
How many wishes
do you wish?
Skip with me...
1, 2, 3, 4...
♡

Say, say oh playmate
Come out and play with me

Teddy Bear, Teddy Bear, turn around,
Teddy Bear, Teddy Bear, touch the ground
Teddy Bear, Teddy Bear, show your shoe
Teddy Bear, Teddy Bear, that will do!
Teddy Bear, Teddy Bear, go upstairs
Teddy Bear, Teddy Bear, say your prayers
Teddy Bear, Teddy Bear, turn out the lights
Teddy Bear, Teddy Bear, say good-night!
♡

A sailor went to sea, sea, sea.
To see what he could see, see, see.
But all that he could see, see,see.
Was the bottom of the deep blue
sea, sea, sea!

How do you spell
Mississippi?
M (cross arms over chest)
I (point to your eye)
Crooked letter (cross legs and jump)
Crooked letter (cross legs and jump)
I (point to eye)
Hunch back
Hunch back
I!

♡

Down in the valley where the green grass grows,
There sat ____, as pretty as a rose.
She sang high, she sang sweet,
Along came ____ and kissed her on the cheek.
How many kisses did she get?
1, 2, 3, 4, 5, 6....

♡

Miss Mary Mack, Mack, Mack
All dressed in black, black, black,
With silver buttons, buttons, buttons,
All down her back, back, back.
She asked her mother, mother, mother,
For fifteen cents, cents, cents,
To see the elephant, elephant, elephant,
Who jumped the fence, fence, fence.
He jumped so high, high, high,
That he touched the sky, sky, sky,
And never came back, back, back,
'Til the Fourth of
July-ly-ly.

Kindergarten

Red, yellow, green and blue
Colors, numbers, letters, too
School's for learning, fun
And friends
Oh, I hope it never ends
-Linda LaTourelle

Today was my first
Day of school
It really is pretty cool
I got new crayons
And school books, too
Oh how I love
Going to school
-Linda LaTourelle

My First Day

See me skip, see me run,
I'm going to school like everyone
See me smile, see me grin,
When the bell rings, I walk in
See me work. see me play,
I'm in kindergarten-my first day!
-unknown

- ⓞ A Kid with Class
- ⓞ ABC-123
- ⓞ All-Star Student
- ⓞ Bookworm
- ⓞ Bus Stop
- ⓞ First Day of School
- ⓞ I Can Read Now
- ⓞ I'm a Big Kid Now
- ⓞ Me and My Teacher
- ⓞ My Artwork
- ⓞ Reading Rainbow
- ⓞ Report Card
- ⓞ School Daze
- ⓞ School Friends
- ⓞ School Rules
- ⓞ School's Cool
- ⓞ Show and Tell
- ⓞ Story Time
- ⓞ Teacher's Pet
- ⓞ The Wheels on The Bus

I'm the happiest child alive
I had a birthday, now I'm five!
Off to school today, I go
To learn the things I need to know!

Big Enough

I waited and I wondered
When I could go to school
Daddy said I couldn't
Cause it's against the rules

He said I wasn't old enough
But one day I will be
And then I'll be a school kid
Just you watch and see

Now that I had a birthday
I'm five years old you see
My mom said I can go now
And I said yip-yippee

-Linda LaTourelle

All I Need to Know
I Learned in Kindergarten

The wheels on the bus go round and round
And my mommy's tears fall to the ground
I'm going on the bus to school today
I told her "don't worry", I'll be o.k.

-Linda LaTourelle

Learning is fun
And I've just begun!
And today is an important day
Today Kindergarten
Tomorrow first grade
Look out world
I'm on my way!

-Thena

- ⓘ My New Friend
- ⓘ My Teacher is the BEST!
- ⓘ Big Kid Now
- ⓘ All Grown Up
- ⓘ My First Day of school my mommy cried, but I went on a fun bus ride!

232

Mommy Went to School

Mommy went to school today
To take her baby boy
With heart full of mixed emotions
None of them including joy!
Mommy went to school today
To take her little son
With backpack on his little frame
He was quite the collegiate one!
Mommy went to preschool
To check the teachers out
Make sure they were nice and sweet
Didn't raise their voice or shout.
Mommy went to school today
Second day in a row
Leaving little one with "lubs"
It was so hard to go.
Can you hear my heart breaking
Can you see inside my heart?
Can you feel the millions of kisses given
Before I tore myself apart?
Tomorrow will be better
I just know that it will be
Mommy is getting use to school
And so is he!
-Thena Smith ©

Dear Teacher...

My baby starts school today. I wonder how he'll do. I
know you don't really know him yet, but he's a precious
little person, filled with curiosity and joy. Please do me
one big favor now—love him as though he were your boy.

Sincerely,

His Momma

Ladybugs

- The Lady of this Garden
- Ladybug Lane
- Ladybugs Welcome!
- Save the Ladybugs

Ladybug, Ladybug Fly away Home

Lady of the Garden

Fluttering wings with black little dots
Adorning your garden with red little spots
Scooting leaf to leaf
Without a worry
Nothing will bother her
So there's no need to hurry
Pretty lady, bright red hues
Flying about, often landing on you
Sweet little lady
What cheer you bring
Spreading your color
Welcoming spring
-Teri Olund ©

Pretty Little Ladybug
Pretty little lady
Dressed in your Sunday best
All dolled up in red
With black dots upon your vest!
I hold you on my hand
Wish I could give a hug
To my dainty little friend
A little ladybug!
-Thena Smith

Ladybugs

Oh, how I love a ladybug
They are special
Don't you see?
They are little ladies
And are so beautiful to me!
Don't like worms or tadpoles
Don't like slimy slugs
But I love the dainty creature
That is called a lady bug!
-Thena Smith

234

Lazy Crazy Summer Days

- Beach Boys
- Beach Bum
- By the Shore
- Cool in the Pool
- Down By the Sea
- Family BBQ
- Firefly Summer
- Fun in the Sun
- Good Day Sunshine
- Making a Big Splash
- It's a sunshiny day!
- Popsicle Paradise
- June Bugs
- Lil' Swimmer
- Ocean of Love
- Shore is Fun
- Slip-n-Slide
- Splish, Splash
- Waterbugs
- Hot Fun in the Summertime

Sunflakes

If sunflakes fell like snowflakes,
gleaming yellow and so bright,
we could build a sunman,
we could have a sunball fight,
we could watch the sunflakes
drifting in the sky.
We could go sleighing
in the middle of July
through sundrifts and sunbanks,
we could ride a sunmobile,
and we could touch sunflakes-
I wonder how they'd feel.
-Frank Asch

Summer

Summer brings us nice warm sun
For swimming, fishing, and lots of fun;
For finding seashells in the sand;
For sunbathing to get a tan;
To do all these things and more
At the beach and seashore.
-unknown

Humming Birds and Honey-Bees
Love the flowers and the trees
I love summer and the sun
Eating ice cream, having fun

235

- A Day In The Sun
- All Wet
- At The Lake
- At The Pool
- Barbeque Time
- Barefootin'
- Bathing Beauty
- Cookin' out
- Dog Days Of Summer
- Down By The Bay
- First Day of Summer
- Goggle Girl
- Good Ol' Summertime
- Got Sun Block?
- Heat Wave
- I'm Walking On Sunshine
- It's Hot, Hot, Hot
- Keeping Cool
- Lazy Days Of Summer
- Little Mermaid
- Little Miss Sunshine
- Makin' A Splash
- Makin' Waves
- Our Little Fish

- Our Little Mermaid
- Our Star Swimmer
- Playing In The Sand
- Playing In The Sprinkler
- Pool Party
- Popsicle Smiles
- Ray Of Sunshine
- S Is For Summer
- Sink Or Swim
- Slip-n-Slide
- Snorkeling Fun
- Soaking In The Sun
- Splish Splash
- Sprinkler Fun
- Star Swimmer
- Stayin' Cool By The Pool
- Summer Fun
- Sun & Fun
- Swimming Lessons
- The Colors Of Summer
- Underwater
- Water Fight
- You Are My Sunshine
- Yum Yum Summer Fun

The Summer Children

I like 'em in the winter when their cheeks are slightly pale,
I like 'em in the spring time
when the March winds blow a gale;
But when summer suns have tanned 'em
and they're racing to and fro,
I somehow think the children
make the finest sort of show.

When they're brown as little berries
and they're bare of foot and head,
And they're on the go each minute
where the velvet lawns are spread,
Their health is at its finest
and they never stop to rest,
Oh, it's then I think the children look
and are their very best.

We've got to know the winter
and we've got to know the spring,
But for the children, could I do it,
unto summer I would cling;
For I'm the happiest when I see 'em,
as a wild and merry band
Of healthy, lusty youngsters
that the summer sun has tanned.

Days are getting' shorter an' the air a keener snap;
Apples now are droppin' into Mother Nature's lap;
The mist at dusk is risin' over valley, marsh an' fen
An' it's just as plain as sunshine, winter's comin'

-Edgar A. Guest

237

Children of Summer

With your sticky popsicle smile,
Racing out the slamming screen door,
Splashing, soaring through the sprinkler,
How could I adore you even more?

With your bare feet tickling in the grass,
Cheeks warmed in the sun, bright pink,
Twirling, whirling, dancing in the heat,
How could you change each time I blink?

With your drowsy head upon my shoulder,
Warm smell of your summer dusted hair,
Wet soggy swimsuit dampening my lap,
How could I need you more than air?

-Donna Linderman ©

Lemonade Stand

Come buy a glass of lemonade
Ice cold and extra sweet
It only costs a quarter
For this refreshing treat!
We guarantee each cupful
Will really cool you down!
Won't you please stop by
Before you head to town?
We're probably the only
Stand for miles and miles
We promise every cupful
Comes with a great big smile!

-Jennifer Byerly © 2004

Fireflies

See the air filling near by and afar,—
A shadowy host—how brilliant they are!
Silently flitting, spark upon spark,
Gemming the willows out in the dark;

Waking the night in a twinkling surprise,
Making the star-light pale where they rise;
Startling the darkness, over and over,
Where the sly pimpernel kisses on the clover;

Piercing the duskiest heights of the pines;
Drowsily poised on the low-swinging vines;
Suddenly shifting their tapers around,
Now on the fences, and now on the ground,

Now in the bushes and tree-tops, and then
Pitching them far into darkness again;
There like a shooting-star, slowly on wing,
Here like the flash of a dowager's ring;

Setting the dark, croaking hallows a-gleam,
Spangling the gloom of the ghoul-haunted stream;
They pulse and they sparkle in shadowy play,
Like a night fallen down with its stars all astray;
They pulse and they flicker, they kindle afar,
A vanishing hose,--but how brilliant they are!
-Mary Mapes Dodge

GLOW LITTLE FIREFLY GLOW!

Lightening Bugs in Pickle Jars
What a sparkling sight!
How I love the fun we have
Collecting bugs at night.
We rub them on our face and arms
And laugh as they make us glow
We love the summer evenings
And the fireflies glittery show!
-Linda LaTourelle

239

Get YOUR Fresh Lemonade

The Lemonade Stand

Get your ice cold LEMONADE,
Hurry, before it's gone!
We made it just this morning
For this table that it's on.
We promise that you'll like it,
And there's sugar in it, too.
(Not like it was the other day
When Mom and Dad said, "Ewwww ...")
Get your ice cold LEMONADE.
Boy, grownups sure are funny.
They smile a lot at little kids
Who are trying to make money.
Thank you, ma'am, and thank you, sir.
You've helped us out a bunch.
(Sissy let's go make some more.
It's almost time for lunch.)
Get your ice cold LEMONADE,
Only fifteen cents a glass!
We've gotta make more money,
And we've gotta make it fast.
Daddy said it wouldn't work,
That people wouldn't stop.
They'd hurry right on past us
And then they'd laugh a lot.
One last glass of LEMONADE.
This was so much fun!
-CJ Heck ©

Manners

Good manners: The noise you don't make when you're eating soup

OOPS!

Brother is in trouble
Sister is a rat
He burped at the table
And Mom did not like that!

Sister told on brother
And then to make it worse by far
Dad sat down in his chair
And found my brother's candy bar!

Mom said we should have manners
And mind our 'peas' and q's
Said we should always sit up straight
And know which fork to use.

Dad said introductions
Mean that we should smile and say
"I'm so glad to meet you
Please have a happy day."

But between you and me
I feel I must confess-
I'm not much for manners
For I feel casual is the best!

-Thena

Mind Your Manners

Mind your manners
if you please
Don't lick your fingers
Chew your peas

Elbows off the table
Napkin on your lap
Spoons are made to eat with
Not to drum and tap

Food fights are too messy
Simply not o.k.
Be thankful for your food
And don't forget to pray.

Listen to these words
I'm trying to say to you
For someday when you're grown
You'll tell your own kids, too.

-Linda LaTourelle ©

The hardest job kids face today is learning good manners without seeing any

241

Me

Just Like Me

I've got eyes just like my Mommy's
A nose just like my Dad's.
My ears are like my Grampa's
But it's really kinda' sad.
Everyone who sees me
Sees some part of me they know
Like my temper from my uncle
Or my smile from 'so and so'.
I just hope when I get bigger
That people stop and say:
"Hi there, glad to see ya...
You sure look like you today!"
-CJ Heck ©

I love my curly hair and freckles
On my face and nose
I like my teeth which are like pearls
And my lips of pinkish rose.

I like my eyes of blue
And that my feet are small
But loving to be who I am
I like the best of all.
-Thena

Me

I'm the only me
The only me there is
The one and only me
That there will ever be!
-Thena

Messy Me

- ☺ What H-A-V-E You done???
- ☺ Being organized interferes with my creativity

Messy Room

Excuse my messy room
But underneath my bed
Live the garbage monsters
Where they like to be fed

I toss them dirty socks
That I've worn on my feet
Because they're always hungry
And needing stuff to eat!

They love the candy wrappers
From chocolate bars the best
That's why I always toss them
Along with all the rest

Mama's always saying
"Your room is looking bad!"
I tell her I can't clean it 'cause
The monsters might get mad!

So I feed the garbage monsters
Every chance I get
But mama says I'm the laziest
Boy she's ever met!

-Jennifer Byerly © 2004

Tidy up your room
Don't forget to make your bed
Put your books back on the shelf
That's what my mother said!

I think my room is beautiful
Just the way it is right now
But no matter what I say
She disagrees somehow!
-Thena

Tidy up!
Mom said today
But I had just
Begun to play.

What I considered
Pleasant to see
She considers
Very Messss-ie!
-Thena

♡

I love my room
It is really cool
With papers and books
And stuff from school.

Mom says it's messy
Dad says it's fine
But I don't really worry
Because the mess is mine!
-Thena

243

Room Cleaning Robot

I'm building a robot to clean up my room
using junk on my floor like this busted balloon.
I'll build it with tee-shirts and three smelly socks,
four wrappers, a rock, and a cereal box,
a handful of worms that were dried in the sun,
my brother's rare comic, a cinnamon bun,
a library book that's a year over due,
a sneaker, a sandal, and Dad's missing shoe.
I'll keep on constructing with old underwear,
used tissues, dried spit balls, and fallen out hair,
a half eaten sandwich, that's half a year old,
a broken umbrella, I can't get to fold.
I'll top off my robot with crushed soda cans,
a jar full of flies, and a bucket of sand.
As I finish my robot, I have to confess,
that my room is now clean, but my robot's a mess.
-Robot Pottle ©

♡

My Invisible Maid

My room was messy
As untidy as could be
But it was suddenly straight
Almost 'auto-magically'.

Did a maid come in
And tidy whilst I was gone
I think she must have-
And her name was MOM!
-Thena

I'm in Love with Mud

I'm in love with mud,
It's sad, I know, but true.
I just can't help but splash in it,
Or stomp a path right through.
It's sticky and it's dirty,
And it covers all my clothes.
But when I see it lying there,
A voice inside me grows...
...You can't resist, you know I'm right,
It's fun to play in mud!
Look at it just sitting there,
I really think you should!
I splatter in the grimy goop,
I can't resist the ooze!
I run, I jump, I stamp about,
It drips into my shoes!
-Gareth Lancaster ©

In Love With Mud

I'm in like with dirt
'Cause a little never hurt
But I love to share with my buddy
My absolute love to get muddy!
-Thena

Mud Pies
For Mom and I

245

Military Brats

Dear Santa
What do you tell your little boy,
When he confides in you,
That all he wants for Christmas,
Is to have his dream come true?
Mama, I had a dream last night,
That Daddy had come home,
That you no longer have to cry,
And spend your nights alone.
That everything was once again,
Just like it used to be,
That I was bouncing once again,
Upon my Daddy's knee.
Will you help me one more time?
To write Santa and ask,
If he can bring my daddy home,
Like Christmas in the past?
I'll be so good and say my prayers,
And never miss a night,
If only you will help me with,
This letter that I write.
So I got a pen and paper,
And helped to guide his hand,
As he ask Santa to bring home,
From a far and distant land,

The father and the husband,
We miss so very much,
And yearn to see and then hold
close,
And feel his loving touch.
And after the letter was written,
In childish and bold hand,
I tried to ease his little heart,
And did the best I can,
To explain that even Santa,
Is a very busy man,
But I know that he will listen,
And do the best he can.
You see son you are not alone,
In this letter that you write,
There are boys and girls all over,
Without their Dads tonight.
Your father is one of many,
Who won't be home this year,
But you must be a brave lad,
Have trust and do not fear.
That next year will be different,
And Christmas will be great,
Your Daddy will be home again,
If only somewhat late.
-Loree (Mason) O'Neil ©

I'll Be Brave

I will be brave, Daddy
When you have to deploy
Although it is so awful
And takes away my joy.

I will be brave for mommy
For she will miss you so

I love you so very much
Do you really have to go?

I will do my very best
To be good while you're away
I will be brave, Daddy
But... just not today!
-Thena Smith

246

Military Kids

God bless the kids of our military men
And those whose mothers serve as well.
God bless the ones who live in fear
And have no parent home to tell.
God bless the little soul
Whose parents have gone to fight
Who has no parent to tuck him in
Kiss him and hold him tight.
God bless the tiny baby too
Who doesn't even understand as yet
That Mommy or Daddy isn't there
To soothe its tiny fret.
God bless those military kids
And bless their parents too
And reunite them all Dear God
For we lift them up to you.

-Thena Smith ©

Daddy, I will pray for you
And in my heart I hug you tight
Asking God to bless you every day
While you're away
Morning, noon and night!
-Thena

♡

Why do Daddies have to go
And fight with other Dads
Can't countries learn to get along?
Why must we all be mad?
-Thena

My son, don't cry or fret
Or worry that I will forget
All of the joy your love brings
In even the simplest things!

Don't forget to do the things
That you love so much to do
Carry on with your daily life
And know that I love you.

The thought of you safe at home
With the people that love you
Keeps me going every day
And will help to get me through.
-Thena

247

Moving

A Goodbye To Your Best Friend

I'm just a little girl but I am old enough to know
It's hard to say goodbye
when my heart just knows "hello"
The hardest thing I'll ever do is say good-bye to you
When the moving van shows up
my heart may break in two
But I'll stand bravely watching you as you drive away
And hope some day
our paths will cross another sunny day
On moving day please turn around
and know forever more
I'll be the girl who's standing brave
and waving by the door!

-Jennifer Byerly © 2004

Moving Day

We are moving again
I never seem to get unpacked
When it's time to
Pack it all back!
Back in the boxes
Back in the van
We pack and unpack
As fast as we can!
But it doesn't really matter
In what house we live or where
Just as long as the ones I love
Are residing with me there!

-Thena

Music Time

- A chorus line
- Band on the run
- Boogie woogie
- Garage band
- Good vibrations
- Hard rock
- High fidelity
- High notes
- I'm just a singer in a rock-n-roll band
- In music there is harmony— in harmony there is peace
- In my heart there rings a melody
- I've got rhythm...
- Jam session
- Juke box Saturday night
- Life is the song, love is the music
- Live and in concert
- Make a joyful noise
- Maestro...
- Mr. Tambourine man
- Music from the heart
- Music has charms to soothe the savage beast
- Music notes
- Music of the heart
- Music teachers give from the heart
- Moosic to your ears
- Piano man
- Pickin' and grinnin'
- Practice makes perfect
- Remember the music
- Strike up the band
- Striking the right note
- The beat goes on
- The gift of music
- The harmony between friends is perfect
- The sound of music

Let the Music Begin

249

Come, my little children, here are songs for you;
Some are short and some are long and all are new.
You must learn to sing them very small and clear,
Very true to time and tune and pleasing to the ear.

Mark the note that rises, mark the notes that fall.
Mark the time when broken, and the swing of it all.
So when night is come and you have gone to bed,
All the songs you love to sing shall echo in your head.
-Robert Louis Stephenson

Early in the morning I hear on your piano
You (at least I guess it's you) proceed to learn to play.
Worthy little minds should take and tackle their piano,
While the birds are singing in the morning of the day.
-Robert Louis Stephenson

I signed up for a music class
To help me learn to play
I would learn piano
If my mom got her way
But I held out for the instrument
That I think I'll like the best of all
I will start my tuba lessons
Sometime early next fall!
-Thena

I'd rather play music than do anything

Naptime

Naps

I've tried to tell my mother,
I don't need a nap for me.
Naps are just for babies—
But we just don't agree.
I'm much too big to take one
And I've tried to tell her that.
But Mom will never understand
Why I don't want a nap.
So, every day I lay here
With nothin' else to do.
Sometimes, I even fall asleep
And I think she does, too.

-CJ Heck ©

Tree House

My Daddy built a tree house
(And he let me help him, too.)
We built it in the old oak tree
And he let me paint it blue.
He made it have some windows
So I can see into the yard
And steps to climb, a rope to swing
Boy, we worked awful hard!
Daddy? Hey where are you?
Now it's done...it's time to play!
Oh, he's sleeping in the hammock
Shhh... (whisper)
I think I wore him out today

-CJ Heck ©

Nickname Nonsense

Nicknames

My mother calls me "sweetie."
My father calls me "champ."
My grandma calls me "dearie."
And it's always "sport" from Gramp.
Aunties call me "honeybun,"
Or "sugarplum," or "doll."
And uncles often call me "kid,"
Or nothing much at all.
My brother, who is bigger,
Laughs and calls me "shrimp."
And stupid bullies at my school
Sneer and call me "wimp."
My sister thinks she's funny,
But she is even meaner.
Just because I eat alot,
She calls me "vacuum cleaner."
Others call me other things
That I won't even mention here.
I do my best to turn my back, and try to disappear.
I'd love to shout and tell the world
To use my real name.
I'm tired of this idiotic aggravating game.
My name, so you will know it, is:
"Albert Alexander Aloysius Poindexter
Charles Nicodemis McGillicuddy."
But you can call me "Buddy."
-Ted Scheu ©

Night Watch

Stardust

At the end of the day
When the sun goes down
When darkness falls
And there's silence all around
Look out your window
And see if you can spy
Sprinklings of stardust
Floating from the sky.
It glitters and shines
On the grass and trees
Casting its sparkle
Over you and me.
It settles on your eyelids
So gently, it seems,
Bringing restful sleep
And pleasant dreams.
-Patricia Osborn Orton ©

♡

There was a monster in my closet
I saw it just last night
It reared its ugly monster head
When Mommy turned out the light!

There was a monster in my closet
But it's not there today
When Daddy came into my room
The monster ran away!
-Thena

253

No Boys Allowed

Girls Only

"No girls allowed!" the sign said
Why that just isn't fair!
Who cares if we should choose
To wear ribbons in our hair?
That's fine" is how we answered
"We'll make our very own"
Clubhouse for GIRLS ONLY!
Where we'll leave yours alone!
But ours will have nice curtains
And flowers on the table
We'll serve hot tea and biscuits
If mama says we're able
So go ahead and keep
Your clubhouse dark and dusty
We'd rather play in one
That doesn't smell so musty!
-Jennifer Byerly © 2004

IT'S A GIRL'S WORLD

Club House

Let's build ourselves a clubhouse
We won't let girls join in
Because the girls are babies
Who cry when they don't win
They smell too much like flowers
And those ribbons in their hair
Are things that we're not wantin'
In our clubhouse anywhere
So let's put up a sign
That says "No girls are allowed"
And put it on the clubhouse
Of which we'll be so proud!
-Jennifer Byerly © 2004

No Girls Allowed

Clubhouse

Rough boards slightly askew
With nails poking out
Created by young boys hands
The workmanship leaves no doubt.
Spaces with no wood covering it,
And weathered beyond belief
With one new sparkling addition
That gives the eyes relief—
A freshly painted sign
That proudly proclaims
In letters bold and loud:
BOYS CLUBHOUSE ONLY!
NO GURLS ALLOWED!

-Thena

The sign on their club house read
NO GURLS allowed
They seemed quite mean
And more than a little bit proud.

But I didn't let it bother me
I just marched up to their door
Let them smell the fresh baked cookies
And that sign fell on the floor!

-Thena

BOYS RULE-GIRLS DROOL!

Pageant Princess

Every time I look at you
My heart swells up with pride
Even though you're so beautiful
What counts is what's inside
And you're the kind of person
Whose inner light shines through
No matter where you are
No matter what you do
So regardless of the outcome
Of the pageants you attend
It's the beauty that you have inside
That determines if you win!
So if you have the title
When the pageant is all done
It doesn't matter either way
'Cause you've already won
-Jennifer Byerly © 2004

Parade of Joyful Memories

There's just something about a parade
That delights and pleases a soul
There's something about all the people
That makes it delightful not dull
But nothing compares to the feeling
When the marching is done by you
The feelings of joyful abandon
That pulling wagons with my friends can do
And strollers with babies and streamers
Smiling and waving along
While the band is drumming and playing
As we marched in step to the song
The laughter we shared will be cherished
With a joy that I'll always replay
Because nothing compares to the memories
That was marched into my heart that day!
-Jennifer Byerly © 2004

Pets

My Dog Hector

I have a dog named Hector
We run and play all day,
But when his bath time comes
My Hector runs away.
I see him peeping 'round the fence
And then he's gone again.
He's here, he's there, he's everywhere
But he knows I'm going to win.
I finally get him in the tub
With brush and soap in hand
But just as things are going swell
He jumps and runs again.
He looks so very funny
With soap from head to toe
But he finally lets me catch him
Then back to the tub we go.
-Patricia Osborn Orton©

Happy Ending

We waved goodbye to kitty
As we watched her drive away
Two girls and their mother
Came for her today!
We're happy yet we're feeling
Just a tad bit blue
Because we loved the kitty
But we're thankful they will too.
-Jennifer Byerly © 2004

Tumbling Doggie

There was a little boy, and he had a little dog,
And he taught that dog to beg;
And that dear little dog all dinner-time
Would stand upon one leg.

One day, to his master's great surprise,
That little dog said, "Here goes;"
And he cocked his hind-legs up in the air,
And stood upon his nose.
-Nursery Nonsense

ZOO SWEET ZOO

School Carnival

I won myself a gold fish
At the carnival last night
I gave the man 5 tickets
Then tossed the ball just right!

I got to bring him home
Inside a paper cup
But then when it was morning
He was floating belly-up!

We gave my pet a funeral
God rest his little soul
And then we said goodbye
As he went down the toilet bowl!
- Jennifer Byerly ©

Kitty in the Basket

Where's my little basket gone?
Said Charlie boy one day;
I guess some little boy or girl
Has taken it away.
And kitty too, I can't find her.
Oh dear, what shall I do?
I wish I could my basket find,
And little kitty too.
I'll go to mother's room and look;
Perhaps she may be there,
For kitty loves to take a nap
In mother's easy chair
Oh, Mother! Mother! Come and look!
See what a little heap!
My kitty's in the basket here,
All cuddled down to sleep.
He took the basket carefully,
And brought it in a minute,
And showed it to his mother dear,
With little kitty in it.

-Mrs. Follen

When The Cat's Away The Kids Will Play

- ⑨ A Breed Above The Rest.
- ⑨ A Dog Is Child's Best Friend
- ⑨ A Dogs Best Friend Is Human
- ⑨ A Dog's Life
- ⑨ A Tail Of Two Cats
- ⑨ All dogs go to heaven
- ⑨ Alley Cat
- ⑨ Animal Farm
- ⑨ Ask not for whom the dog barks ... It barks at thee
- ⑨ Assistant to my dog/cat
- ⑨ Attack Cat
- ⑨ Bad Dog/Good Dog
- ⑨ Beauty And The Beast

259

- All creatures great and small, the Lord God made them all
- Birds Of A Feather Flock Together
- Bow-Wowing The Night Away
- Busy as a beaver
- Butterfly Kisses
- Cat and mouse
- CAT-i-tude
- CAT-napping
- Cats are purrrr-fect
- Cool Kitty
- Cow-nt Your Blessings
- Cute And Fuzzy As A Bunny
- Dandy-lion dude
- Don't bite the hand that feeds you
- Every dog has it's day
- Feeding Time
- Fish Tales
- Free as a Bird
- Friends Fur-ever
- Fur Ball
- Fur-ever Friends
- Get a Wiggle on
- Good Dog
- Here Kitty, Kitty

- Home's Where The Cat/Dog Is
- Home Tweet Home
- How much is that doggie in the window
- Hunny Bunny
- I am lion, hear me roar.
- I Ruff you very much
- I tawt I taw a Puddy tat
- I Toad You So
- If I could talk to the animals
- I'll get you my pretty and your little dog too!!!
- I'm a tweet widdle bird
- I'm Not Rude, I've Got Cat-i-tude
- I'm the cats meow, even if I am the dog
- In the Doghouse
- It's A Dog's Life
- It's raining cats and dogs
- Just bee-boppin' around
- Just Me and My Dog
- Kitty, Kitty
- Let sleeping dogs lie
- Licks of Love
- Love Me, Love My Cat/Dog
- Paw prints On My Hearts

New Puppy

There's a puppy at our house, we got her last week.
She's chock full of smarts, and never does leak.
Well, not in the house, at least, she lets us know,
With a whine, or a yelp, that means "I gotta go."
So, we rush out the door, and cheer when she squats,
Then she licks me to tell me she loves me lots.
Yep, smartest dog ever, she knows what to do!
"Hey Mom, what's this spot on my new rug?
Peeeewwwww!"

-Ted Scheu ©

- Lucky Dog
- Girl's/Boys Best Friend
- Meow Spoken Here
- Monkey see, monkey do
- My dog's bigger than your dog
- My name is No No, Bad Dog. What's yours?
- Old MacDonald Had a Farm
- Pets "R" us
- Pitter Patter Of Little Paws
- Puppy Love
- Purrr-fect Pals
- Raining Cats And Dogs
- Sittin' Pretty With My Kitty
- Some Bunny loves you
- The Cat In The Hat

- The Cat's Meow
- The Life Of A Dog/Cat
- The pick of the litter
- This place is a ZOO!
- Toad-ally Awesome
- Visit To The Vet
- Where The Animals Roam
- Will Work for Tuna
- Woof Woof
- You quack me up!
- You're So Dog-Gone Cute
- You're Some Bunny Special

WHO'S IN THE DOGHOUSE?

Picnic

Picnic in the Park

Oh what fun to picnic in the park!
Oh what a wonderful way
To enjoy the sun and have some fun
And spend a lovely day!
Oh what fun to sit in the grass
And drink lemonade in the shade!
What fun to eat from a picnic basket
Things so lovingly made!
But the most special thing
That ever I could do
Is to go on a picnic
In the park with You!

-Thena ©

- ⊕ Ant Go Marching
- ⊕ Backyard Barbecue
- ⊕ Barbecue Bash
- ⊕ Bar-B-Q Time
- ⊕ Cookout
- ⊕ Family BBQ
- ⊕ Fun, Food, and Bar-B-Q
- ⊕ Life's a Picnic
- ⊕ Lunch In The Park
- ⊕ Picnic in the Park
- ⊕ The Teddy Bear Picnic

I love to picnic
in the park
play and swing
Until it's dark
With you each day
Is lots of fun
A picnic time
For everyone

WEENIES and
S'MORES
PICNICS GALORE

Pirates

The world of waters
was our home, and
merry men were we!
Sweet and low, sweet and low,

Wind of the western sea,
Low, low, breath and blow,
Wind of the western sea!
-Tennyson

It's a Pirate's Life For Me

Ole' Blackeye

Ole' Blackeye was a pirate,
But he wasn't very good.
He wore patches over both eyes,
And a parrot on his foot!
His rotten ship and fraying flag,
Had seen much better days.
And his crew had all but left him,
'Cause they were not getting paid!
Ole' Blackeye couldn't read a map,
Or sail a route by star.
So he floated round in circles,
For near to not too far!
His wooden leg was broken,
And his beard a tangled mess.
The only help he had these days,
Was a scruffy dog called Jess.
Ole' Blackeye was a pirate,
And he knew at that he stunk.
So he packed it in and sold his boat,
Before he'd gotten sunk!
-Gareth Lancaster ©

The Jolly Band of Pirates

Oh we're a jolly band of pirates
Who sail the seven seas
But years of yo-ho ho-ing
Has caused fluid on your knees
Upon our ship, The Skinny Dog
We roam the Spanish Main
Where the creaking of our rigging
And our shoulders, sound the same
Our gallant captain, Cross-Eyed Jake
Is known to suffer much
With a bad case of lumbago
And wood-worm in his crutch
You see we're not the youngest crew
That ventured out to sea
The average age amongst us all
Is almost sixty-three
So as we sail towards the sun
To chase the pirate dream
Not for us a treasure chest
We need a pension scheme.

-Rob Erskine ©

- Yo-Ho-Ho & a Bottle of Soda
- Aye Aye, Mate's
- Man Overboard
- Walk the Plank
- Polly Wanna Cracker?
- Fire the Cannons

- Ships Ahoy
- Pirates Cove
- The Pirate Patch
- The Treasure Map
- X Marks the Spot
- Shiver Me Timbers
- Looking for Lost Treasure

264

Rain

- A Walk in the Spring Rain
- And Me without my Umbrella
- And the Heavens opened up
- And the Rain Came Down
- Any one who thinks only sunshine brings happiness has never danced in the rain!
- April Showers Bring May Flowers
- Bring on the Rain
- City Slickers
- Come Rain or Shine
- Days of thunder
- Fun in the Mud
- Have You Ever Seen the Rain
- I'm No Stranger to the Rain
- It's a Wonderful Rainy Day
- Let it Pour
- Let it Rain, Rain, Rain
- Mommy's Little Mud Puddle
- Mud Bath
- Mud Pies 10¢
- Nobody Here But Us Ducks

- Oops! My Name is Mud
- Puddle Jumper
- Rain or Shine, You're a Friend of Mine
- Rain, Rain Go Away
- Raindrops Keep Falling on My Head
- Showers of Blessings
- Soft is the Rain
- Splish, Splash
- The Sun'll Come Out Tommorrow
- When It Rains...It Pours
- Who'll Stop the Rain

I Love Dancin' in the Rain together

When it Rains

When it rains it seems as though
The tiresome day would never go.
Indoor games and indoor toys
Are more for girls 'n they are for boys.
Not much fun for me to play
In the house the livelong day,
Building blocks and 'tending store—
When it rains it's such a bore!

COME RAIN OR SHINE—
YOU ARE A FRIEND OF MINE!

Puddle Stompin'

I like saying, spring has sprung.
I like the way it sounds.
And spring brings with it lotsa rain,
(God's wringing out his clouds).
Rain means puddle stompin'!
After rain, they're everywhere.
No shoes or socks, I'm barefoot.
I get wet, but I don't care.
I don't think my mommy likes it
'Cause I get muddy, (ewww),
But puddles just can't help it.
Somehow mud gets in there too.
Uh oh. Here comes Mommy.
Hey, look at Mommy run.
Mommy's puddle stompin', too?
Now, it's really fun!
-CJ Heck ©

Color me a rainbow

Color me a rainbow,
When the sun comes out to play,
After the dark of storm clouds,
Have all been blown away.
Include the brightest yellow,
To look like smiling faces,
Of loved ones and good friends,
Who live in far off places.
Bright green is very pretty
And is like all growing things,
While red is for the sunset,
That the evening hour brings.
Blue is not for feelings
That you wish would go away,
But instead is the color
Of a bright and cloudless day.
Next time I see a rainbow,
I think I'll not forget,
That it was colored just for me,
By someone that I've met.
-Loree (Mason) O'Neil ©

SOMEWHERE OVER THE RAINBOW

- A rainbow is a promise
- A Cloudy Day is No Match for a Sunny Disposition
- After the rain goes— Rainbows
- All the Colors of the Rainbow
- My End of the Rainbow
- Over the Rainbow
- Rainbows are proof that God keeps his promises.
- Rainbows End
- If there's no pot of gold at the end of your rainbow, maybe you are at the wrong end

267

Remember When

The Days Gone By

O The days gone by! O the days gone by!
The apples in the orchard,
and the pathway through the rye;
The chirp of the robin,
and the whistle of the quail
As he piped across the meadows sweet
as any nightingale;
When the bloom was on the clover,
and the blue was in the sky,
And my happy heart brimmed over,
in the days gone by.
-Unknown

The moments of today
Will one day be tomorrows
Treasured memories

- ☺ Back in Time
- ☺ Sweet Scents of Childhood
- ☺ The Good Ol' days
- ☺ Where were you when...
- ☺ When I was (age)...
- ☺ You and Me
- ☺ Way Back When
- ☺ Happy Times

- ☺ The year _____ Was President
- ☺ When Mom was a girl
- ☺ I Remember When...
- ☺ Today In History
- ☺ The History Books Will Read...
- ☺ I will remember you
- ☺ Memories to treasure

Remember When We Were Kids...

There's a place within our hearts where we keep our favorite memories. Memories that make us smile. Here are some things that will bring back thoughts of a different time. Share them with your children as you make memories of your own.

Take some time and sit down with your kids and talk about how things are now and then tell them about what it was like when you were a child. You'll have fun being nostalgic and perhaps they'll realize that life was fun in simpler times. And maybe you'll even be able to inspire them to appreciate it.

Make the time to play and laugh and be together. The years fly by and the memories only happen when you choose to make it a priority.

LAUGH, LOVE AND LIVE— YOUR LIFE WILL BE BLESSED!

Remember when...

- Games you played...
- Hide and Seek
- Freeze Tag
- Red Light, Green Light
- Mother May I?
- Dodge Ball
- Flying Kites
- Red Rover
- Playing Jacks
- Hula Hoops
- Blowing Bubbles
- Climbing Trees
- Cowboys and Indians
- Hopscotch
- Kickball
- Double Dutch
- Sling Shots

269

Family time was...

- Eating supper together
- Going to Church was family time
- Catching lightning bugs in a jar
- Running through the sprinkler!
- Saturday morning cartoons
- Sunday dinners with Grandparents
- Going on family vacations
- Eating supper together
- Mom packed your lunch
- Drive-in Movies

THOSE WERE THE DAYS...

You wore...

- Mary Janes
- Buster Browns
- Keds
- PF Flyers
- Saddle shoes
- Ribbons in your hair
- Crew cuts
- Pony tales
- Capris
- Pegged Pants

Things you ate...

- Sunflower Seeds
- Laughy Taffy
- Tootsie Rolls
- Lollipops
- Jawbreakers

You laughed at...

- Pillow Fights
- Jumping on the Bed
- Being Tickled

Remember when...

- ☺ Going downtown was a great way to spend a Saturday
- ☺ Going out for dinner was a special treat
- ☺ Going to the principle's office was trouble
- ☺ Dad coming home and finding out was bigger trouble
- ☺ You played outside past dark and didn't want to come in
- ☺ Grandma and Grandpa's house was a fun place to go
- ☺ Mom's were there when you got home from school
- ☺ Dad was your hero and you listened when he spoke
- ☺ Holidays were truly a time to have fun
- ☺ Your sister/brother was your best friend
- ☺ Going shopping was a privilege
- ☺ Families ate supper together

There are so many other memories that I can share (but that's for another time). Remember these memories and let them evoke new ones. Treasure them, share them with your children. Begin today to make the time to create memories for your children. Time goes by too fast and our kids grow up so very fast—savor the moments. Write them down and know that one day your children will be saying to their children... I remember when I was a kid...

**Cherish every moment
Memories are wonderful
Give your kids a present for the future**

Rocket Ships and Space

Sailing Out to Space

I dream of sailing out to space,
Upon a yacht of stars.
With port holes all along the sides,
I'd gaze amazed at Mars.
With mast made strong with spider webs,
And sail of fluffy cloud,
I'd watch the Earth go sweeping past,
As out to space I ploughed.
With stars in front and stars behind,
And planets far and near,
I'd sail my yacht around the rings,
Of Saturn with a cheer.
And onwards passing Jupiter,
To watch the big, red storm.
Then far around its outer moons,
And through an asteroid swarm.
I dream of sailing out to space,
To catch a star or two.
Exploring through the universe,
And just take in the view.
-Gareth Lancaster ©

I'm off to see the Universe
On a rocketship tonight
Planets are flying by me
Oh what an awesome sight!

Rocket Ships and Space

Rocket Ship

I made myself a rocket
I used a cardboard box
It has a viewing window
And a door that really locks
I'm working on the engine
So it will fly real fast!
Soon I hope to launch it
Into orbit with a blast!
Mother says that I have
A grand imagination
But I'm just a little boy
Headed for the lunar station!

-Jennifer Byerly © 2004

Beam me Up Daddy

Slingshot

I'm gonna take a ride
On a slingshot made for two.
I'll be nice and take my sister
We'll be flung to Timbuktu.
I'm gonna get back home
On a slingshot made for one.
With my sister stuck in
Timbuktu
My life will be more fun!

-Robert Pottle ©

Outta Here

I'm leaving soon
For the moon
Get on board
There's lots of room!
We'll fly in space
A rocket race!
There may be aliens
We'll have to face!
But we'll be brave
And simply wave
As we fly through
The star filled cave
Let's zoom away
Through the Milky Way
Just you and me
We'll fly all day!

-Jennifer Byerly © 2004

TO INFINITY AND BEYOND!

273

Royalty

- ...Happily Ever After
- A Court Fit for Kings
- A Feast Fit For Kings
- A Grand Castle
- A Hall as Grand as Versailles
- A Knights Adventure
- A Royal Proclamation
- Almighty King
- Almighty Queen
- As You Wish
- Climbing the Tower Walls
- Do not meddle in the affairs of dragons, they get hungry
- Hear Ye, Hear Ye
- Her Majesty
- His/Her Royal Highness
- I am a child of the King
- I Believe...
- In a Far Away Land
- King Love A Lot
- King of All Kings
- Kiss A Frog
- Locked in the Tower
- My Knight in Shining Armor
- Now All We Need are Six Mice, a Rat, and a Lizard
- Once Upon A Time
- Our Little Princess
- Prince Charming
- Queen For a Day
- Queen of the Fairies
- Sir Lord _____
- The Clock Strikes Twelve
- The King in His Castle
- The Royal Jester
- The Thistle Queen
- The Tiny Princess
- Up the Castle Walls
- Wearing a Dragonly Smile
- When You Wish Upon a Star
- Where's my Pumpkin?
- Your Grace
- So Saith the King...

School Days

- A + Memories
- ABCDEFG—Tell Me What You Think of Me
- A Kid with Class
- A No-Brainer
- A school is a building that has four walls - with tomorrow inside.
- A Touch of Class
- ABC-123
- Adding It All Up
- After School Special
- All Booked Up
- All I Need to Know I Learned in Kindergarten
- Ahhh Mom!
- Back to Class
- Back to School
- Be True to Your School
- Big Man on Campus
- Book Buddies
- Book Worms
- Brain Overload
- Brainiac
- Caught Thinking
- Chalk It Up!
- Class Mates
- Do the Math
- Elementary School Days
- Fast Times at _____
- First Big Day
- First (1st) Day of School
- Go Figure
- Good Old Fashioned School Days
- Hall Pass
- Head of the Class
- Homeschool Kid
- Honor Roll
- In a Class of His Own
- Intellectual Property
- It's as Easy as 1-2-3
- It's as Easy as A-B-C
- Kindergarten Cutie
- Kudos and Distinctions
- Learning Curve
- Letter Perfect
- Live and learn
- Math Really Adds Up

275

New School Day

With the first day of school approaching
My stomach is feeling in knots
New clothes await in the closet
By the school supplies that we bought

My children are tan and well rested
My garden is welcoming rain
It's nearing the last part of August
The pool awaits to be drained

Soon the bus will be coming
Scooping up my youngest girl
I'll wave from the window watching
As my emotions erupt in a swirl

My husband will be driving our oldest
In the morning when he leaves for work
The chance to connect with each other
Offers them one extra perk

I'll turn on some music and hope that
The day will go by rather fast
So I can welcome my children
Back into my arms at last!

I'll pray that they'll come home with smiles
And stories that they'd like to tell
Until we awake in the morning
In response to the next school bell!
-Jennifer Byerly © 2004

Homework makes you Ugly!

- A Wise Teacher Makes Learning Fun
- A Year to Remember
- Art Class
- Back to School
- Field Trips
- Honor Student
- My Classmates
- My Favorite Subject
- My Favorite Teacher
- My Little Genius
- My School Picture
- Learn, Dream, Grow
- Homework Heartaches
- School Memories
- Student of the Month
- Recess—My favorite subject

Learning is boring at times
Unless I make up some rhymes
That help me remember
How many days in September
Or the tables I call my "times."
-Thena

We are so proud of you
And excited to say
That you are the student
Chosen for this week
To be honored as a star
Even as we speak!

Show and Tell

The love of learning
The sequestered nooks
And all the sweet
Serenity of books.
-Longfellow

School Days

Still sits the schoolhouse by the road,
A ragged beggar sunning;
Around it still the sumacs grow,
And blackberry vines are running.
Within, the master's desk is seen,
Deep scarred by raps official,
The warping floor, the battered seats
The jack-knife's carved initial;
The charcoal frescoes on its wall;
Its door's worn sill, betraying
The feet that, creeping slow to school,
Went storming out to playing!
-Whittier

The Junk Box

My father often used to say:
"My boy don't throw a thing away:
You'll find a use for it some day."

So in a box he stored up things,
Bent nails, old washers, pipes and rings,
And bolts and nuts and rusty springs.

Despite each blemish and each flaw,
Some use for everything he saw:
With things material, this was the law.

And often when he'd work to do,
He searched the junk box through and through
And found old stuff as good as new.
-Edgar Guest

What I've Learned at School

At school I've learned a lot of things
I really like to do.
Like running in the hallway
and eating gobs of glue.
I've learned I'm good at making pencils
dangle from my nose.
I've learned to hum and pop my gum.
I practice and it shows.
I've learned I like to cut in line
and love to cut the cheese.
I've learned to fake a burp, an cough
and even fake a sneeze.
You'd think with all this learning
I'd be doing well at school.
But everything I learn to do
seems to break a rule.
-Robert Pottle ©

The Race

With the bell the race begins.
All will run. One will win.
Murphy's running first with pride.
He doesn't know his shoe's untied.
When he crashes in the hall,
he takes out Tasha, Keith and Paul.
I steer around the wreck with skill.
I'm gonna win. I can. I will!
I'm moving fast with super-speed.
Hey, I'm first. I'm in the lead.
I round the corner. There's the bus.
All those behind are eating dust.
I'm on the bus. I'm first. I win!
Tomorrow we will race again.
Playtime's great, but not as cool
as when we get to leave the school.
-Robert Pottle ©

279

First Day of School

New socks, new shoes
New shirt and pants, too!
Mommy's all excited –
It's my first day of school!

My back pack is heavy
So many new things!
Crayons and glue
New notebooks too!

Mommy's now crying
When I ask "why?"
She smiles and says:
"Time, how it flies!"

This school is big
I'm sure to get lost
Mommy takes my hand
-I will be just fine!

She's more worried 'bout
The bus ride!
This day has gone by fast
I love my new class!

This Bus is sure bumpy
Not like our car,
It's a real good thing
I don't live very far!

We've been riding an hour
Only to stop once
Now I really wish
I had eaten my lunch!

This is my stop –
I'm so glad to be home!

Tomorrow I do this –
ALL ON MY OWN!!!
-Teri Olund ©

It's time to go back to school
I don't like it but that is the rule
Summer is over and done
And that's the end of my fun
No more time in the sun
It's time to go back to school!
-Thena

OFF TO SEE THE WORLD

8:29 A.M.
I'm sitting in the time-out chair.
I think I'm here to stay
because I gave our classroom pet
a carrot made of clay.

10:42 A.M.
Here I am time-out again.
I guess it isn't funny
to perform a disappearing act
on the classroom bunny.

1:06 P.M.
I'm in the time-out chair again
which isn't really fair.
It's not my fault that Peter
Wanted me to cut his hair.
-Robert Pottle ©

I Cut My Hair at School Today

I cut my hair at school today,
but only on one side.
I was going to do the other
'til a tattletaler cried,
"Teacher, teacher, hurry, quick,
a rule is being broken."
The teacher pointed to the door,
not a word was spoken.
I'm off to see the principal.
I'm not afraid of him.
I'll bring my scissors, just in case
I think he needs a trim.
-Robert Pottle ©

I'm Late for School

I got up late for school today,
And nearly missed the bus!
I hurried down the stairs,
Wolfed my toast, and caused a fuss!
I quickly threw books in my bag,
My pens, my lunch and shorts.
Grabbed my coat from out the cupboard,
Took my bat and ball for sports.
I slid across the kitchen floor,
And hopped around the cat!

Then expertly rolled over,
Jumped back up and grabbed my hat!
I belted out of our front door,
Spun round and swung it shut.
Saw the bus was waiting for me,
I felt I had time to strut!
I climbed aboard and then froze still,
And knew that things weren't right!

My friends fell down in fits of fun,
And pointed with delight!
My face went red, I couldn't breathe,
For in my haste I knew!
I'd forgotten to wear trousers,
Jumper, shirt, my socks and shoes!

-Gareth Lancaster ©

- ① Magic School Bus
- ① Making the Grade
- ① Me and My Big Ideas
- ① My favorite subjects are lunch and recess!
- ① My Old School

282

When's Recess?

Back to School

The alarm clock rings
And you open your eyes
The morning's beginning
It's time to rise

Get up, get ready
New clothes, new shoes
Pack your lunch
It's off to school

Get in your seat
The bell's going to ring
Teacher is talking
I can't hear a thing

The kids are so noisy
They're happy today
But they better be quiet
Or we won't get to play

-Linda LaTourelle

283

The Night Before School

Twas the night before school
When all through our house
The children were sleeping
With their dog, cat and mouse

The parents were praying
For the blessings that day
They loved their dear children
In a powerful way

Tomorrow was a new day
The kids were revved up
Teacher's were ready
To fill the learning cup

The lunches were packed
And school supplies, too
Clothes were laid out
Nothing more to do

So Mom settled down for
A nice restful sleep
Her husband was snoring
The kids not a peep

The dreams and the night
So quickly flew by
The alarm didn't work
And no one knew why

Then all of sudden
Things became clear
We're off to the start
Of a crazy new year

-Linda LaTourelle © 2005

284

Elementary Graduate

We're mighty proud of you son
That's why we like to boast
That you are such a great kid
Who deserves a sparkling toast
So here's to your success and
We raise our glass with cheers
You're now a graduate of
Your elementary years!

-Jennifer Byerly © 2004

SCHOOL LUNCH–
NOW I APPRECIATE MOM'S
HOME COOKING

School Lunch

Cold and wrinkled peas
served upon a tray.
Crunchy tuna, sour milk,
I threw it all away.

Lunch at school is gross,
makes me want to gag.
Tomorrow I will pack my own
and bring it in a bag.

Next day, I make my lunch.
I won't get a tray.
Get to school, the menu's changed
to pizza-bar-buffet.

-Robert Pottle ©

Cafeteria of Wonder

Grab my tray
Milk carton and juice
Plastic silverware
Can I sit next to you?

Mystery meat,
Tuna casserole
They say it's good for us
It's food (NOT!) for the soul.

Poke it with a fork
Is it dead or alive?
Best part's the pudding cup
With my spoon by my side.

Hey, who threw that?
Look out here it comes,
A handful of potatoes
Whoo-hoo this is fun!

Throw it here, throw it there,
Food fights are fun and simple,
Better hide and pray real hard
'Cause I just hit the principal!
-Nicole McKinney ©

☆

Standing in line
Waiting for the food
Boy, am I hungry
I sure hope it's good
Watch out for the chicken
It's really dog meat
And don't eat the veggies
They smell like brother's feet
-Linda LaTourelle

286

Scripture about Children

ⓘ Sons are a heritage from the LORD, children a reward from him. -Psalms 127:3

ⓘ Children's children are a crown to the aged, and parents are the pride of their children. -Proverbs 17:6

ⓘ He settles the barren woman in her home as a happy mother of children. Praise the LORD. -Psalms 113:9

ⓘ Even a child is known by his actions, by whether his conduct is pure and right. -Proverbs 20:11

ⓘ Let not mercy and truth forsake you; bind them around your neck, write them on the tablet of your heart and so find favor and high esteem in the sight of God and man. -Proverbs 3:3-4

ⓘ Train up a child in the way he should go, and when he is old he will not depart from it. -Proverbs 22:6

ⓘ Children, obey your parents in all things, for this is well pleasing to the Lord. -Colossians -3:20

ⓘ Children, obey your parents in the Lord for this is right. Honor your mother and father which is the first commandment with promise. -Ephesians 6:1,2

ⓘ And your fathers...bring them up in the training and admonition of the Lord. -Ephesians 6:4

ⓘ Discipline your son and he will give you peace; he will bring delight to your soul. -Proverbs 29:17

Behold children are a heritage from the Lord, the fruit of the womb is a reward.
-Psalms 127:3

Siblings

- Brotherhood/Sisterhood
- Sisterly/Brotherly Love
- Sisters are the Best/Brothers are the Best
- Brothers from the start, Friends from the heart
- Brothers make the best friends
- Brother's are a pest—they bug you
- Brother's together
- Celebrating Sisterhood
- Celebration of Sisters
- Chance made us sisters, hearts made us friends
- Each of our lives will always be a special part of the other
- First a Brother, Now a Friend
- Forever my Brother, always my Friend
- Giggles, Secrets, and Sometimes Tears
- Having a sister is like having a best friend that will always be there. You know whatever you do, they love you anyway.
- How do people make it through life without a brother/sister?
- I Love My Brother/I Love My Sister

THAT'S MINE!

Sibling and Friend— two words that mean the same

If You Two Don't Stop Fighting

Our mother yelled, I'll stop this car
If you two don't stop fighting!
Of course, we just ignored her words,
But then it got exciting.
She hit the brakes pulled off the road,
And handed us her phone.
Call me when you settle down.
For now, you're on your own.
She drove away, and we both cried,
We're sorry! Come back please!
She didn't, so we ordered up
A pizza, extra cheese.
We still feel pretty badly though—
The situation stinks.
Next time we order pizza,
We won't forget the drinks.

-Ted Scheu ©

- ① Two of a Kind

- ① We acquire friends and we make enemies, but our siblings come with the territory

- ① What's the good of news if you haven't a sister to share it?

- ① When brothers/sisters stand shoulder to shoulder, who stands a chance against us?

- ① When I'm big, I'll get even **BUT MOM!**

- ① When My Sister and I are Old We Shall...

- ① You can kid the world, but not your sister/brother

- Just Like Big Sister/Little Brother
- Like branches on a tree we grow in different directions yet our roots remain as one
- More than Santa Claus, your sister knows when you've been naughty and nice
- My Brother, My buddy, My Sister, My girlfriend
- My sister taught me everything I really need to know
- My Brother, My Friend
- Near and Dear
- No Chance of Escape
- Of the two, one is the dancer and one is the watcher
- Oh, Brother
- Peas in a Pod
- Quit Touching Me
- She's My Sister
- Sibling Harmony
- Sibling Rivalry
- Brother/Sister Act
- Sister and Friend - two words that mean the same
- Brothers/Sisters - Gotta Love 'Em!
- Sisters Are a Special Kind of Friend
- Sisters are Forever
- Brothers are Special—Especially Mine
- Sisters are the Best Kind of Friends
- Sisters are the blossoms in the garden of life
- Sisters are the crabgrass in the lawn of life
- Sisters are two different flowers from the same garden
- Sisters by Chance, Friends because Mom Said So!
- Sisters make the best friends

SHE HIT ME!

290

Sick Days

Chicken Pox

The strangest thing occurred
On a weekend none the less
I woke up feeling rather punk
And my skin was just a mess
There were all these itchy red dots
That wouldn't let me be
My mother says it's Chicken Pox
That's what was ailing me!
-Jennifer Byerly © 2004

I 've got the sniffles
Feeling very blue
Mom say's I'm o.k.
And I must go to school

Skating

Skating

Frozen hard, Ice cold,
blue lake.
Tinted swirls, like frosted
icing upon a Gleaming
Birthday Cake.
Will you hold up
underneath me while
I glide about
wearing my new skates?
-Lottie Ann Knox

C hicken soup
Ginger Ale
Feeling sick
Looking pale

Mom's my nurse
Oh what fun
But she can't wait
Until day is done

To school tomorrow
Mom said I must go
I said, "I'm sick"
She said, "not so"

But I know better
I'm feeling ill
My tummy's sick
I need a pill

And then I remembered
My class field day
I can't stay in bed
While my friends go play

So I hollered to Mom
I'm feeling quite well
I'll be at school
Before the first bell
-Linda LaTourelle

Sleepovers

The boys are in the basement
I can hear them as they play
I won't really know the
damage
Until the break of day
Is that a lamp I hear crashing
On the tile below
Oh, my goodness gracious
I really don't want to know
I hear my doggie barking
And the cat let out a meow
That had the sound of pain
Rather like a howl
I must keep my promise not to peek
But I hear the sound of mischief brewing
Even as I speak...

-Thena

Boys—
Don't
Make me
Come
down
There!

Staying up all night
Having pillow fights

10 Pizza's — $100
5 cases of soda — $25
1 can of carpet cleaner —$10
1 roll of film development —$5
Bribing you sister and her friends with
pictures of them in their facials — priceless!

-Teri Olund ©

Oops...Here Comes the Kids!!

The cars are driving up
And bikes are racing in
There goes the telephone
And the doorbell rings again!
Parents are calling me
To make sure that I'm home
Kids are constantly text-messaging us
On the family's three cell phones.
We have plans for the evening
And the kids are rushing to the door
To invite all the buddies inside
For a sleepover on the basement floor!

-Thena ©

- ☺ Ghost stories, Junk Food and Tag, Oh, My!

- ☺ Who needs girls? I'm hanging with my buddies

- ☺ Sleepover At My House!

- ☺ Where's The Floor...All I See Are Kids!

- ☺ Pull an All-Nighter

NO GIRLS ALLOWED

- ☺ Chillin' with my Buddies
- ☺ Bragging & Boasting
- ☺ Scary Movies
- ☺ Telling Jokes
- ☺ How to have a sleepover
- ☺ Video Games
- ☺ Play until you drop
- ☺ Beware: Truth or Dare
- ☺ It's a Guy Thing
- ☺ Sports Center
- ☺ Wrecking the House
- ☺ Backyard Campout

Slumber Party

I wasn't born a princess,
but if the Tiara fits!

♡

Nails and Hair and Makeup, Oh, My!
Manicures, Mud faces and Make-overs, Beautify!

- Nothing but giggling—smiles galore

- Dressed to impress—Cover Girl in Training

- Who needs boys? I'm dancing with my friends.

- Slumber Party At My House Tonight!

- Where's The Floor...All I See Are Kids!

- Up All Night—Sleep all Day

- I Get to be the Mom!

- Sharing beauty secrets

- Games and Sports and Movies, Let's Go!

NO BOYS ALLOWED

- Me & My Girlfriends
- Chit chat
- Boy talk
- Prank calling
- Chick flicks
- How to have a sleepover

- Pillow Fight
- Bedtime stories
- Pedicure Party
- Jammie Girls
- Junk food junkies
- Sweet dreams

Slumber Party Tonight

Come with a pillow
(We call it a cloud)
And a bedroll or sleeping bag
(Although no sleeping allowed!)
We will have lots of snacks
And stay up all night
No one will go to bed
Until we see daylight!
So come on and join us
As we giggle, laugh and dance
For if you want a night of fun
This is your best chance!!
-Thena ©

It's a Party

Girls are coming
Giggling as they arrive
On chips and dips
And soda and laughter
They all seem to thrive!
They are armed with pillows
And have hair dryers in tow
It's a girls slumber party
In case you didn't know!
-Thena

Girls Rule—Boy's Drool

The Slumber Party

One, two, three now four
Girls come giggling through the door
I look up there's even more!
My parents start getting a little up-tight
"How many girls did you invite?"
I had a limit? I must have forgot!
The Pizza Man is at the door
Sleeping bags fill the floor
Just then the phone starts ringing
The music cranks up
And the girls start singing.
Fashion shows, hair and nails
Secrets and very tall tales
Fill the air until deep in the night
My parents praying the bed bug would bite.
All too soon the doorbell again
A stream of parents picking up this time
The house looks like a big pig pen
Now the clean up must begin
So we can get ready for next weekend!

-Shanda Purcell 2005

Good friends come to your Slumber Party,
Best friends stay to clean up.

♡

Mr. Sandman bring me a dream!

♡

You should not be the first one
to fall asleep at a Slumber Party.

Smiles— /smil/ v. to show pleasure, amusement, or affection by an upward curving of the corners of the mouth and a sparkling of the eyes

Smiling

Smiling is infectious,
You can catch it like the flu.
When someone smiles at you
You'll start smiling too.

A simple little smile
Comes from inside out
It feels so warm and good
You no longer want to pout

So when you feel like crying
Remember, don't look down
Just put a happy smile on
And throw away that frown

Keep a cheerful attitude
And give those you know a lift
And when you do you'll find
It was you who got the gift
-Linda LaTourelle

◉ Giggly Grin

◉ A Laugh Is A Smile that Bursts

◉ A Smile Can Brighten even the Darkest Day

◉ A Smile is a Curve that Sets Everything Straight

◉ Love begins with a smile

Your Sweet Face

Not a single expression
Of happiness or glee
Of tantrum or frustration
Is wasted on me!

I see them all
And I marvel 'tis true
At all of the expressions
That decorate you!

Your face like a canvas
Holds them all in delight
And I inwardly record them
Each wonderful sight!
-Thena

SHINE!

◉ Smile—You're on "Mom's Camera"

◉ A Smile is a Frown Turned Upside Down

◉ A Smile is a Language Understood By All

◉ Smile, God Loves You

◉ A merry heart makes a cheerful countenance
-Proverbs 15:13

Sneakers, High Heels & Shoes

So Strong

I took them to the Laundromat,
Then washed them in the sink.
I've tried powders, sprays, and foamy pads,
But still my sneakers stink.
-Robert Pottle ©

I love my sneakers
I wear them everyday
They make me run so very fast
And feel good when I play.
I don't mind wearing sandals
If I am at the beach
But my trusty comfy tennies
Are always kept within my reach.

-Thena

If the shoe fits— buy it in every color

Sneakers come in many sizes
From the simplest to the priciest
Some have rings
And some have springs
So many shoes
So hard to choose
Oh well, I'll take
Them all!

-Linda LaTourelle

From high-tops to flip-flops There's sneakers for everyone

Cinderella is proof that a new pair of shoes can change your life

High Heels

Pretty little girl of mine
Growing up before your time
These High Heels you beg to wear
As you walk about with flare
It has taken years of practice
In Mom's closet you did venture
Until now upon your feet
Your first pair of heels, what a treat!
-Shanda Purcell 2005

Princess Red Shoes...

I look like a kid, but I'm a princess you see
Little Princess red shoes, that's me!
They call me Cynthia 'cause they don't know
I'm a princess but my crown doesn't show.
My Grandmommy buys me lovely red shoes
That make my day and chase away all my blues
For when I put them on, the whole world can see
That it brings out the princess in me!
Teasing comes from my brothers
And they deny my princess-ship to others
But as long as I know that I am royalty
I will just smile, bow and sweetly curtsey.
I love being a princess
There is so much to do
For one thing I must polish
Each little red shoe!
-Thena Smith

I wasn't born a princess, but if the shoe fits

Special Kids

Behind The Smile

What do you see when you look at me
A person or a disability?
I know I live within this home
But my hopes and dreams are still my own
Although they're locked inside my head
It doesn't mean that they are dead
I'd like the same as any of you
I'm capable of choices too
Many people quietly say
It would be much kinder if they were locked away
Then we'd be safe as we walked the street
And ensure that everything is neat
To them we say, "We have rights too
There, but for the Grace of God, go you
We will not go quietly into the night
But we'll stay and be counted, here in the light
We hope the message will sink home
Just treat us as you would your own
And look beyond the disability
Because there, behind the smile, is me.
-Rob Erskine ©

Daring to be different
In my own way
I am a special child
Who loves to laugh and play

Let Love

God made so many children
In varying shapes and sizes
He made them very precious
From simple to the wisest

Each and every child
Is a treasure from above
He made them all so special
And sent them here to love

So, no matter who the child
Just know he is God's best
Be sure to give him all you have
Let love take care of the rest

-Linda LaTourelle

The Perfect Home

I believe that in God's plan
He searched the whole world through
And in the twinkling of an eye
He found the perfect home for you

A home with parents
Whose patience runs so deep
With hearts full of love
Waiting for you, their child to keep

He knew you were so special
And would need a tender touch
So he found the perfect parents
Who would love you very much

-Linda LaTourelle

301

God Made Her Special

I know a little girl
Who has a charming way
Her silly little antics
Can bless a person's day

Her eyes are shaped like almonds
She may not speak so well
But still her heart speaks volumes
And it isn't hard to tell!

Each morning when she rises
She takes a special bus
But when she gets to school
It's she who teaches us

For I know her heart is open
It stretches far and wide
She only seems to care about
The beauty that's inside

God made her very special
When he placed her on this earth
More precious then a diamond
Her loving soul is worth!

-Jennifer Byerly © 2004

There's something
special about You
That made my dreams
At last Come true

My Dear Chosen Parents—

I've loaned to you My Special Child for you are among the few
that I could trust to raise with love, this gift I've given you.
At first each problem you must face, you will not understand,
but if you'll place your trust in Me, I'll bless you as I planned.
I saw the bitter tears you've cried, the heart constrained with pain,
and with compassion I wept too with teardrops like soft rain.
You will survive this perilous time and one day look back in awe,
for I will give you hope and peace and strength on which to draw.
Now when you feel discouraged do not bow your head in shame,
for I'll be there to help you each time you call My name.
This precious little child of yours is blessed with inner joy,
and he will charm and gladden you...he is yours to enjoy.
He's created in My likeness, yet in a slightly different way,
so take pride in watching your son develop other skills each day.
He may not walk or talk the same as other children do...
but I've given to him lots of hugs to give right back to you.
You both will be his teachers, and sacrifices will be made,
but the rough times that you now face, in time will gently fade.
The special way he tilts his head, the gentle way he'll smile
will make the job you have to do all the more worthwhile.
And as you watch him grow and play, you won't hear a complaint,
for I gave him a great capacity to love without restraint.
You are My chosen parents and I've equipped you for this task,
so when you don't know what to do, don't be afraid to ask.
Now shelter him with tenderness and encourage him to see
the love you both have for him...for he's a special gift from Me.

Love,

Your Heavenly Father

-Dorothea K. Barwick © 1998

My View

My view of the world
May be different than yours
For you stand on two sturdy feet
While I see the world from a different view
I see it from a wheelchair seat!

But I see the world and I love what I see
And I love sharing my world with you
For I don't fret and won't ever forget
That you are the best of my view!

I may see the world from a seat that's low
And peer through bars at places I can't go
But I always see and recognize
The love for me that is held in your eyes.

I hope someday to see the world
From a taller and stronger frame
But until that dream comes true
I love looking at the world with you
And I love it just the same!

-Thena
(written for Sonda's Baylee)

I See

When I look at you
I see a smile
That brightens my world
I don't see any disability
I see my beautiful little girl!

-Thena

304

Sports & Activities

ALL SPORTS

- All-Star
- Are you Game?
- Backyard Soccer
- Beat the Clock
- Center circle
- Champions All-State
- Champions to Beat
- Close, But No Prize
- Defense
- Fake / Foul
- Family Game Night
- Far and Wide
- Faster, Higher, Braver
- Game Over
- Go for the Gold
- Go Team Go, Fight Team Fight
- Goal Keeper/Kicker
- Goal!/Goalie
- Great Game
- I Get a Kick Out of Soccer
- I Love Soccer
- In a league all your own
- Inch by inch my goal is a cinch
- Instant Replay!
- It's not over til it's over
- I've/We've got you covered.
- I've/We've got your back.
- Just for Kicks
- Kick and Run
- Kick back and have a great time!
- Kick-off
- Let the Games Begin
- Let's Volley
- Little Sport
- Mid-fielder
- MVP
- My favorite season is
- Never Quit
- No Pain, No Gain
- On your mark get set GO!

- Out of Bounds
- Penalty Area
- Playing By The Book
- Playoffs
- Prime Time Sports
- Ready, set, goal!
- Rookie of the Year
- Side Tackle
- Stealing First/Second/Home
- Sweep the series/Clean sweep
- Sweet Smell of Victory and stinky socks
- Taste of Victory
- Team Player
- Team Spirit

- The Agony of Defeat
- The Best Team In the West/East
- Tie-Breaker
- Undefeated Champions
- Victory Seekers
- Watch your Offsides!
- Way to Go!
- We Are The Best
- We Are The Champions
- We've Got Spirit
- What a kick!
- Winning With Style and Grace
- You're my Hero
- Zone Defense

CYCLING

- Born to Bike
- Where the rubber meets the road
- If you don't like my driving, get off the sidewalk
- On a bicycle built for ME!
- Where the Blacktop Ends
- Cycling ROCKS!

FOOTBALL

- We interrupt this school day for football season!
- Football ROCKS!
- Touchdown!
- First and 10
- Go for the whole nine yards!
- Half-time
- SuperBowl Here We Come

306

HOCKEY

- Face Off
- The Puck Stops Here
- Slapshot
- Chicks With Sticks
- Play For The Glory
- Heart Of A Champion
- My World, My Life, My Game
- I'm a hockey Dad/Mom!
- I'd rather be playing hockey!

RACING

- Go speed racer
- Kid Hot Rod
- Racing Rocks!

SKIING

- Chill Out!
- Ski Bum
- Cold feet, Warm heart
- I'd rather be skiing
- Slip sliding away
- Bumping down the bunny trails

SOCCER

- I'd rather be playing soccer
- I'm the Proud Coach
- School? It's soccer day!

MISC. SPORTS

- Skateboarders Rule!
- Gymnasts beam!
- Swimmers make a big splash
- Little Sport Fan
- It's a big win
- Sports are cool
- Team Super Star
- Rah, Rah, Ziz Boom Bah
- Cheer for the team
- Varsity Kids
- We came to play!
- We came to win!
- Victory is ours
- We won! We won! We won!
- Sports Fanatic!
- Press on to the goal

I press toward the goal for the prize of the upward call of God in Christ Jesus

BOWLING

- Bowlers Always Have Time to Spare
- Grip It and Rip It
- Strike it Up

MARTIAL ARTS

- Karate Begins and Ends With Respect
- Float Like a Butterfly— Sting Like a Bee

RUNNING

- Born to Run
- Running Like the Wind
- Slow and Steady Wins the Race
- The Race is On
- Your Mark, Get Set, Go

SURFING

- Hang ten
- Surf's Up
- Ridin' the Waves

WRESTLING

- Go to The Mat
- Pin to Win
- Pin'em Down

MISCELLANEOUS

- Let the Games Begin
- No Pain, No Gain
- It's a Real Nail Biter!!!
- Instant Replay!
- Grudge Match
- Game Day
- You're My Hero
- Winning Isn't Everything, It's the Only Thing
- Kick the ball
- Jump High
- Win for the Team
- Mean, Mad & Movin'
- Stretch and Bend
- Reach for the Prize
- Gold Medal Winner

I love to be outdoors playing with my friends
No matter what the weather, we love to just pretend
That we're running at the track or kicking for the goal
Climbing up a mountain or sliding down the pole
Sports are just a way to help us grow up strong
Whatever we may do, we'll play the whole day long

-Linda LaTourelle

W orking as a forward
Or playing at mid-field
Soccer is a game in which
Your feet must wheel and deal
Running like the wind
Your eyes upon the goal
You have to work to keep the ball
Under your control
-Jennifer Byerly © 2004

KARATE

- ① Above the Belt
- ① Alive and Kicking
- ① Getting our Kicks
- ① I get a kick from karate
- ① It's a Kick
- ① Karate Kid
- ① Kick Back
- ① Kick It!
- ① Kick the Habit
- ① Quest for the black belt
- ① What a kick!

Coaching

Thank you for your time coach
You simply are the best
Your patience and your willingness
Really passed the test
We know that you'd prefer that
We wouldn't make a fuss
But we wanted you to know that
You sure scored big with us!
-Jennifer Byerly © 2004

Let's hear it for the Winners & still Champions

The goalie blocks the goals
She gets to use her hands
Sometimes she takes a kick
Or on the ground she lands
Defenders have a job
The sweeper makes the call
The referee call's "penalty"
If you're pushed before you fall
But out of all the teammates
On the team you see
The ones that I prefer the most
Are my parents cheering me!

-Jennifer Byerly © 2004

Soccer Guardian Angel

Soccer is a game
Where it's good to use your head
Whether on a ball
Or preventing cards of red
But one thing that's for sure
I think you will agree
A special little angel
Is the best defense for me!

-Jennifer Byerly © 2004

Boys Play Football - Intelligent Boys Play Soccer

- ① Soccer Dad

- ① Soccer is a kick

- ① Soccer Mom and Proud of It

- ① Soccer Season

- ① Soccer's a Ball!

- ① Get the Goalie

- ① Spread out, Spread out...

- ① Watch your Offsides!

- ① What a kick!

The Athlete

An athlete is a special person
With strength of body and soul.
It takes a lot of inner strength
To retain his outer control.

His mind is sharp and his body strong
His focus never wavers
As he starts for his final goal.
And every moment he savors.

Whether in a practice session
Or in a scheduled meet
Or running countless marathons
He's ready to compete.

We applaud our son the athlete
And admire his courageous, competitive spirit
And in our hearts we cheer him on
And know that within his heart he can hear it!
-Thena Smith ©

Ask not what your teammates
can do for you—
Ask what you can do
for your teammates!

There are four seasons:
Football Season
Hockey Season
Basketball Season
Baseball Season

Sun, Moon & Stars

- Hitch your wagon to a star

- I will love the light for it shows me the way, yet I will endure the darkness for it shows me the stars

- If I had a star for every time you made me smile I would be holding the night sky in my hand!

- Reach for the stars

- Let the sun shine in

- Turn your face to the sun

- We can't all be stars, but we can all twinkle

- Twinkle Twinkle Shine on Me

- When you wish upon a star

- You are my shining star

- You are my Super Star

- You are my sunshine

- Sunshine in my heart

Keep your face toward the sunshine and the shadows will fall behind you

Good friends are like STARS—
You don't always see them,
but you know they are always there

Stars are the daisies that began the blue fields of the sky
-D.M. Moir

Starlight Starbright
Wish I may, wish I might

The Sun

Don't you think the sun is bright?
I wonder where it goes at night?
Does it sleep or does it hide?
Or is the moon its other side?
Does it hide behind the hills?
Late at night as outside chills?
Do you think it needs to rest?
From all that warming it does best?
Could it even have a home?
Maybe in London or even in Rome?
Or does it just float around?
Moving slowly from town to town?
Yes, I think it must do that!
After all the earth's not flat.
So the sun goes round and round
Spreading sunshine on the ground!
-Gareth Lancaster ©

Man from the Moon

There once was a man from the moon,
Who dusted the sky with a broom.
He cleaned it at night,
To keep the lights bright,
And scooped out new stars with a spoon!
-Gareth Lancaster ©

Catch a falling star
Hold it close to you
Dream about the day
All your wishes come true

MY STAR

STARS

Look at the stars,
Way up there,
So very far away.
High in the sky,
They shine so white,
And never seem to stray.
Like little dots,
Or specks of paint,
Just floating up above.
I wonder,
What they do up there,
And what they are made of.
Are they just holes,
Poked out the sky,
By giants long ago?
Or maybe they're,
Electric lights,
Strung up to make a show!
So far up there,
I'd like to be,
To take a look first hand.
To just get close,
And have a peek,
That really would be grand!
-Gareth Lancaster ©

I threw a coin in the wishing well
But my wish did not come true.
I wished upon a star
And that one fizzled, too

But I have learned one thing—
Before I make another
Wishing on a star
Is cheaper than the other

313

Sunday School

The Books of the Bible

You know it starts with Genesis
And ends with Revelations
You've learned that Jeremiah
Comes before Lamentations
Matthew, Mark, Luke and John
Followed then by Acts
All start off the New Testament
As one of your bible facts
You've worked so hard to learn them all
And now you've passed the test
We're so very proud of you
What a great success!

-Jennifer Byerly © 2004

♡

Sunday Go to Meetin' Clothes

Got on my suit and tie
Shoes are shiny and bright
Sister has on her best dress
And something she calls tights.
Daddy wears a suit and has his Bible
And Mom looks pretty in her hat
As she instructs us to behave
And not act like a brat.
When we are dressed like this
No fun and game thing goes
For we are all dressed up for church
In our Sunday Go to Meetin' clothes!

-Thena

Super Scouts

- As Eagles We Can Fly
- Boy Scouts Jamboree
- Boy Scouting Brothers
- Brownie Basics
- Campfires and S'more
- Cub Scout Day Camp
- Cub Scouting Brothers
- Do Your Best
- Eagle Scouts Soar
- Earning the Badge
- Experience Wildlife...Be a Scout Leader
- I Will Do My Duty...
- Scouting Is Great!
- On My Honor
- Scouting Rocks
- Trail to Eagles
- We've Got Cookies

MAKE NEW FRIENDS-BUT KEEP THE OLD

Scouting Poems

I'm a Junior Girl Scout
I value my self-worth
There's nothing I won't try
Anywhere on earth
My uniform holds badges
To reflect the work I've done
They also mark good memories
Of laughter, love, and fun

-Jennifer Byerly © 2004

I'm proud to be a member of Studio 2B
I believe my family is also proud of me!
My uniform holds badges
To mark the work I've done
They also hold good memories
Of laughter, love and fun!

-Jennifer Byerly © 2004

315

Daisy Scouts

I'm a Daisy Girl Scout
I'm learning lots of things
I'm working towards my first badge
I've learned new songs to sing
I'm making brand new friends
And having lots of fun
I feel so good about myself
When every day is done!
-Jennifer Byerly © 2004

Brownie Scouts

I'm a proud young Brownie
That's why I promise you
I will be respectful
In everything I do
When serving God and country
If I am put to test
I promise I will always
Pledge to do my best
I love to wear my uniform
And I want you to know
You can always count on me
Everywhere I go!
-Jennifer Byerly © 2004

- ⓘ Scouts Honor
- ⓘ Be Prepared
- ⓘ Scout It Out

- ⓘ Hiking to New Heights
- ⓘ We Belong
- ⓘ Cookie Time

Teeth

I've Just Lost My Two Front Teeth

I've just lost my two front teeth
Now there's just a hole
They came out during break time
I was chewing a cheese roll
My friends all come and ask me
Can we have a peek
Mum says that it's lucky
The school photo was last week
But I don't care about the gap
Just one thing makes me bristle
It's when I talk to anyone
It comes out with a whistle

-Rob Erskine ©

My Tooth

The tooth fairy took my tooth lath night
And left thome money, too.
But now I can't thay wordth too well
And I don't know what I'll do.
What if my friendth all laugh at me
Becauth I thpeak like thith?
What if they won't come over
And thereth no one to play with?
Hey gueth what? My friend juth called.
He lotht hith tooth today!
You know what elth? He thoundth like me!
He wanth to come and play!

-CJ Heck ©

317

Went to my dentist
Mom said I had to go
I thought I would skip it
And she wouldn't know
But soon my teeth were ugly
I mean total disgraces
Soon I was back to the dentist
But this time for braces!

-Thena

Wiggle it, pull it,
Wrap it up tight
Put it under your pillow
For the tooth fairy tonight

-Linda

My, what big teeth you have!

- ① Dentist—the Boss of Floss!
- ① A Time To Brush
- ① Be true to your teeth and they won't be false to you
- ① Brush Brush Brush
- ① Check-Up Time
- ① Dentists get to the root of the problem
- ① Flossing is Fun
- ① Hug a Dentist
- ① Look Mom, No Cavities
- ① Looth Tooth
- ① Lost All Wisdom
- ① Open Wide
- ① Pearly Whites
- ① Smiles for miles
- ① Something's Mithing
- ① The Tooth Fairy was Here
- ① Tooth or Consequences
- ① Toothless Wonder

- ① All I Want For Christmas is My Two Front Teeth
- ① The Tooth, the Whole Tooth and Nothing but the Tooth
- ① Toothache: the Pain That Drives You to Extraction
- ① You Don't Have to Brush All Your Teeth, Just the Ones You Want to Keep!

318

Teachers

The unexpected courtesy,
The thoughtful, kindly deed,
A hand reached out to help me
In the time of sudden need
Thank you, Teacher

- If You Can Read This, Thank A Teacher

- Leading a Child to Learning's Treasures...Gives a Teacher Untold Pleasures

- Of All the Gems on This Earth, Teachers are the Most Precious!

- Teacher—A Kids Best Friend

- Teachers Are In a Class Of Their Own

- Teachers Can't Live on Apples Alone

- Teachers Favorite Months: June, July & August

- Teachers Have Class

- Teachers Make Kids Count

- Teachers Make the Grade

- Teachers Make the Little Things Count

- Teachers Rule!

- Teachers Task: To Take a Lot of Hot Wires and Make Sure They Are Well Grounded

- The Best Teachers Teach From the Heart, Not From the Book

- What the teacher is, is more important than what he teaches

- The Mediocre Teacher Tells...the Good Teacher Explains...the Superior Teacher Demonstrates...the Great Teacher Inspires!

- To Teach Is To Touch the Future

- When All Else Fails Ask A Teacher

I LOVE MY TEACHER

319

Wisdom on Teachers & Education

- Education is not the filling of a bucket, but the lighting of a fire

- The student becomes the teacher, so teach them well, for they will pass it on to the next generation.

- Kids don't care how much you know as a teacher until they know how much you care about them

- For a teacher to live forever in the memory of even a single child is the best tribute of all

- Be such a teacher, and live such a life, that if every teacher were like you, and every life such as yours, every classroom would be a child's paradise

- The only teachers who don't make mistakes in the classroom each day are those in retirement

- There are two ways of spreading light to your students -- you can be the candle or the mirror that reflects it

- The aim of education should be to teach us how to think, rather than what to think

- It takes so little to make a student happy. Just a smile, a caring comment, an encouraging word, an attentive ear

♡

Here's a special bookmark
to mark your page for you
Place it in your book
when your reading time is through
Every time you use it
we hope that you will know
You taught someone to read once
which helped a mind to grow
-Jennifer Byerly

Teachers are the tenders in the gardens of their care
That keep a classroom happy with children blooming there

Thanksgiving

- A Day of Thanks
- A Happy Heart Is A Thankful Heart
- A Time for Giving Thanks
- America the bountiful
- Apple pies...
- Be thankful always
- Be ye thankful
- Bless this food
- Bountiful Harvest
- Cornucopia of family
- Count your blessings
- Cup of Blessings
- Family & Turkey & Football...Oh My!
- Family gathering
- Family Traditions
- Feast with the Pilgrims
- Give thanks in all things
- Give us this day our daily bread
- Giving thanks
- Gobble 'til you wobble

- Gobble! Gobble!
- God is Great...God is Good
- Harvest Delight
- Horn of Plenty
- I am thankful for _____
- In everything give thanks
- It's turkey time!
- Let us be thankful unto the Lord
- Let us Give Thanks
- Let's Get Stuffed
- O, the Lord's been good to me

Thanksgiving time is getting near
And Mom bought a turkey
She will cook it in the oven
With stuffing made with care
So that all the relatives can come
And our Thanksgiving share.

-Thena

Enter His gates With Thanksgiving And Praise!

- Pilgrim's Progress
- Pumpkin Pie
- Sharing the Harvest
- So much to be thankful for
- Take time to be thankful
- Thankful for family
- Thankful Hearts
- Thanksgiving Bounty
- Thanksgiving traditions
- The Feast
- There shall be showers of blessings
- Turkey Day!
- Turkey in the straw
- Turkey Tunes and Holiday Wishes
- Turkey, dressing and pumpkin pie
- We Are Gathered Here...
- We are Thankful For...
- We gather together to ask the Lord's blessings
- We Give Thanks
- What a Bunch of Turkeys!
- What We Are Thankful For:

Thanksgiving
Turkey and pie
My mom cooks so good
We are so thankful
For family and food

Thanksgiving is—
Family together
Gobs of good food
Cool winter weather
A thankful mood

As we express our gratitude, we must never forget that the highest appreciation is not to utter words, but to live by them.
-JFK

He who thanks but with the lips
Thanks but in part;
The full, the true Thanksgiving
Comes from the heart.
-J.A. Shedd

Thanksgiving is—
Love
Family
Friends
Turkey
Blessings
Pumpkins
Thankfulness

We Are Truly Blessed!

For flowers that bloom about our feet;
For tender grass, so fresh, so sweet;
For song of bird, and hum of bee;
For all things fair we hear or see,
Father in heaven, we thank Thee!
-Ralph Waldo Emerson

Forever on Thanksgiving Day
The heart will find the pathway home.
-Wilbur D. Nesbit

Theme Parks

- A Fair to Remember
- A Family Affair
- A Land Of Imagination
- A Thrill a Minute
- A World of Adventure
- Always an Adventure
- Around And Around
- Beat the clock
- Bump Um! Crash Um!
- Cliff-Hanging Fun
- Clowning Around
- Coaster Fanatics
- Coaster Zombies
- Coastertown
- Coastin' the Coasters

- Coney Island
- County Fair
- Disney or Bust
- Do it again!
- Don't Look Down
- Drive Safely, No Bumping
- Fast, Faster, Fastest!
- Front Row Seats
- Funtabulous Adventure
- Give it a whirl!
- Hang On Tight
- Help Me Find My Stomach
- Hi Ho the Pirates Life
- Hurl-a-Whirl
- I'm going too fast!

- It's a Jungle Out There
- It's a Small World
- Let the good times roll
- Look Mom, No Hands
- Loop the Loop
- Lost His Lunch
- Our favorite thrills
- Our State Fair
- Put the petal to the metal
- Ride the Carousel
- Round and Round they Go
- Scream and Shout
- Sliding Into A Day of Fun
- Splash Down
- State Fair
- Take me to the top
- The Barf Mobile

- The Big Adventure
- The Merry-Go-Round
- The Ultimate Thrill Ride
- The Vomit Comet
- This is a FUN house?
- Thrill Ride
- Thrill Seekers
- Ticket to Ride
- Top Speed
- Twirler Whirler
- Twist And Shout
- Up, Up, Up
- We're Getting Goofy
- Whee! Faster!
- White Knucklin' It
- View From the Back
- World of Adventure

You Must Be This Tall

She ran to the ferris wheel
And squealed out in delight
Jumped up and down in giggles
It was a funny sight.

I watched her being giddy
And I understood it all
As she proudly stood beside the sign
Proclaiming—"You Must Be This Tall!"
-Thena

324

Toy Box

The Toy Box Ate My Brother

The race was on to get a toy
And Thomas was the winner
He beat me to the toy box
But he ended up as dinner
The toy box ate my brother
'cuz he made a tragic blunder
He entered with a head-first dive
And quickly got pulled under
He kicked his feet and called my name
While our toy box drooled and slurped
I knew dear Thomas was no more
When that toy box loudly burped
No toy box can be trusted
So I make this solemn promise
I'll rid the world of all of them
In memory of poor Thomas
I know you must be frightened
So I will help you, girls and boys
Just ship your toy box off to me
—along with all your toys!
-Jeff Mondak

Dear Kids...
Please pick up all your toys
And put them away!
The toy box is hungry!
Love, Mom

Tree House

A platform hidden high above,
in a giant maple tree,
Far back in branches that were spread,
Was special world to me.
One day it might be penthouse,
For visitors so elite,
While next day it was 'campfire'
Where we sat with grubby feet.
I held some parties high above,
Served tea to 'Mrs. Brown',
And even hid, for hide and seek,
From searchers on the ground.
A place where distance knew no bounds,
Imagination soared,
Where I could be a 'Queen' with crown,
A 'man' was called 'My Lord.'
A special place made for escape,
From cruel world down below,
Where wishes, dreams, and just plain thoughts,
Like seeds, sprang forth to grow.
I think back now, to younger days,
Of many hours spent,
In high above the ground,
Perfumed with nature's scent.
For it was there, among the leaves,
My dreams were free to roam,
'Til Mother's voice called out to me,
'Come down, time to come home.'
-Loree (Mason) O'Neil ©

**My tree house was a
place where distance knew no bounds,
And my imagination soared**

Twist and Giggle

A penny saved is...not much.

As you make your bed so shall you...mess it up

Don't bite the hand that...looks dirty.

Kind words, linger warmly about us
and fill us with delight and inspiration

Forget the cake, go for the icing!

I love to give homemade gifts.
Which one of my parents do you want?

Laugh and the whole world laughs with you,
cry and you have to blow your nose!

Never smart off to a teacher
whose eyes are twitching!

One of the luckiest things
that can happen to you in life is,
I think, to have a happy childhood.
-Agatha Christie

Quick tip:
Sleep in your clothes
so you'll be dressed in the morning.

There is only one pretty child in the world—
and every mother has it. –Chinese Proverb

Who are these parents
and why are they calling me Son?

You can't teach an old kid new...math

Vacations—/ve ke shEn/noun/time devoted to food, fun and folly; playtime; whooping it up; family togetherness; makin' memories

- (Your name) Travels
- Adventure Time
- American the Beautiful
- Among My Souvenirs
- Another Day In Paradise
- Are we ever going to get there?
- Are we lost?
- Are We There Yet?
- Ask for directions—who me?
- Big Yellow Taxi
- Bon Voyage!
- Diary of Our Road Trip
- Did you remember the suitcase?
- Different Worlds
- Distant Shores
- Do you know where we're going?
- Don't touch your sister!
- Down By the Sea
- Driving Ms. _____
- Face In A Crowd

- Family Reunion
- Fantastic Voyage
- Far Away Places
- Flying High
- From Here To Eternity
- Gateway To The World
- Going Places
- Great Adventure
- Having A Wonderful Time
- Head For The Border
- Heartbreak Hotel
- Here we go again
- Home at Last
- Home Away From Home
- Homeward Bound
- I gotta go to the bathroom
- I know where we're going!

Daddy, I think you missed the turn

Our Dream Vacation

- I smell a skunk
- Incredible Journey
- Laundry Time
- Leaving on a Jet Plane
- Let's Get Away From It All
- Life's A Journey, Not A Destination
- Memories Are Made Of This
- Mom, does Dad knows where we're going?
- My Travel Story
- Next Stop (destination)!
- No Computers, No Phones, No Faxes
- O, Beautiful For Spacious Skies
- Off We Go, Into the Wild Blue Yonder
- Oh, the Places We'll Go
- On the Bonny, Bonny Banks
- On The Road Again
- On Vacation

- Our Family Vacation
- Our Summer Home
- Our Winter Home
- Out of this World
- Over The Mountain, Across the Sea
- Pack Your Bags and Leave Tonight
- Packing Day
- Paradise Hawaiian Style
- Peaceful Easy Feeling
- People I Know; Places I Go
- Planes, Trains and Automobiles
- Road Hog
- Road Trip
- Room with a View
- Sail Away
- Ships Ahoy!
- Skiing to the Top
- South of the Border
- Summer Vacation

ALL ABOARD!

Travel \trav·el\ n. 1. journey: 2. trip or tour

It's not how fast you get there, but how much fun you have!

- Rollin' Down the Rails
- Sand-tastic Beaches
- Sweet Home (state name)
- Thanks for the Memories
- That's What I Like About the South
- The Big Apple
- The Golden State
- The Joy is in the Journey
- The Maine Event
- The Time Of Our Lives
- The Wise Man Travels to Discover Himself
- Ticket to Ride
- Ticket Please
- Today in Paradise
- Tourist Trap
- Traveling Together
- Turn Here

- Two Tickets to Paradise
- Under the Skies of _____
- Unofficial Beach Bum
- Up a Lazy River with You
- Van-tastic Vacation
- We're Off
- Westward Ho!
- What a View!
- What a Wonderful World!
- What I Did On My Summer Vacation!
- What's that over there?
- Where are we?
- Where in the World Are We?
- Where Are We Going?
- We're in the middle of nowhere!
- Wish You Were Here
- World Traveler
- X Marks the Spot

Let's take a trip together—

PLAYING THE LICENSE PLATE GAME

Vacation

We're having a vacation
A special getaway
That's why we chose the ocean
So we could rest and play

Mama said "wear sunscreen"
As she reaches in her sack
She makes me sit beside her
Then she rubs it on my back

Daddy takes his shirt off
Sets up the low beach chairs
I wade into a tide pool
The wind blows back my hair

Brother builds a castle
Using lots of sand
Then he kicks it over
And starts to build again

The tide licks at the shoreline
Leaving shells along the beach
I see a pretty starfish
Just beyond my reach

Oh how I love the ocean
The waves, the sand the sun
Every time we go there
We have a lot of fun!

-Jennifer Byerly © 2004

My favorite thing is to
go where I've never been
☆
Strong and content
I travel the open roads
-Walt Whitman

Vacation

Oh the road as we travel the highway
Is a long one that stretches for miles
I ask my dad "are we there yet"
He answers "No, not for awhile!"

I watch out the window and wonder
Why the things that are close go by fast
Except for the time to get where
We're going seems to last and last

The sun in the sky shines so brightly
But my mother says it will be night
Before we reach our destination
So boredom starts picking a fight

I wonder if this is all worth it
'Cause sitting here sure is a pain
Next time I hope that my father
Will consider our taking a plane!
-Jennifer Byerly © 2004

**Anything, everything, little or big
becomes an adventure
when the right person shares it.**
-Kathleen Norris

☆

The joy is in the journey,
not at the journey's end

☆

**Two roads diverged
into a wood,
and I took the one
less traveled by**
-Robert Frost

Valentine's Day

- Be Mine
- Bunches of Love
- Forever Yours
- Gimme a Kiss
- Heart Throb
- How Do I Love Thee
- How Sweet it Is

- Let Me Call You Sweetheart
- Love Me Tender
- Loves Me...Loves Me Not
- Only You
- Sealed With a Kiss
- You Belong to Me
- XOXOXOXOX

Why Was Cupid A Boy

Why was Cupid a boy,
And why a boy was he?
He should have been a girl,
For aught that I can see.
For he shoots with his bow,
And the girl shoots with her eye,
And they both are merry and glad,
And laugh when we do cry.
And to make Cupid a boy
Was the Cupid girl's mocking plan;
For a boy can't interpret the thing
'Til he becomes a man.
'Twas the Greeks' love of war
Turn'd Love into a boy,
And woman into a statue of stone—
And away fled every joy.
-William Blake

HEART OF MY HEART

333

- 100% Lovable
- A Heart Full Of Love
- A Heart of Gold
- Basketful of Love
- Be My Cupid
- Bunches of Love
- Call Me Cupid
- Candy Kisses
- Chocolate Day
- Color the World with Love
- Cupid's Cuties
- Cupid's Kisses
- First Love
- Flowers and Candy And Hearts, Oh My
- Forever Yours
- Funny Face, I Love You
- Gimme a Kiss
- Happy Hearts Day
- Happy Valentine's Day
- Heart Beat
- Heart Throb
- Heart to Heart
- Heart's Desire
- How Sweet It Is!
- Hugs and Kisses!
- I'm Sweet on You
- Just 4 U
- Kiss-Able Kids
- Let It Be Me
- Let Me Call You Sweetheart
- Love Bugs
- Love Letters
- Love Ya Valentine
- Mad About You
- My Funny Valentine
- My Girl
- My Sweethearts
- My SweetTart
- Only You
- Puppy Love
- Sealed With a Kiss
- Some Bunny Loves You
- Sweeter Than Candy
- Sweetie Pie
- The Key To My Heart
- Will You Be My Valentine?
- You Belong to Me

334

Vive la difference

We're Different

The kids at our house number three,
as different as they can be;
And if perchance they numbered six
Each one would have particular tricks,
And certain little whims and fads
Unlike the other girls and lads.
No two glad rascals can you name
Whom God has fashioned just the same.

-unknown

Just Me

I'm Not Different
I'm just me
You're not different
As far as I can see!

We are not alike
For we are each unique
But each person that we know
Helps to make our world complete!

-Thena

**Dare to be different
Dare to be new
Dare to be special
Dare to be you!**

Water World

- (_#_) Little/Big Fishes
- (Name), Row the Boat Ashore
- A Canoe for You
- A Day at the Beach
- A Day at the Races
- A Human Cannonball
- A Need for Speed
- A Quick Dip
- A Splashing Good Time
- A Walk On The Beach
- A Whale Of A Time
- Ahoy Matey's
- All Aboard
- All Wet
- Aqua Kid
- At One With The Sea
- At The Lake
- Attack of the Crabs
- Back To The Beach
- Bathing Beauty
- Beach Boys
- Beach Bums
- Beach Combers
- Beauty and the Beach
- Beyond The Sea
- Big belly flop!
- Blue Bayou
- Building Sandcastles
- By The Sea
- By The Shore
- Castle Crashers
- Castles In The Sand
- Catch A Wave
- Catchin' Some Rays
- Come sail away
- Cool Clear Water
- Cool fun in the Hot sun
- Coolin' off in the Pool
- Crazy about Kayaking
- Dig This
- Discover The Wonder Of Waves
- Dive Right In

Swimming

I'm swimming! I'm swimming!
Oh boy, look at me.
I'm swimming! I'm swimming!
Way out in the sea.
I'm swimming! I'm swimming!
I just learned today.
I'm swimming! I'm swimming!
It's easy I say.
I'm swimming! I'm swimming!
Just jumped off the boat.
I'm swimming! I'm...
Oh no!
I forgot to float.
-Robert Pottle ©

- Divin' Diva
- Diving Board Dare Devil
- Don't Rock the Boat
- Down By The Bay
- Down By the Sea
- Down the Shore
- Escape to the Cape
- First Dip Of Summer
- Friends By The Sea, Just You And Me
- Fun in the sun
- Getting Their Feet Wet
- Going For A Swim
- Hair-larious
- Hand in hand, through the sand
- Hang Ten
- Hangin' On For Dear Life
- Happy as Clams
- Having A Sand-Sational Time
- HELLLLO Sunshine
- Here Comes the Sun
- In the Swim of Things
- It Came from Beneath the Sand
- Junior Lifeguard
- Just Add Water

- Just Beachy
- Just Floatin'
- Just keepin' my head above water
- Kerplunk! Kersplash!
- Lakeside Adventures
- Let's Go Surfin' Now, Everybody's Learnin' How
- Let's Sail Away
- Life Is The Beach
- Lifeguard in training!
- Life's A Beach
- Lil' Sandman

- Living and Laughing on the Beach
- Looney Dunes
- Makin' Waves
- Making A Big Splash
- Making Waves
- Mr. Sandman
- Ocean Adventures
- Ocean Fun
- Ocean Wonders
- Official Beach Bum
- On the Boardwalk

Waterpark

Brother rides the big slide
And screams the whole way down
I think I am a mermaid
As I splash and swim around
Mother finds a lounge chair
Then she works on her tan
Sometimes she shades her eyes by
Holding up her hand
Daddy has a cold drink
He brought into the park
I hope we stay forever
At least until it's dark!
-Jennifer Byerly © 2004

SAILING, SAILING, OVER THE OCEAN BLUE

- On the Waterfront
- Our Little Fish
- Peek A Boo, I Sea You
- Playing In The Sand
- Pool Fun
- Pool Party
- Pool School
- Pool Time
- Red Sails in the Sunset
- Ride the Wave
- Riding the Rapids
- Row, Row, Row Your Boat
- Sailing Away
- Sailing Takes Me Away
- Sand Everywhere
- Sandcastles
- Sand-Sational Summer
- Sand-Tastic Surf
- Sea, Sand And Surf
- Seashells By The Seashore
- Seaside Treasures
- She Sells Sea Shells, By The Sea Shore
- Shell Game
- Shell Seekers
- Shore Is Fun
- Sink Or Swim
- Sittin' On The Dock
- Snorkeling Fun
- Sliding into Fun
- Snorkeling in the Sun
- Splash Dance

Swimming Lesson

Swimming is an easy thing,
If you know how to do it
You push the water wide apart
And then you just go through it!
-unknown

339

Waterslide

The sun on my skin is stinging
I can't wait 'til I can cool down
As I sit on the edge and let go
Of the best water slide around
The splash of the water feels awesome
As I slip down and I start to slide
I can't wait to climb back up the staircase
And give it another ride!

-Jennifer Byerly © 2004

- Splashing Good Fun
- Splat! Belly Flop!
- Splish Splash
- Stayin' Afloat
- Staying Cool In The Pool
- Still Waters Run Deep
- Summer At The Shore
- Sun-Bathing Beauty
- Surf City
- Surf, Sand, Fun
- Surfer Boy / Girl
- Surfin' Safari
- Surfin' U.S.A
- Surf's Up
- Swimming In The Fast Lane
- Swimming Lessons
- Swimming With The Fishies
- Swims Like a Fish
- Takin' A Dip
- Taking The Plunge
- Testing The Waters
- That Sinking Feeling
- The Beach Boys/Girls
- The Big Wave
- The Jewel Of The Pool
- The Sand And The Sea
- The Surf, The Sand—Ain't Life Grand?
- The Unsinkable (Name)
- Toes In The Sand

- Totally Tubin'
- Tropical Breezes And Blowing Palm Trees
- Under The Boardwalk
- Under The Sea
- Underwater Fun
- Unofficial Beach Bum
- Water Boy/Girl
- Water Bugs
- Water Fight
- Water Fun
- Water Wars
- Waterworld
- Wave Reviews
- We Love The Beach
- Wet 'N Wild
- Whale Of A Time
- What Are You Wading For?
- Whatever Floats Your Boat
- Where The Ocean Meets The Sky, I'll Be Sailing
- Where's The Sunscreen
- Whitewater

- Wide Ocean Spaces
- Wipe Out
- You Rule The Pool
- You're All Wet

Swimming

I wanted to go swimming
So I went down to the lake
But there sunning on a rock
Was a great big ugly snake!
I hustled to the ocean
Before it would get dark
But feared a massive tidal wave
Or a humongous hungry shark!
Then I had a great idea
I know what will be cool
I will just go swimming
In my blow-up plastic pool!!

-Thena

BEACH BUM

Weather—Winter

The birds are gone, The ground is white,
The winds are wild, They chill and bite;
The ground is thick with slush and sleet,
And I barely feel my feet.

−Unknown

Weather, weather
Rain and storm
Where is it nice
And sunny and warm?
Cold as an icebox
Wet as a stream
Where is the weather
Of my sunny dreams?

-Thena

- ⓐ All Bundled Up
- ⓐ Arctic Blast
- ⓐ Baby It's Cold Outside
- ⓐ Brrrrr...It's Cold
- ⓐ Chillin' Out
- ⓐ Chilly Weather

DASHING THROUGH THE SNOW

Frosty

The branch above my head is white
covered by the snow last night.
I listen to the icy breeze
and watch the fluffy dancing trees.
Then all that snow drops from the tree
and lands, of course, on top of me.
Snow down my boots, between my toes.
Snow down my pants, and on my nose.
Snow in my ears, I can not hear.
I am a snowman now I fear.

-Robert Pottle ©

342

Winter

- Cold Hands, Warm Heart
- Cool Cats
- Cuddlin' with Cocoa
- Descends the Snow
- Digging Out
- Dressed To Chill
- Dressed Up Like Eskimos
- Dry Socks and Mittens...
- Fabulous February
- Feeling a little Frosty
- First Snow
- First Snowball of the Season
- First Snowfall
- Frostin' on my windowpane
- Frosty and Friends
- Frosty the Snowman
- Frosty's Winter Wonderland
- Fun in the Snow
- Glisten and Glide
- Have Snow, Will Shovel
- Hitting the slopes
- Hug a Snowman
- Ice Wars
- In the Frosty Air
- It's Snowtime!
- It's Winter
- Keeping Warm
- Let It Snow
- Michelangelo of Snow
- Mitten Weather
- Northern Exposure
- Old Man Winter
- Once There Was a Snowman
- Our Snow Angel
- Our Snow Day
- Ready for Winter
- Sleigh Ride
- Slip Sliding Away
- Snow Adventure
- Snow Angels

Jack Frost nipping at your nose

Winter

- Snow Angels
- Snow Ball Fight
- Snow Buddies
- Snow Bunny
- Snow Day
- Snow Flakes are Angels kisses
- Snow Fun
- Snow Happens
- Snow Is Glistening
- Snow Kidding
- Snow King/Queen
- Snow Much Fun
- Snow-one Else Like You!
- Snow Picasso
- Snow Play
- Snow Prince/Princess
- Snow, Snow, Snow
- Snowball Fight
- Snowballs for Sale
- Snowbody loves you like I do

- Snowcones for Sale
- Snowed In
- Snowflakes
- Snowflakes Are Angel Kisses
- Snowflakes for Sale
- Snowmen will melt your heart
- Snowy Day
- The Perfect Storm
- The Polar Express
- Think snow
- Warm and Cozy
- Warm Woolen Mittens
- Wet Mittens
- Will Work for Freezer Space
- Winter Blues
- Winter Fun
- Winter Playground
- Winter White
- Winter Wonderland
- Winter's Dawn

In the meadow, we can build a snowman...

Weather—Spring

**Springtime brings new babies
Robins, squirrels and deer
Everything is pretty
It's my favorite time of year**

- A bouquet of springtime
- A Great Day To Fly A Kite
- A Smile As Sweet As Spring
- A Very "Buzzy" Spring!
- April Showers Bring May Flowers
- As Fresh As Springtime
- Better get an umbrella!
- Celebrate Spring
- Cinco de Mayo
- Colors Of Spring
- Enchanted April
- Everything Sprouts In Spring
- First Signs Of Spring
- Happy Spring
- Hop Into Spring
- Hurrah For Spring
- In Like A Lion and Out Like A Lamb
- It's Always Spring In A Mother's Heart
- It's Spring and Look Who's Blooming
- Let's Go Fly A Kite
- Love Bugs and Crazy Daisies
- Love In Bloom
- May Day
- New Beginnings
- No Matter How Long The Winter, Spring Is Sure To Follow
- One Fine Day
- Out Like a Lion, In like a Lamb

Between Winter and Summer, Lies A Beautiful Spring

Spring

A Green Growing Garden,
A Good Cup Of Tea,
A Day Touched By Sunshine,
A Warm Memory

- Puddle Jumper
- S is for Spring
- Spring Ahead, Fall Back!
- Spring Break
- Spring Chicks
- Spring Cleaning
- Spring Days
- Spring Fever
- Spring Fling
- Spring Happy Spring!
- Spring Has Sprung
- Spring is Bustin' Out All Over
- Spring Is Full Of Sweet Days And Roses
- Spring Is In The Air
- Spring is Just Ducky
- Spring To Life
- Spring, Happy Spring!
- Springtime Pleasure
- Swing Into Spring
- Take time to smell the flowers
- The Essence Of Spring
- The First Sign Of Spring
- The Flowers Are Blooming
- Thinking Of You Is Like The Spring, You Bring Love And Joy To Everything
- Twixt Winter and Summer
- Winter is History!
- Winter is Past

Imagination is... the highest kite that one can fly

Weather—Summer

The Queen of Hearts,
she made some tarts,
all on a summer day:
The Knave of Hearts,
he stole those tarts,
and took them quite away!

-Lewis Carroll

- A Bright, Sunshiny Day
- A Day In The Sun
- A Little Taste Of Summer
- A Place In The Sun
- A Quick Dip
- A Sip Of Summer
- A Slice Of Summer
- A Summer Place
- A Summer To Remember
- A Summer's Day
- A Taste Of Summer
- At The Lake
- At The Pool
- Backyard Barbecue
- Barefootin'
- Beatin' The Heat
- Beyond The Sea
- Blowing Bubbles
- Catchin' Bugs
- Catching Rays
- Celebrate Summer
- C'mon And Swim
- Cookout
- Cool Clear Water
- Cool Fun In The Hot Sun
- Cool In The Pool
- Diving Darlings
- Divin' Diva
- Diving Into Summer
- Dog Days Of Summer

Summer isn't over until the school bell rings

Summer

- Down By The Bay
- Dreaming Of Summer
- Endless Summer
- Firefly Summer
- First Swim Of Summer
- Flip-Flop Days
- Floating Into Summer
- Fun In The Sun
- Girls Just Want To Have Sun
- Going For A Swim
- Gonna Soak Up The Sun
- Good Clean Fun
- Good Day Sunshine
- Good Morning Star Shine
- Got Sun Block?
- Gotta Wear Shades
- Happy Summer Days
- Heat Wave
- Hello Sunshine
- Here Comes Summer
- Here Comes The Sun
- Hot Fun In The Summer Time

- I'm Walking On Sunshine
- In The Good Ol' Summertime
- In The Heat Of The Night
- It's A Beautiful Day
- It's A Sunshiny Day
- It's HOT! HOT! HOT!
- Jump Into Summer
- Jumpin' June
- June Bug
- June Is Bustin' Out All Over
- Kastles, Kites And Kids
- Keeping Cool
- Lakeside Adventures
- Lazy Days Of Summer
- Lazy Summer Days
- Let The Sunshine In
- Lil' Swimmer
- Little Mermaid
- Little Miss Sunshine
- Look At Them Goggly Eyes
- Lounging By The Pool
- Make A Big Summer Splash

Summertime and the swimming is cool!

Summer

**A perfect summer day is
when the sun is shining,
the breeze is blowing,
the birds are singing,
and the lawn mower is broken**

- My Future's So Bright, I've Gotta Wear Shades
- Oh, Those Summer Nights
- One Crazy Summer
- One In A Melon
- Popsicle Weather
- Run In The Sun
- S Is For Summer!
- Sailing Away
- School's Out For Summer
- Seasons In The Sun
- Sink Or Swim
- Sizzlin' Summer
- Slide Ruler
- Sliding Into Fun
- Sliding Into Summer
- Slip N' Slide
- Slippery When Wet
- Slippin' And A Slidin'
- Snorkeling Fun
- Splish Splash
- Splishin' And A Splashin'
- Summer Days Are Here Again
- Summer In The City
- Summer's Child
- Summer Sun
- Sunsational
- Suntan Surprise
- Sunshine On My Shoulder
- The First Day Of Summer
- The Boys/Girls Of Summer
- Too Much Fun In The Sun
- You Are My Sunshine

You Are The Sunshine Of My Life

Weather—Autumn

Autumn

Sing a song of seasons!
Something bright in all!
Flowers in the summer,
Fires in the fall!

-Robert Louis Stevenson

- A Festival of Fall Colors
- A Golden Fall
- A Harvest of Memories
- 'A' Is For Autumn
- A Rainbow of Colors
- A September to Remember
- Adieu to Summer
- All of Autumn
- Amazing Autumn Days
- Another Autumn
- Apple of My Eye
- As Autumn Leaves Turn
- Autumn at the _____'s
- Autumn Awareness
- Autumn Colors
- Autumn Days Are Here Again
- Autumn Festival
- Autumn Glory
- Autumn Harvest
- Autumn in all it's Glory
- Autumn is Nature's Pallet
- Autumn is Pumpkins and Piles of Leaves
- Autumn Leaves Are Falling
- Autumn on My Mind
- Autumn Splendor
- Autumn Treasures
- Autumn's Glory
- Autumn's Here
- Autumn's In The Air
- Awesome Autumn
- Bonfires of Autumn!
- Bushel of Blessing

Hi-Ho, Hi-Ho, It's Off To Rake We Go

Autumn

Pumpkins Come
And Pumpkins Go,
But A Jack-O-Lantern

- Crisp Fall Air
- Crisp, Cool Autumn
- Dancing Leaves, Falling Down On Me
- Don't Leaf Me!
- Drifting Into Fall
- Fabulous Fall
- Fall "Leaves" Me Happy
- Fall Family Fun
- Fall Festival of Colors
- Fall is Here!
- Fall Memories
- Fall With Friends
- Falling Down with Friends
- Falling into Fun
- Falling Leaves
- Fall's Coloring Book
- Fall's Harvest
- Five little pumpkins
- Flavors Of Fall
- Forever Fall
- Found The Great Pumpkin
- Frolic in the Fall Leaves
- Frost on the Pumpkins
- Glorious Days of Autumn
- Golden Days
- Golden Memories
- Happy Fall, Y'all
- Harvest Happenings
- Harvest Moon
- Harvest of Happiness
- Harvest Time
- Have A Good Fall, Y'all

Everyone Must Take Time
To Sit And Watch The Leaves Turn

Autumn

- Hayrides and Pumpkin Pie
- Horn Of Plenty
- I'm A Pleasing Pumpkin
- In Search Of The Perfect Pumpkin
- Indian Summer
- It's Fall, Ya'll
- It's Pumpkin Time
- It's The Great Pumpkin, Charlie Brown
- Jump Into Fall
- Jumping in the leaves
- Just A Little Bit Corny
- Kaleidoscope Of Colors
- Lazy Autumn Days
- Leaf It To Me
- Leaf Your Troubles Behind
- Leap into Leaves
- Leaves Come Tumbling Down
- Leaves of Time
- Let's go Cow-tippin'
- Never Fear... Autumn Is Here
- October Fest

- October Fun
- Oh, Those Autumn Colors!
- Orange, Brown, Red & Gold
- Our Basket Overflows With Autumn Memories
- Pick Of The Patch
- Picking Pumpkins
- Piles of Autumn Smiles!
- Piles Of Leaves
- Piling Up The Memories
- Playing in The Leaves
- Preserving our Harvest
- Pumpkin Faces And You
- Pumpkin Hall Of Fame
- Pumpkin Parade
- Pumpkin Patch
- Pumpkin Pie
- Pumpkins 4-Sale
- Pumpkins For Sale
- Rainbow Of Autumn Colors
- Rake, Dump and Jump!
- Rakin' In The Fun
- Raking Leaves

A Whirlwind of Color

Autumn

- Pumpkin Parade
- Reap the Harvest
- Red and Gold and Orange, Oh, My
- Rolling in the leaves
- Scarecrow For Hire
- Seasonal Splendor
- Shades of Autumn
- Share Your Bountiful Harvest
- Shine On, Shine On Harvest Moon
- Silly As A Scarecrow
- So Many Pumpkins, Which One Do I Choose?
- Something To Crow About
- Spring Ahead Fall Back!
- Summer Falls Into Autumn
- Sweet September
- The Apple Dumplin' Gang
- The Beauty Of Fall
- The Great Pumpkin Caper
- The Great Pumpkin Venture
- The Perfect Pumpkin
- The Pick of the Patch
- The season has changed,
- Thirty Days Hath September
- Time for Fall Fun
- Too Corny
- Turning over a New Leaf
- Unbe-leaf-able
- Walking in a Fall Wonderland
- Way Down Yonder In The Pumpkin Patch
- We Live For The Bounties Of Fall, But The Harvest Of Friendship Is Blessed Above All
- We Rake, We Pile...We Jump!
- Welcome To Our Patch
- We're 'Haying' a Good Time
- What Did One Pumpkin Say To The Other Pumpkin?
- When Autumn Leaves
- When Autumn leaves Fall
- Who You Gonna Call, Leaf Busters!
- You COLOR my World

And the leaves came tumbling down

Weather—All
The Ground Has Gone All Crispy

The ground has gone all crispy
The grass has all turned white
Jack Frost was very busy
While we slept through last night
There's ice upon my window frame
And in the puddles too
The time has come for mellow mists
Shivers and the flu
So wrap up warm this winter
Avoid the snow and slush
And if you can escape a cold
Enjoy the Christmas rush!
-Rob Erskine ©

Losing

Sure is windy out today.
There goes my hat. It blew away.
At least I've got my glasses on.
Oh no! Where are they? Darn they're gone.
And now I'm getting quite a scare,
atop my head there is no hair!
This fate is worse than all my fears.
The wind just blew off both my ears!
Oh no, I must? I must? ACHOO.
My nose is gone 'cause off it flew!
Excuse me now, I have to cough.
Goodness me my wips fwew off!
Wifout my wips it's hahd to tawk.
Escuse me as I take a wawk.
-Robert Pottle ©

Unsuitable Weather

It's raining, it's boring,
I feel like exploring.
But I'm stuck here,
My face a sneer,
Just staring at the flooring!

It's thundering, it's lightning,
My misery is heightening.
There's nothing to do,
But sit here and stew,
As there's no sign it is brightening!

It's hailing, it's snowing,
My boredom is growing.
I might go to bed,
And rest my head,
There's just no hope of it slowing!

It's misty, it's foggy,
And outside's really soggy.
If I don't move,
And eat some food,
I'll end up faint and groggy!

It's sunny, it's clearing,
This sudden change is cheering!
But I'm having fun,
The TV's on,
And I'm not disappearing!
-Gareth Lancaster ©

Winter is an etching, spring a watercolor, summer an oil painting and autumn a mosaic of them all

Worms In Spring

When the earth is turned in Spring
The worms are fat as anything.
The birds come flying all around
To eat the worms right off the ground
They like worms as much as I
Like bread and mild apple pie
And once when I was very young
I put a worm right on my tongue
I didn't like the taste a bit
So I didn't swallow it.
But OH! It makes my Mother squirm
Cuz she thinks I ate this worm.

-unknown

Windy Days mean Kiting Days

- A Kite, a Sky, and a Good Strong Wind
- Blowing in the Wind
- Brace Yourself
- Breezy Days
- Flyin' Away
- Fly the Friendly Skies
- Gone With the Wind
- Higher and Higher
- Let the Four Winds Blow
- Let's Go Fly a Kite
- Oh, Go Fly a Kite
- Ride the Wind

- The Wayward Wind is a Restless Wind
- Tree Topper
- Up to the Top
- Up, Up and Away
- Up with the wind
- Wayward Wind
- What a tail!
- When the Wind Blows
- Windy Day

FLYING HIGH

356

Why and other questions?

How bright is the moon?
How far to the west?
How much sand on the beach?
Oh, when does God rest?

How many stars in the sky?
How hot is the sun?
How deep is the ocean?
Ah, look what God's done!

At the end of the rainbow
Or up in the clouds
The world in its wonder
Shows God's love abounds.

-Linda LaTourelle

Why?

Why is the sky so high?
So hard for me to reach?
The clouds look like cotton candy
I want to grab and eat!
Why are the trees so tall?
and their leaves why do they fall?
Why won't you let me climb them
to the very top?
Why is the grass so green,
so soft under my feet?
Why is the water blue?
I can see me and you!
Why does it rain so long?
I want to go outside!
Why do you get so flustered
each time I ask you "WHY?"

-Teri Olund ©

Winners Like Me

Woe is Me

Woe is me! I seem to be
Always left behind
I might as well be a worm
Wiggling in my slime
No one seems to notice me
No one seems to care
I'm always last at everything
And that just isn't fair!
So I'll just be a piece of dirt
Chopped liver and the such
I'm sure that no one cares for me
At least not very much!

-Jennifer Byerly © 2004

I press toward the mark for the prize of the high calling of God

-Phil. 3:14

I'M A WINNER—
MOM TOLD ME SO!

I'm being
The best that
I can be
It's really
Very simple
I'm just
ME!

Winners don't whine
And whiners don't win
A whiner will be a loner
And drive away a friend.
Don't be a whiner
Or you will be ignorable
For most of us,
Find whining
to be deplorable!!

-Thena ©

358

Words of Wisdom—humor and other prophetic words on the raising of a child; or rather a child raising you!

Lessons In Life

Look both ways when you cross the street
When you come indoors, wipe your feet
Dot your I's and cross your T's
Remember to say thanks and please
Clean your teeth when you go to bed
Comb the hair upon your head
Always eat up all your sprouts
They do you good; there's no doubt
Say Goodnight to Mum and Dad
They love you if you're good or bad
Don't feed the animals in the zoo
After all they don't feed you
Put your litter in the bin
Paper, cardboard, gum and tins
Savour sunsets and the dawn
For one day it may all be gone
Respect the views of other men
In times of anger, count to ten
Remain relaxed in times of strife
And may you have a peaceful life
-Rob Erskine ©

Children are one-third of our population and all of our future

A Very Wise Prayer to Live By

Lord, make me an instrument of your peace.
Where there is hatred...let me sow love
Where there is injury ...pardon
Where there is doubt...faith
Where there is despair...hope
Where there is darkness...light
Where there is sadness...joy

Divine Master,
grant that i may not so much seek
To be consoled...as to console
To be understood...as to understand,
To be loved...as to love
For it is in giving...that we receive,
It is in pardoning, that we are pardoned,
It is in dying...that we are born to eternal life
-St. Francis of Assisi

Children's Logic and more...

Never ask your 3-year old brother to hold a tomato.

No matter how hard you try, you can't baptize cats.

There is a point where you aren't as much mom
and daughter as you are adults and friends.
-Jamie Lee Curtis

When your Mom is mad at your dad,
don't let her brush her hair.

The trouble with children is that they are not returnable

Blessed are the young for they shall inherit
the national debt. –Herbert Hoover

A family is a little kingdom,
torn with factions
and exposed to revolutions
-Samuel Johnson

A great man is he who does not lose his child's heart
-Mencius

Children in a family are like flowers in a bouquet.
There's always one determined to face in an
opposite direction from the way the arranger desires.
-Marcelene Cox

If you have never been despised by your child,
you have never been a parent
-Bette Davis

A life spent making mistakes is not only more honorable,
but more useful than a life spent doing nothing.
-George Bernard Shaw

I am not young enough to know everything.
-Oscar Wilde

Every child is born a genius.
-R. Buckminster Fuller

If your sister hits you, don't hit her back
They always catch the second person

I'm so proud of you!

Never be afraid to try something new.
Remember, amateurs built the ark;
Professionals built the Titanic

A Family is—Love that's always Home!
-Linda LaTourelle

You Are Special!

Be the wonderful and unique individual you are!

- Be all you can be and then try harder
- Be happy in all things
- Believe in the impossible
- Don't sweat the junk
- Don't Worry
- Dream Big
- Dress how you like
- Express yourself
- If you want a kitten, start out asking for a horse
- If you want it, ask for it

- Color outside the lines
- Lighten up—Have Fun!
- Look for the Fun
- Make up the rules along the way
- Making your bed is a waste of time
- Share with your friends
- Use your imagination
- You gotta cry a little
- You gotta laugh a little
- Keep asking why 'til you get it

Imagination is more important than knowledge.
-Albert Einstein

A hunch is creativity trying to tell you something.
-Frank Capra

All I ever needed to know, I learned in kindergarten
-Robert Fulghum

I have no greater joy than to hear that
my children are walking in the truth
-III John 4

Kids go where there is excitement.
They stay where there is love.
-Zig Ziglar

You Are...

- ☺ A gift from God
- ☺ A jewel dropped from heaven
- ☺ A beam of sunlight from God
- ☺ My heart, my soul, my love, my life
- ☺ The sweet peas in the garden of life

You are...

The wonder of my life
My sweet and shining star
The best of all there is
Pure love is what you are

My heart's one true desire
The joy in the morning sun
With each daily breath of life
You are my reason to go on

From the moment of your birth
Each day is a priceless treasure
My life has changed forever
I am blessed beyond measure

-Linda LaTourelle
(For my girls!)

THANK YOU LORD
FOR CHILDREN!

363

Zoo-rific Good Time–I wanna walk
like the animals do...take me to the zoo

- A Day Among The Animals
- A Day at the Zoo
- A Trunk Full Of Love
- A Wild and Crazy Place
- A Zooper Day
- A Zoope-rific day
- A Zoo-tiful Day
- All Creatures Great & Small
- An Elephant Never Forgets
- And God Created...
- Animal House
- At The Zoo
- Choo Choo To The Zoo
- Critter Country
- Dandy'lions'
- Day At The Zoo
- Doctor Dolittle
- Doin' the Elephant Walk
- Don't Feed the Animals
- Everybody's Zooing It!
- Fun at the Zoo
- Giraffic Park
- Going Wild
- Hangin' Around
- I Am Lion, Hear Me Roar
- I Work for Peanuts
- I Zoo, Do You?
- I'm Just Wild About...
- In the Jungle
- In the Swing of Things
- It's a Jungle Out There
- It's a Zoo Around Here
- It's All Happening At The Zoo
- Just Hangin' Out
- Just 'Lion" Around
- Just Monkey'n Around
- Kids at play
- Lions and Tigers and Bears, Oh My!
- Look Who's At The Zoo
- Monkey Business
- Monkey See, Monkey Do

ZOO BI DO BI DO–WE LOVE YOU

Dear Dorothy—
Hate Oz!! Took shoes!
Find your own way home!!!!
-Toto

- Monkey'n around
- Noah was God's first Zoo Keeper
- Our little monkey
- Our Private Zoo
- Peanut Gallery
- Please Do Feed the Animals
- Please Don't Feed the Animals
- Rain forest Cafe
- Safari Hunt
- Swing like a monkey
- Talk to the Animals
- Tall Tails
- The Lion Sleeps Tonight
- The Mane Attraction
- The Reptile House
- The Zoo Crew
- This Place is a Zoo
- Trip to the Zoo
- We're off to see the...
- Welcome to my zoo

- Welcome To The Jungle
- Welcome to the Zoo
- What a Zoo!
- Where the Wild Things Are
- Wild and Crazy
- Wild and Wooly
- Wild Thing
- Wild!
- Wonderful Zoo
- You're Grrrrrrreat!
- Zippitty "Zoo" Da
- Zoo Crew
- Zoo pidi do dah
- Zoo Time
- Zoobilee
- Zoo'pendous Day
- Zooper Zoo
- Zooperstars
- Zoorassic Park
- Zoorific

COME ON A SAFARI WITH ME

Sid The Chimpanzee

Crashing into branches
As he swings from tree to tree
All the jungle knows he's coming
It's Sid the Chimpanzee
He's really not the brightest chimp
His eyes are not the best
And if he has to climb too far
He has to stop and rest
He suffers with lumbago
Arthritis on his knees
His bum is bald and purple
And his coat is full of fleas
But he didn't always look like this
In fact, when in his prime
His triple back-flip somersault
Won bananas every time
So all you youthful chimpanzees
Who are little more than kids
Be respectful to your elders
For we all end up like Sid
-Rob Erskine ©

Where the Wild Things

The Rhinos Statement

I weigh the best part of a ton
My skin is armour-clad
Sometimes my temper is quite short
I get that from my Dad
My pointed horn is often poached
But surely you must see
That after all is said and done
It looks its' best on me
-Rob Erskine ©

UP
ON THE
WOOF TOP

The Elephant

The elephant goes like this and That,
He's terribly big and terribly Fat.
He has no fingers, he has no Toes,
But goodness, gracious, what a NOSE!

Elephants Bogies

There's a question I would like to pose
Are there bogies up an elephants nose?
The nose is very long and thick
So there's lots of places they could stick
To clean his nose would take much trouble
You'd have to do it with a shovel
Climb inside and dig away
It would take the best part of a day
Could it be done? No-one knows
So we'll leave the bogies up the elephants nose
-Rob Erskine ©

ZOO-OLOGIST IN TRAINING

The Forgetful Flamingo

I'm a pretty pink flamingo
Who stands about all day
With one leg tucked beneath me
I've always stood that way
Until the day that I forgot
I really did feel dumb
I lifted both my legs at once
And fell flat on my bum!!
-Rob Erskine ©

367

Your Favorite Quotes

Use this space to write down your favorites or create your own!

Your Favorite Quotes

Use this space to write down your favorites or create your own!

_____

_____

_____

_____

_____

_____

_____

_____

_____

_____

_____

_____

_____

_____

_____

_____

_____

Your Favorite Quotes

Use this space to write down your favorites or create your own!

Your Favorite Quotes

Use this space to write down your favorites or create your own!

Biographies

We are so honored to share these wonderful writers with you and hope that their works will not only inspire you in your creativity, but bless you with joy, wisdom and love. We thank them so much for their tremendous generosity in sharing their poems and thoughts with us. I am so blessed to know them and pray tremendous blessings for each of them for sharing their passion. (All works are used with permission from the author.) and now...

♡

Frank Asch known for his Moonbear picture books, Frank has written in almost every category of children's literature including poetry, concept books, juvenile nonfiction, and children's novels. It is Bluegrass Publishing's honor to include *Sunflakes* in this publication. Written while vacationing in Montana, Sunflakes is only one of the many works by Frank Asch. With a creative career that spans four decades, Frank Asch has contributed greatly to America's youth and those that love them. To learn more about this remarkable man, his current projects, and available titles, please visit www.frankasch.com.

Brenda Ball communicates with innocent words of wisdom the writings that will touch your heart and soul. First published at age 23, Brenda has been blessed with a great literary talent. Professionally, her career choices have been enriched by her ability to communicate with the written word. Now living in Castlewood, Virginia (a small, rural town nestled beautifully at the foothills of the Blue Ridge Mountains) with her husband, Butch, and her youngest sons, she loves being a stay-at-home wife, mother, poet and writer.

Over the years writing has become a passion for Brenda; she believes that, 'Poetry is God's way of writing upon one's soul." The author of over two-hundred poems, Brenda is presently working on her first novel. She is also developing a new series of children's books based on the antics of her five year old granddaughter. Readers can look forward to seeing more of her work in upcoming publications.

Dorothea K. Barwick is the owner of Handmaiden Creations in Hopkins, SC. She has been sharing her poetry on Faith, Hope and Encouragement for many years. She says, "Sharing my poems is my way of honoring God and thanking Him for what He has done for me." Published works and handmade cards by Dorothea can be found by searching the web or emailing her directly at DBARWICK!@sc.rr.com.

Carla Birnberg has been rhyming since she can remember. What began as a way to tease and torment her two sisters grew into little tokens she would bestow upon friends and family. When Linda LaTourelle came into her life Carla finally found a way to share her poems with people outside of her immediate world. Carla lives in Austin, Texas with her two dogs and her non-rhyming husband.

Jennifer Byerly was born in Oregon where she and her husband, of 21 years, reside. The couple adopted two beautiful children at birth and Jennifer counts herself as blessed to be able to stay home full time with them. Jennifer has dabbled in poetry since she was a child, but it wasn't until 2003 when her youngest daughter was diagnosed with a very perplexing and heart-breaking disorder that she really began to write. "Writing poetry has become a wonderful therapeutic outlet for me." The author credits her modest talent as a direct gift from the Lord. "I do not know how long God will place these words in my heart, but I do plan to write until He tells me I am finished." Jennifer finds herself especially inspired at the idea of placing a smile on the face of another. "It is like an Rx for my soul." If you have a special request for a poem, you can reach Jennifer at jenjoy3@comcast.net.

Rob Erskine lives in the United Kingdom with his wife and two daughters. He works as a manager in an organization that supports adults with special needs and teaches them to learn to live independently. His hobbies include golf, fishing and playing the guitar. His writing began as a gift to his daughters. On sleepless nights he would recite his poems to help them into slumber-land. More of his endearing poetry can be found on his website at www.postpoems.com/members/camlann.

Nicholas Gordon was born in Albany, New York and now lives in Fort Lee, New Jersey. He is married and has three children. He earned a B.A. in English from Queens College, an M.A. and PhD from Stanford University. He taught English at New Jersey City University, as well as other colleges and universities. Currently, he is retired from teaching, but has an active website that generates thousands of hits per day. His website is a collaboration of several hundred works from the last fifteen years. www.poemsforfree.com.

CJ Heck, a native of Ohio, lives in New Hampshire with her husband George. She has three married daughters and five grandsons. A published poet and children's author, CJ also writes essays, fiction and non-fiction, and poetry for adults from her inner feminine side. Her work has been published by Teaching Point, Inc., McGraw-Hill, Little and Brown, National Wildlife Federation,

Writers Digest Books, St. Anthony Messenger Press, Oxford University Press, Dane Publishing House, and New Hampshire Magazine. CJ is busy promoting her book through school visits, poetry workshops and other personal appearances. Visit her website at: http://pages.prodigy.net/myaquas.

Tom Krause, the author of "Touching Hearts-Teaching Greatness—Stories From a Coach That Touch Your Heart & Inspire Your Soul" published by Andrews-McMeel. Tom is also an International Motivational Speaker whose poetry has been read by over 3 million people worldwide. Tom is also known for his contributions to several books in the "Chicken Soup for the Soul" series. Tom currently lives in Nixa, MO with his wife, Amy, and sons, Tyler and Sam. To learn more, check out his website: www.coachkrause.com.

Gareth Lancaster writes poetry mainly for his children's entertainment and publishes them on his own website "FizzyFunnyFuzzy" http://fizzyfunnyfuzzy.com. He lives in Derbyshire, in the United Kingdom. Gareth has had some short stories published in the past and spent four years working as a journalist for several UK internet magazines.

Linda LaTourelle has been writing since her childhood. In writing this book, she hopes to enable others to see how all children are precious to the Lord. In her own words, "I hope that through scripture, the writings of others' and my own words, this book will be a blessing to all who read it..."

Linda is a single mother, of two beautiful and talented daughters and the owner of Bluegrass Publishing, Inc., a leading publisher and creator of tool books for journaling, scrapbooking, rubberstamping, cardmaking and other crafts. She truly loves the opportunity to introduce the works of other writers to her readers. Her books offer sentiments, quotes, poems, teaching and tips on a wide array of topics. Full of joy, thought, wisdom, humor, life and love, her books reach the human heart from 5 to 105. The feedback is often, "We just love to sit and read them."

Her passion for writing, publishing and sharing the Lord through it all, has enabled her to have a business that has touched lives all over the world—showing that heartfelt words can reach across oceans and continents. Look for more wonderful and insightful books to come from Linda LaTourelle.

Donia Linderman currently lives in Michigan with her husband, Gavin, and their 2 daughters, Elyssa and Olivia. Poetry has been a means of self-expression for her since she was in the 1st Grade. As an avid Scrapbooker, it only seemed natural to use poetry as a form of journaling. "I greatly enjoyed writing these poems and I am thrilled to have the opportunity to share them with others."

Nicole McKinney is a classy young lady of 18! She has been writing poetry for as long as she can remember. To share her love of the arts with others, is her life's desire. She has a joyful spirit and is active in the local community theater.

Jeff Mondak is a children's poet who lives with his wife, two sons and two dogs in Tallahassee, Florida. Many of Jeff's poems have appeared in magazines such as "Cricket," "Spider," and "Spellbound." You can read more of his poems at: "Jeff's Poems for Kids," http://garnet.acns.fsu.edu/-jmondak.

Loree Mason O'Neil was born on November 7, 1935, in the tiny town of Driftwood, Oklahoma which is located just south of the OK/KS state line. Her parents were dairy farmers. Aspiring to be a writer, Loree took two years of journalism while in high school. After graduation, she married and had four sons. As things go, she put her writing on hold and then in 2000, a Canadian greeting card site posted one of Loree's older poems. It was well received, and at that point she started pumping them out. Loree learned that she truly enjoyed sharing her thoughts and experiences through poetry. Loree's website, www.poetrybyloree.com, is truly an experience.

Teri Olund was born in Louisiana, but transplanted to Texas at a very early age. With her maternal grandparent's encouragement, she began to write little limericks at the age of 10. She is married to a wonderful man, David, and has a beautiful little boy, Michael, who inspired most of the poems in this publication. Working as a Commercial Escrow Officer, Teri began scrapbooking when her dear friend, Dana, introduced her to the "art" about six years ago. That is when Teri began to blend her love of poetry with her love of telling stories through photographs. More of her poems can be found at her website: www.teribugdesigns.com.

Patricia Osborn Orton lives with her husband in Decatur, AL and has been writing poetry for the past 16 years. Her poems have been published in numerous poetry anthologies and other publications. She is a member of the National Library of Poetry and has won Editor's Choice awards for her poems in the past. More of her wonderful poems for children can be found at her website: http://angelwings-ggtg.com/patsmagic/children.htm.

Robert Pottle is a parent, a poet, a presenter, and a former first grade teacher. He enjoys traveling to schools across the country to share his contagious enthusiasm for poetry. Robert lives in Maine with his wife and two children. When not writing or performing at schools, he enjoys camping with his family and other outdoor activities. To learn more about Robert, visit his website at www.robertpottle.com. You can also order his books with the order form in the back of this book.

Ted Scheu is a children's poet from Middlebury, VT who brings giggles and smiles to kids, ages 3 to 300, with his rollicking performances and roller-coastery poems. Scheu's poems are borne of his own childhood memories, and his experience as an elementary teacher and parent. Scheu (pronounced "shy") travels the world as a visiting author. In addition to his performances, he conducts poetry writing workshops in schools for grades K-6. Scheu's poems are published in several popular anthologies in the US including, "I Invited a Dragon to Dinner" by Philomel, NY (2002), and "If Kids Ruled the School" "Miles of Smiles," and "Rolling in the Aisles" by Meadowbrook Press, MN (2004), and in the UK, in three anthologies published by Macmillan Children's Books. He also has a self-published CD of his poems called, "Warning, Don't Eat More Than Three!" A new collection and CD are due out early in 2005. His work may also be found at his web site at: www.poetryguy.com.

Thena Smith was born in a tiny farming community in western Kentucky where she remained until she married her college sweetheart in 1965. For the last 20 years she has lived in Coronado, California with her husband, Ron and her daughter, Melissa. Thena remembers writing her first poem at the age of 7 for a class Christmas project. Her mom sent it to the local newspaper and it was published. For many years, she wrote, but failed to save her writings. Finally encouraged by a friend to save her work, they presented a collage of poetry and music that was televised on a local cable station. She also co-wrote a children's musical that was presented locally. Thena has always been a scrapper. And, as the hobby began to catch on she began to share verses with others. A local on the scrapbooking message boards, Thena has written hundreds of poems to share with her friends. More of Thena's writings can be found in her two best selling books, "Where's Thena? I need a Poem about..." and "Whispers". Watch for more of Thena's works to come at www.bluegrasspublishing.com.

Shanda Purcell has a great love for life. She feels just as comfortable managing the business of Bluegrass Publishing, Inc. as creating and designing craft projects or writing. She is truly blessed to be part of an industry where she can use all her God given talents. In her own words, she says, "The craft industry is based on sharing; your ideas, designs and family, any little bit I can contribute makes me happy." Shanda lives in Western KY with her husband Matthew and four children; Neil, Hannah, Jackson and Emma.

SPECIAL THANKS

To my Mother—thanks for paying attention to all the little details! You did an awesome job. I love you so much, you're the BEST! I Love having you here to share this with. I thank you for raising me to have the values that I have. Your love is wonderful. Thanks for all you do.

To the children, parents, and staff of South Marshall Elementary, Lone Oak Elementary, and St. Joseph Elementary of Western Kentucky, "thank you." We are grateful for your participation in our first children's poetry contest and humbly appreciate the contributions of poetry. It is our honor to support you as you introduce and foster a love of literature in these young minds.

Ultimate Kudos To: Mrs. Cindy Marks, Mrs. Whitis, Mrs. Nancy Wilson, Mrs. Rosa, and Mrs. Kim Smith and to Emily Baker, Kayla Carrico, Conner Lee English, Lawson Grider, Austin Shane Jones, and Miranda Prater and to their parents!

LINKS TO SOME OF OUR FAVORITE SITES

- Be sure to visit the websites of all our contributing writers. You can find a link to more of their sites on our website at: www.BluegrassPublishing.com.

- Our favorite place for fonts is www.letteringdelights.com. Doug and his company have the greatest selection of fun, funky and fabulous fonts for all your scrapbooking and crafting needs and wants. Be sure to tell them we said, " Hello."

- Need a website created? Visit Holly VanDyne our great web-designer. She is a joy to work with and will do all she can to help you develop the site that fits your needs. www.scrapbookinsights.com.

OUR BEST SELLERS!

We have the <u>Largest Collection</u> of poems &quotes
for the scrapbookers and cardmakers ever created!

The Ultimate Guide to the Perfect Word
(Our biggest seller—over 200,000 copies sold!)
Linda LaTourelle

The Ultimate Guide to Celebrating Kids I
(birth through preschool-384 pages)
Linda LaTourelle

Introducing the first book in our new
"Perfect Words Worth Repeating" series...
LoveLines
(artistic quotes to be used time and again)
Linda LaTourelle

Where's Thena? I need a poem about...
(insightful & witty poems)
Thena Smith

Whispers
(passionate poetry & words of love)
Thena Smith

Be sure to watch for all of our books
on Shop At Home Network!

MORE SURPRISES
COMING SOON!

NEW BOOKS
NOW AVAILABLE

The Ultimate Guide to the Perfect Card 2nd Ed.
(Bigger and better—newly revised-384 pages)
Linda LaTourelle & CC Milam

COMING ATTRACTIONS

A Mother's Heart—A Father's Wisdom
(Book 2 in the series "Perfect Words Worth Repeating")
Linda LaTourelle

Season's Greetings
(Book 3 in the series "Perfect Words Worth Repeating")
Linda LaTourelle

A Taste of Paste
(poems for the classroom)
Thena Smith

Board Smartz!
(learning quips & bulletin board tips)
Thena Smith

C is for Christmas
(poetry for the season)
Thena Smith

What Can I Say?
(words with an artistic flair!)
WendiSue

WATCH OUR WEBSITE FOR NEWS!

The End

♡

In all this life
the greatest blessing
is the love of a child.
May your life be
overflowing wth this
incredible gift from above.
And may you cherish and nurture
that love and be forever
full of gratitude for it.
Serve that love well
by the giving of
all that you have—
your time, your heart
your love, yourself and
you will discover
Ultimate Joy.
Through loving a child
you will know
just how much
God loves you
And you will be
Twice blessed!

If you enjoyed the poems written **by Robert Pottle** in *Celebrating Kids II*, you can order signed copies of his two books **Moxie Day and Family** and the sequel **Moxie Day the Prankster** with the form below.

ORDER FORM

Name _____

Address _____

City _____ State _____ Zip_____

E-mail _____

Phone ( ) _____ - _____   Signed Book? Yes ☐ No ☐

If signed, to whom? _____

Qty	Title	Unit Cost
	Moxie Day and Family *by Robert Pottle*	9.95
	Moxie Day and the Prankster *by Robert Pottle*	8.95
	Subtotal	
	Flat Rate Shipping & Handling	1.99
	5% Sales Tax (Maine only)	
	TOTAL	

Make check or money order payable to:

Blue Lobster Press
Dept. S
RR1 Box 509
Eastbrook, ME 04634
Checks must be drawn from a U.S. Bank

Thank You For Your Order!

BLUEGRASS PUBLISHING, INC.
ORDER FORM

NAME		DATE

ADDRESS

CITY/STATE

CREDIT CARD #	EXP. DATE

PHONE ( ) —	

E-MAIL

QTY	TITLE	EACH	TOTAL
	The Ultimate Guide to the Perfect Word BY LINDA LATOURELLE · OUR BIGGEST SELLER	$19.95	
	The Ultimate Guide to the Perfect Card BY LINDA LATOURELLE · NEW/BIGGER-384 PG	$19.95	
	The Ultimate Guide to Celebrating Kids I BY LINDA LATOURELLE · BIRTH TO PRESCHOOL	$19.95	
	The Ultimate Guide to Celebrating Kids II BY LINDA LATOURELLE · NEW/GRADE SCHOOL	$19.95	
	LoveLines—Beautifully designed quotes BY LINDA LATOURELLE · NEW/COPY & USE	$12.95	
	Where's Thena? I need a poem about... BY THENA SMITH	$19.95	
	Whispers: Passionate Poetry BY THENA SMITH	$12.95	

SEND ORDER TO: **BLUEGRASS PUBLISHING, INC** PO BOX 634 MAYFIELD, KY 42066 (270) 251-3600 FAX (270) 251-3603 **WWW.BLUEGRASSPUBLISHING.COM**	6% TAX KENTUCKY	
	$2.95 Per Book	
	TOTAL AMOUNT	
	$	

BP

Thank You
FOR YOUR
ORDER

May God Bless You

In His Love,
Linda

Bluegrass
PUBLISHING

www.theultimateword.com
270 · 251 · 3600